How Students Write: A Linguistic Analysis

How Students Write: A Linguistic Analysis

Laura Louise Aull

Modern Language Association of America
New York 2020

85 Broad Street, New York, New York 10004
www.mla.org

To order MLA publications, visit www.mla.org/books. For wholesale and international orders, see www.mla.org/bookstore-orders.

The MLA office is located on the island known as Mannahatta (Manhattan) in Lenapehoking, the homeland of the Lenape people. The MLA pays respect to the original stewards of this land and to the diverse and vibrant Native communities that continue to thrive in New York City.

POD 2023 (first printing)

Library of Congress Cataloging-in-Publication Data

Names: Aull, Laura, author.
Title: How students write : a linguistic analysis / Laura Louise Aull.
Description: New York : The Modern Language Association of America, 2020. | Includes bibliographical references. | Summary: "Analyzes sentence-level patterns in first-year and advanced student writing, comparing thesis-driven argumentative papers and analysis-driven explanatory papers. Examines text features including diplomatic evidentiality, explicit cohesion, and compressed detail to consider how course assignments shape students' choices. Includes suggestions for assignment design and activities for student analysis"—Provided by publisher.
Identifiers: LCCN 2019053952 (print) | LCCN 2019053953 (ebook) ISBN 9781603294683 (hardcover) | ISBN 9781603294522 (paperback) ISBN 9781603294539 (EPUB) | ISBN 9781603294546 (Kindle)
Subjects: LCSH: English language—Rhetoric—Study and teaching (Higher) | Report writing—Study and teaching (Higher) | Academic writing—Study and teaching (Higher) Classification: LCC PE1404 .A9235 2020 (print) | LCC PE1404 (ebook) | DDC 428.0071—dc23
LC record available at https://lccn.loc.gov/2019053952
LC ebook record available at https://lccn.loc.gov/2019053953

For Bethany, sister and sage

Contents

List of Tables

Appendix

List of Figures

Acknowledgments

Given my choice of superpowers, I would speak all the world's languages. My ideas would expand so much more, I think, and I would never accidentally get sweetened condensed milk in my coffee in Indonesia. Yet, in the course of writing this book, I have felt I already have something like this superpower in the people I know. So many supportive folks, only some of whom I have space to name here, help me think and write far beyond the bounds of my limited language and ideas.

A Spencer Foundation postdoctoral fellowship through the National Academy of Education provided time for research as well as generative conversations with National Academy members, including Shirley Brice Heath and Sarah Freedman, and postdoctoral fellows, including Sarah Levine.

Large corpora of student writing, which depend on the work of students, linguists, computer scientists, faculty, and administrators, provide rare resources for macroanalytic insights about student writing, and I am grateful for access to the two corpora I analyze in this book. The upper-level corpus benefited from the work of students and scholars under the excellent guidance of Ute Römer and Matt O'Donnell, and it is freely available. The first-year corpus was made possible by an award from the National Science Foundation (1544239) titled "Collaborative Research: The Role of Instructor and Peer Feedback in Improving the Cognitive, Interpersonal, and Intrapersonal Competencies of Student Writers in STEM Courses," and benefited from student writers at the University of South Florida and the collaboration of Joe Moxley, Alex Rudiny, and Norbert Elliot.

I am grateful to have several colleagues who read my work and round upward—they imagine its best version, and they make it better. Norbert

Elliot rounds up the most: he was a visionary and unfailing supporter of this project from its earliest stages. Dylan Dryer provided crucial feedback throughout the project, from early, informal conversations through a full manuscript review. Collaborators on concurrent projects, including Zak Lancaster, David West Brown, Val Ross, and my students Madison Mosely, Darby Deutsch, Mutong Zhou, and Caroline Welch helped me develop and rethink ideas, as did Chad Whickman, editor of *Written Communication*, and editors of special issues and collections Paul Butler, Star Vanguri, Brian Ray, Tiane Donahue, Benjamin Miller, and Amanda Licastro. As ever, ongoing conversations with Anne Ruggles Gere, John Swales, and Anne Curzan make my work better. My Modern Language Association (MLA) editor Jaime Cleland and several anonymous reviewers helped me develop and revise the manuscript and in particular think about my hope to reach a broad audience concerned with student writing. Erika Suffern and Dana Symons at MLA were meticulous readers during the copyediting stage.

I am grateful as well for my family and friends in the Cayman Islands and the United States. My thanks to Randall, Paul, Lucy, Sarah, Jay, Suzy, Devon, Jessica, Susan, Shona, Morna, Lynn, and Ellen. My thanks to my parents, Jerome and Cricket, and siblings, Jake, Nika, Geneva, Talia, Bethany, and their partners and children. Bethany Aull, to whom this book is dedicated, offered her incisive intellect in reading and responding to the entire manuscript. To all of you: thank you for your generosity. Finally, my enduring thanks to my twin soul James, whose sincere efforts to approximate my level of excitement about phrasal and clausal detail provided one more happy observation in the course of this project.

Introduction: Discourse and Student Writing

In 2016, I completed a study initially unrelated to the divisive presidential election happening the same year. The study focused on generalizations in first-year college writing: sweeping statements such as "People today have lost the ability to communicate" or "Everyone will cheat to get ahead." It might not surprise regular readers of first-year writing that claims like these were prevalent, appearing in over 95% of the essays I analyzed and usually extending far beyond what could be supported.

Amid the discursive climate of our time, though, adequate support did not capture the issue. Many generalizations privileged one perspective above possible exceptions. They emphatically closed dialogic space, the sorely needed space for discussion or alternative views. A more prescient implication, it seemed, related to a lack of what Krista Ratcliffe called rhetorical listening: our stance of openness in relation to other texts and views. Common in first-year writing by strong and struggling students alike, generalizations did not open space for civil, judicious exchange.

A possible explanation was developmental. Perhaps generalizations fell away with added knowledge and experience, as students gain maturity and writing practice. Indeed, first-year students seem to generalize much more than upper-level students or expert academic writers.[1] More analysis, however, showed that first-year writers were significantly more circumspect in their reports and summaries, where their claims were more often qualified and narrow in scope, than in their argumentative essays.[2] First-year argumentative essays in particular were characterized by high levels of certainty and generality.

A more apt explanation, therefore, seemed discursive: institutionalized discourses, Michel Foucault argues, produce discourse and habituated ways of thinking (131–32). Emphatic generalizations somehow form a socially recognized way to understand and articulate the world in first-year argumentative essays, even if instructors balk when they read them. This explanation casts writing assignments as *genres* in the sense theorized by Carolyn R. Miller ("Genre as Social Action"; "Genre as Social Action (2014), Revisited"; "Rhetorical Community") and by John Swales (*Genre Analysis*; *Research Genres*) —as typified rhetorical situations that, through recurring discourse patterns, reproduce roles and topical structures that become both rules and resources. Contrasting previous views of genre as a taxonomy or classification system, this conceptualization stresses that genres are a fusion of substance, form, and social action. "Instead of being 'in' a genre, texts are transformative instantiations of genres" (Frow 1633), and these instantiations create and recreate genres according to the accepted language features and shared communicative purposes of corresponding discourse communities (Swales, *Genre*).

Whether or not we think about student writing this way, we experience this discursive reification all the time: in genres from news articles to wedding invitations, recurring discourse enacts implicit and explicit societal values. It makes genres recognizable, constraining and simplifying the set of options for writers. Through patterned discourse—recurring language-in-use—genres enable readers and writers to recognize and reproduce social practices, relations, and identities (Bawarshi, "Genre Function"; Foucault 109–33). In such discursive reproductions some genre users have more power and resources than others to recognize, use, and challenge normative choices (Gee; van Dijk).

Thus *school genres*, those sanctioned by institutions and used repeatedly in student learning, are important examples of institutionalized truth and power: they mediate communicative activity and shape each writer's school-based writing "will," as students adapt their individuality and subjectivity to recognizable, typified discourse (Deacon 437; Bakhtin 78; Bawarshi, "Genre Function" 348). Those students who shape their school-based discourse and "will" according to accepted norms—whether consciously or not—are those most likely to succeed in school. A general example includes the privileging of standardized English above other dialects; more specific disciplinary examples include the active voice in humanistic writing, which privileges writer reasoning, and the passive voice in scientific writing, which privileges research processes and outcomes. To return to the opening example of generalizations, certain discourse patterns reinforce one's own position at the expense of others' views, or, alternatively, create space for multiple perspectives.

It is not a far leap to see patterned discourse in successful student writing as evidence of what one must acquire to succeed in school—academic language, note Pierre Bourdieu and Jean-Claude Passeron, is not anyone's mother tongue (115–16). But this book also approaches patterned discourse as evidence of how school genres operate as semiotic systems. It argues that acknowledging the constitutive power of student discourse patterns in school genres means investigating discourse not as a manifestation but as a generative force in how writers and readers (often tacitly) construct knowledge and relate to one another. And it offers an example of what it looks like to systematically analyze student discourse in school genres along these lines.

In theory, this is an endeavor already at the heart of English studies, where multiple fields critically analyze the discursive construction of truth, knowledge, and identity. By this I mean that, at least theoretically, the constitutive power of the discourse students read and write is widely accepted, particularly in rhetorical genre studies. Rhetorical genre theory underscores that genres are constituted through recurring discourse that helps structure both the way individuals conceptualize and experience rhetorical situations and what counts as "appropriate and possible" responses to them (Bawarshi, "Genre Function" 339–40). A related threshold concept in composition is that genres are enacted by writers and readers through habitual responses to recurring rhetorical situations (Hart-Davidson 39). As discussed in chapter 1, these ideas highlight the theoretical importance of discourse in school genres, suggesting school discourse maintains institutions and helps shape how we understand those institutions and associated communicative actions (Devitt, "Generalizing" 583).

In application, though, studies of student writing in the United States rarely explore patterned discourse because of institutional and methodological developments in English composition studies during the second half of the twentieth century. Developments then and since have moved English composition studies almost exclusively toward the analysis of individual texts and contexts and away from linguistic analysis of writing across texts and contexts. In particular, the contextualist paradigm and qualitative, ethnographic composition research reviewed in the next chapter has led to important context-rich examinations of student writing, but it has also diminished systematic attention to discourse patterns. Even as there is theoretical emphasis on discourse in composition and many instructors and students are alert to factors that influence language, composition research and teaching tend to focus on genre contexts and macrolevel constructs like audience and purpose and to see them as more indicative than microlevel discourse patterns.

As an important addition to context-rich studies of student writing, this book endeavors not only to theorize but also to analyze the constitutive power of discourse choices repeatedly rewarded in student writing in higher education. To do so, I identify student discourse patterns within and across genres and levels that, in their persistence across texts and contexts, reinforce sociocognitive practices and attendant discursive identities. In so doing, I make the case that we—the people assigning student writing in higher education—benefit from knowing something about what students tend to write, not only in individual writing examples but also across them. The reason we know little about patterned student discourse is not because we do not have the curiosity and theoretical support for such an endeavor but because of particular disciplinary developments we can reasonably challenge today.

Why Student Discourse Matters Now

There are at least two reasons more systematic attention to discourse patterns in school genres is especially valuable right now. One is to support diverse learners in higher education. These efforts are aided by descriptive investigations that make privileged discourse expectations transparent and knowable, rather than the common alternative: depending on unconscious assimilation as the primary way students must make the connection between assignment expectations and the written choices they make.

The goal of exposing privileged discourse patterns is not to suggest they are better than others but to identify and describe written choices repeatedly valued in higher education so they are evident and alterable for those implicated in their use. People can acquire a given social language, James Gee describes, "only if they come to recognize how certain grammatical devices and patterns of those devices correlate with (match up with) certain sorts of communicative functions, social practices, and even attitudes and values" controlled by "a group of people who share and 'police' these functions, practices, attitudes, and values" (14). Many such discourse patterns are understandably tacit for students and instructors alike, not least because instructors are usually far from their own academic socialization by the time they assign and evaluate student writing.

The other, related reason is the important role of higher education in modeling thoughtful dialogue. Urgent concerns about discourse—the need for civil discourse, the demise of public discourse—are framed as a particular responsibility of higher education, the humanities, and composition more specifically.[3] Such concerns offer valuable possibilities for the continued relevance of departments of English, wherein students' reading and writing are forms of inquiry and objects of analysis. In sum, investigating student discourse in school genres creates opportunities for exposing and interrogating what is expected from students and for understanding how school genres operate as privileged semiotic systems, efforts theoretically and practically at the core of English studies.

Analyzing Student Discourse

Because meaning-making patterns are often implicit, we need innovative ways to identify and analyze them. In this book, I combine human and computer-aided insights—close and distant reading—to offer a unique view of student writing according to repeating lexical and grammatical choices and effects. The two ways of reading complement one another: together, close and distant views illuminate discursive practices reinforced in school assignments within and across texts and contexts.

By shedding additional light on student discourse, such analysis can support efforts to examine and revise writing assignments and feedback in higher education, recognizing that it is not only in theory but also in the cumulative effect of patterned discourse that school assignments shape writing and thinking. Along these lines, the book adds to developments in corpus linguistic analysis and digital humanities, which challenge false dichotomies between humanistic and empirical methods that limit textual understanding (Elliot et al.). Such analysis advances possibilities for humanistic and empirical study and educational equity, because exposing recurring discourse helps uncover tacit writing expectations, providing opportunities for democratizing pedagogical forms.

Three Qualities Constituted in Student Discourse

Ultimately, the analysis that inspired this book circled back to contemporary concerns about public discourse, though in more complicated ways than I anticipated. Some discourse patterns I discuss in the book facilitate judicious, civil exchange. At the same time, some patterns make academic writing inaccessible for a range of readers, and these two qualities are sometimes at odds. For instance, argumentative writing, especially by first-year writers, contains lexical patterns that repeatedly close dialogic space, leaving no room for alternative views. Yet it also contains grammatical patterns that are interactive and familiar for a range of readers.

In particular, discourse patterns discussed in chapter 5 point to three rhetorical qualities rewarded in student writing development: civility, cohesion, and compression. These three qualities seem both concerning and worthwhile, for they make academic writing at once inaccessible and diplomatic. They are constituted by persistent, significant discourse patterns in upper-level writing regardless of discipline or assignment. I outline them briefly below and return to them in detail in chapter 5.

Perhaps most heartening is that several upper-level discourse patterns contribute to civility, what I describe as diplomatic evidentiality, by blending open-mindedness with well-informed conviction. Discourse patterns constitute civility by balancing the opening and closing of dialogic space: opening dialogic space to acknowledge possible concerns, limitations, and disagreements and, slightly less often, closing it to endorse substantiated ideas. This balance is not characteristic of most first-year, especially argumentative, writing, which tends to close dialogic space much more than open it; but it does characterize upper-level writing, regardless of assignment genre. Specific discourse patterns that create civility include balanced hedging and boosting, concessive and countering clauses, and grammatical structures that help writers critique ideas rather than people.

A second rhetorical quality is *cohesion*, or explicit coherence across parts of a text. The upper-level patterns show a range of cohesive ties that draw attention to how the parts of a text relate. Discourse patterns that create cohesion include text connectives and reformulation words, often in predictable moves, which showcase writers' reasoning and help create a shared understanding between readers and writers. In that such ties illustrate an attentiveness to the reading needs of an audience, they too contribute to written civility.

A third rhetorical quality is *compression*, or the use of dense, phrasal detail. This quality makes upper-level writing particularly difficult to read and write, especially for those whose lexical and grammatical habits are distant from standardized written academic English. Discourse patterns that create compression include complex noun phrases (composed, e.g., of articles, attributive adjectives, and prepositions) instead of unpacking the same detail in lengthier dependent clauses more characteristic of conversational or interactive language (Biber; Biber and Egbert 50–71). For example, this means upper-level writers might write something like *Syntactically dense phrases make academic writing challenging to parse*, rather than a clausal description that includes more explicit grammatical relationships, such as *Many students find it challenging to parse academic writing, because it includes phrases that are syntactically dense*. Compressed writing aids concision: notice that in this example the phrasal iteration is about half as long. But compressed detail can also obscure grammatical relationships, and cognitively, it is more taxing to read. Compressed phrases make academic writing unlike the English language use that students encounter most in conversation and informal writing. They make upper-level writing unlike what many early—even successful—college students write.

Together, these three qualities illuminate how patterned academic discourse engages interpersonal, intrapersonal, and cognitive domains of writing, from strategies that balance open-mindedness and conviction and cue rhetorical relationships to strategies for selecting and parsing information. They also underscore that identifying macroanalytic patterns across texts and contexts adds to what we know about student writing in higher education. By illuminating these patterns, this book aims to add linguistic insights to our understanding of school genres. It strives to offer an English studies audience the first analysis-driven account of student writing that attends to the constitutive power of patterned discourse.

Chapter Outline

Chapter 1, "What We Know (and Don't Know) about Student Writing," reviews contemporary composition research, which places theoretical and pedagogical importance on genre and suggests students who can recognize and adapt to different genres are most successful. Writing instruction and assignments accordingly aim to clarify genre-specific expectations, and composition research strives to understand student responses to familiar and unfamiliar genres. Since the twentieth-century "social turn" in composition, genre-based research and instruction especially emphasize context-rich, qualitative methods and macrolevel rhetorical principles, which means we know a good deal about genre contexts and activity systems and the challenges of transferring knowledge across them. This contextualist paradigm also means we know little about microlevel, recurring discourse in student writing or how it illuminates and constitutes school genres. As important context chapter 1 outlines a notable consequence of the particular development of composition studies since the mid–twentieth century: without linguistic attention in composition research and teaching, discourse patterns in student writing have primarily been measured in assessments, not analyzed by compositionists.

The chapter clarifies this book's theoretical lens and methodological approach by suggesting that a needed next step is examination of patterned discourse as part of understanding school genres and student writing. Beginning with the view that patterned discourse helps constitute a communicative consciousness for how writers and readers relate and make knowledge, the book combines corpus linguistic analysis and close textual analysis to uncover lexical and grammatical patterns in student writing in different school genres and at different student levels. Chapter 1 closes with a brief exploration of the themes addressed throughout the book: the nature of common writing assignments in higher education, discourse patterns across student levels and school genres, and implications for student discourse patterns in different genres and levels.

Chapter 2, "School Genres," provides further context with a historicized review of writing assignments in higher education. The chapter highlights assignment genres and writing constructs (abilities or proficiencies) common in first-year and upper-level curricular writing. The first part of the chapter addresses past and present first-year composition assignments, which have been institutionalized since higher education in the United States expanded in the late nineteenth and early twentieth centuries. This section delineates thirty-six tasks and four constructs shared across first-year writing assignments. The second part of the chapter reviews upper-level writing assignments documented more recently. This section outlines thirty-one tasks and four constructs common in upper-level writing assignments from English and across the curriculum. Following these level-specific overviews, the chapter offers a synthesis of common assignments in higher education according to genre family, genre, rhetorical characteristics, and example tasks.

As the synthesis shows, common across first-year and upper-level writing assignments are two genre families analyzed in the subsequent chapters: argumentative writing assignments, or thesis-driven tasks, in which showcasing persuasive reasoning is a primary rhetorical purpose, and explanatory writing, or analysis-driven tasks, in which showcasing interpretive reasoning is a primary rhetorical purpose. These are evoked regularly in assignment research but underexamined in terms of the discourse patterns and rhetorical aims that constitute them within and across student levels. This chapter thus offers a genre-based context for the linguistic analysis in subsequent chapters which illuminates these assignment genres in new ways.

Chapter 3, "Student Discourse in First-Year Genres," offers a corpus linguistic and close textual analysis of patterned discourse in first-year writing. The first section outlines assignment details and institutional information related to the first-year writing I analyze in the chapter: over six hundred A-graded papers by first-year composition students at a large public institution in the United States, in response to argumentative assignments (argumentative essays) and explanatory assignments (analytic reports and research summaries). The second part of the chapter includes two analyses of aggregate patterns and individual choices in first-year writing. The first identifies lexical and grammatical patterns that distinguish first-year argumentative writing relative to first-year explanatory writing. The second analysis examines stance words in first-year writing—discourse-level choices providing explicit textual and epistemic framing in academic writing—that highlight genre-specific expectations related to stance and cohesion.

The analysis shows that first-year argumentative writing is characterized by interactive, persuasive discourse patterns; an emphasis on human behaviors and needs; and stance word patterns that convey relatively certain and generalized claims, for example, to emphasize the importance of an issue or the broad applicability of a claim. First-year explanatory writing is characterized by a more informational discourse pattern, an emphasis on sources and objects of study, and less generalized claims. Thus the findings do not show a strong empirical relationship between first-year argumentative essays and traditional academic discourse practices. At the same time, explanatory writing shows a more narrow and exclusive set of lexical and grammatical patterns. Furthermore, both kinds of first-year writing show stance word patterns that tend to close dialogic space, leaving little room for exceptions or disagreements.

Chapter 4, "Student Discourse in Upper-Level Genres," offers a parallel analysis of patterned discourse in upper-level student writing. The first section contextualizes the upper-level writing I analyze: over seven hundred A-graded papers written across discipline-specific courses by students in their final year of undergraduate or first three years of graduate school at a large selective research institution. The writing represents sixteen academic disciplines and the two genre families also analyzed in chapter 3: argumentative writing (argumentative essays and critiques), and explanatory writing (reports and research reports). As in chapter 3, the analysis offers a distant view of aggregate patterns across texts alongside a close view of examples that illuminate individual uses of the patterns. Likewise, the analysis identifies key lexical and grammatical patterns in argumentative versus explanatory writing and also examines stance word patterns in each.

The analysis shows that several lexical and grammatical patterns distinguish upper-level writing in argumentative versus explanatory assignments. In argumentative assignments, discourse patterns create a more persuasive and conversational style, with more emphasis on human ideas and needs. In explanatory assignments, discourse patterns create a more informational style, characterized by more noun phrases and passive constructions, which foreground research processes and outcomes and omit explicit information about grammatical agents and relationships. These discourse patterns enact some genre-specific values vis-à-vis what and who constitutes knowledge. At the same time, upper-level argumentative and explanatory writing are both characterized by grammatical patterns relatively unique to academic writing, including noun phrases that add concise but compressed detail. Both also include stance word patterns that show attention to audience objections and reading needs, including balanced hedging and boosting and explicit cohesive clues.

Chapter 5, "A New View of Student Writing," extends chapters 3 and 4 by identifying genre-specific discourse shared across student levels, and level-specific discourse shared across school genres. The first analysis underscores the impact of school assignments regardless of student level. For instance, in argumentative writing, both first-year and upper-level students emphasize human subjects, offer generalized observations, make a case, and add detail in dependent clauses. In explanatory writing, both first-year and upper-level students emphasize research processes and outcomes, offer less generalized conclusions, and present detail in phrasal descriptions.

Especially revealing is what makes upper-level writing distinct from first-year writing. This analysis shows that regardless of the assignment, upper-level discourse patterns include more emphasis on processes versus general observations; more explicit textual connections and comparisons; a closer balance between opening and closing dialogic space (versus primarily closing dialogic space); more compressed, phrasal detail (versus clausal detail); and, when human subjects are emphasized, more emphasis on human ideas and needs (versus human behaviors). Some patterns show the discursive influence of both genre and level. First-year writing intimates more certainty and generality regardless of assignment genre, but first-year argumentative essays show still more certainty and generality than first-year explanatory writing.

Along these lines, chapter 5 offers several considerations for student writing in higher education: first, whether or not students and instructors are consciously aware of them, specific discourse choices are repeatedly rewarded in different school assignments, and these choices reinforce particular sociocognitive habits; second, regardless of what they write, successful student writers appear to undergo a degree of development in which they qualify and specify statements more and use more dense, phrasal syntax; and, third, some upper-level discourse patterns point to both worthwhile and concerning qualities of writing valued in higher education. In particular, upper-level discourse patterns constitute three rhetorical qualities discussed in the chapter: compression, civility, and cohesion. Based on these three qualities, the chapter offers a taxonomy that connects macrolevel assignment expectations with microlevel discourse choices, which together illuminate interpersonal, intrapersonal, and cognitive domains of writing.

The chapter closes by connecting compression, civility, and cohesion to two current discussions: calls for improved contemporary discourse and expectations for ethical student writing practices. Both discussions concern discourse in higher education but neither yet includes systematic attention to patterned language in school genres. I suggest that by connecting these discussions, we can more accurately conceptualize student writing and make our calls for a different kind of public discourse more clear.

The afterword offers applications for instructors and students, directly addressing these two audiences in their own sections. The first section is for instructors, particularly for use as they select and describe assignments with attention to discourse used in those assignments. The second is for students, particularly to support their ability to recognize, analyze, and make informed decisions about common academic discourse patterns. This section unpacks concepts for students, including stance words, grammatical patterns, and rhetorical moves, and offers examples so students can recognize various linguistic and rhetorical strategies as they examine their own and others' writing. The book thus ends with practical guidance for classroom approaches, with added attention to the role of patterns in written discourse.

Notes

1. See Aull et al. for full study.

2. See Aull, "Corpus," for initial study.

3. See, e.g., Leskes, as well as recent articles in *The Chronicle of Higher Education* by June and Mooney, respectively. See *Inside Higher Education* for the 2016 statement signed by college presidents ("Presidents' Message"). Some universities have launched research and community centers for addressing public discourse and civil discourse, e.g., the University of Connecticut (humilityandconviction.uconn.edu) and the University of Arizona (nicd.arizona.edu/). Earlier evidence from the twenty-first century includes the University of Pennsylvania president Judith Rodin's coauthored book with Stephen P. Steinberg, *Public Discourse in America: Conversation and Community in the Twenty-First Century.* See also Davies; "Post-Truth Politics"; Duffy, "Post-Truth."

1

What We Know (and Don't Know) about Student Writing

What We Know: Macrolevel Expectations for Student Writing

Sixty years of composition research has identified multiple components of successful student writing. Components related to a comprehensive writing process are probably most familiar: students are most successful when their writing includes a recursive process that incorporates instructor feedback, adequate time for composing, and substantial revision (e.g., see S. Graham et al.; MacArthur et al.; Lea and Street). Other components, especially emphasized in recent decades, focus on students' genre awareness and analysis: students are most successful when they can analyze genres and adapt to unfamiliar writing situations (Odell and Katz; Ramage et al.; Trimbur; Bean; Melzer; Thaiss and Zawacki; Clark and Hernandez; Johns, *Genre*).

Genre awareness is hence championed across levels of writing in higher education. The *Framework for Success in Postsecondary Writing* names *genre* as a key rhetorical concept that students must learn and practice. The Council of Writing Program Administrators' *WPA Outcomes Statement for First-Year Composition* indicates that first-year college writers should understand "how genre conventions shape and are shaped by readers' and writers' practices and purposes." Genre analysis informs guiding principles of popular instructional approaches for first-year, undergraduate, and graduate-level writing (e.g., Devitt et al.; Hyon; Swales and Feak). These approaches strive to "assist students in developing the rhetorical flexibility necessary for adapting their sociocognitive genre knowledge to ever-evolving contexts" (Johns, "Genre Awareness" 238). An emphasis on genre analysis and awareness aims to foster students' ability to adapt, given that no writing course can anticipate every genre students will need to read or write well. It also underscores ideas valued across English studies, including the ability to critique powerful, institutionalized semiotic systems.

To facilitate genre awareness, writing instruction is tasked with clarifying "what constitutes good writing for a specific purpose and audience" (Cassidy et al. 4), and assignment descriptions and rubrics are now customary in higher education (P. Anderson et al. 207). An important implication is that specified expectations highlight the genre-specific nature of writing and support students' writing processes more than open-ended term paper assignments (Bean 91). Another implication is the importance of the particular genres assigned in schools. Students are less likely to learn those genres and related strategies that are ignored or rejected in their school writing courses (Applebee and Langer 23; Bazerman et al. 356); by contrast, the genres students practice the most constitute their communicative consciousness, not least because students have difficulty evaluating familiar genres critically (Bakhtin 80; Bastian 27). Students, particularly those still developing as writers, maintain ideas about writing from the genres they practice most (Wingate), and common genre expectations directly shape their writing and their understanding of writing (Devitt, *Writing*). Absent an alternative approach, those assigning writing often understandably draw on their own academic socialization and reproduce common school genres.

Because genres are constructions that generally depend on "the implicit or explicit sanction of organizational or institutional power" (Hart-Davidson 40), we can think of school genres as examples of Bakhtin's typical forms that enact and maintain discourses and behaviors, socializing students into producing not only particular texts, but also ways of being (Bakhtin 78–79). Guided by sociocognitive processes and implicit and explicit values, these differences enable and constrain writers' options. Put another way, even if the ultimate goal is genre awareness, students especially learn to notice and practice the strategies privileged in school genres, those sanctioned by institutions and evaluated as part of students' grades. Students are observant, and their success often depends on how well they approximate these sanctioned discourse practices.

Thus the stakes are high for the genres we assign in higher education, though we know little about what distinguishes them in terms of patterned discourse. What discourse choices are repeatedly rewarded in different assignments? At what points, and to what end, are these choices privileged in higher education? What cognitive, interpersonal, and intrapersonal practices do such patterns reinforce? These questions are difficult to answer, and most current answers are driven by the particular disciplinary development of English composition since the mid–twentieth century.

Social Turn Composition and the Contextualist Paradigm

Research in education and composition has especially explored school genres vis-à-vis individual students' writing performances, qualitative study of writing contexts and strategies, and what I refer to as macrolevel rhetorical principles. The first emphasis—on student writing performance in education research—has been reinforced by decades of large-scale writing assessments, even as many composition scholars advocate for more locally controlled and innovative assessments (Adler-Kassner and O'Neill; Huot, *Rearticulating*; Huot and Neal; Poe et al., *Writing*). Cognitive domains of writing, versus inter- or intrapersonal ones, have been easiest to identify and consistently test, and most standardized writing assessments consider writing a cognitive practice, wherein genre knowledge is gained and mastered by individual students according to a narrow set of writing constructs (White et al.; Vojak et al.).[1] As an extreme example, using standardized testing scores (from, e.g., Advanced Placement [AP] or SAT exams) is a convenient, inexpensive way to sort students into (or exempt them from) composition courses, even though these timed exams capture very specific and limited writing skills. This practice is often fueled by scenarios in which underprepared English departments are expected to offer general introductory writing courses for most or all incoming first-year students at a given institution.

The other two emphases—qualitative research and macrolevel principles—have characterized composition studies since the late-twentieth-century social turn in the field. Motivated by theoretical disenchantment and empirical refutation of the overgeneralized process period, as well as by resistance to reductive, formalistic approaches to textual analysis, the social turn in composition shifted primary emphasis to the social contexts and actions of writing. In contrast with some earlier, microlevel attention to linguistics and grammar in composition research and teaching, research in social turn composition has focused on contexts of writing and macrolevel—or, whole-text—rhetorical principles, such as audience and purpose (Connors, "Erasure"; MacDonald, "Erasure"; Micciche; Duncan and Vanguri; Aull, *First-Year University Writing*).

In turn, ethnographic, qualitative research methods have been refined and retailored specifically to illuminate those aspects of writing processes that influence individual students and whole texts. For instance, composition research has investigated how individual students attempt to transfer genre knowledge from first-year writing to other courses, or how a class of students navigates curricular assignment genres (e.g., Beaufort; Downs and Wardle; Driscoll and Powell; Sullivan). Likewise, composition approaches to assessment especially underscore macrolevel aspects of writing such as the use of evidence and imagined audience (Anson and Dannels; Dryer). For example, contemporary composition assignments might specify an audience (e.g., "your senator"; "other students") (Smagorinsky 31–50), and first-year assignment rubrics often reward writing described as "appropriate for the audience" and that "flow[s] logically" (Dryer 13), rather than draw attention to discourse-level clues that relate to audience or flow (Aull, "Connecting").

These developments provide an important context for understanding English composition studies today and possibilities for its future. Influenced by forces within and beyond the field, a clear divide evolved in the twentieth century between the two disciplines most concerned with teaching postsecondary written English in the United States: composition and linguistics. Early separation between these fields was primed by the particular formation of higher education departments in the late nineteenth and early twentieth centuries. In broad strokes, composition was historically part of English departments that treated language use as an art, whereas linguistics was a separate department that treated language as a science (Payne). In the 1950s and 1960s, Noam Chomsky's linguistic approach, with its exclusive focus on theoretical versus actual uses of language, became renowned, leading many compositionists to view linguistics as supporting "an extremely narrow, noncontextual notion of what it means to be a user of language" (Crowley, "Linguistics" 499). Social turn composition, by contrast, was interested precisely in actual uses of language in authentic contexts, and the field "decenter[ed] . . . language and text" in favor of "a stronger focus on the social patterns of activity revolving around the interpretation and (re)production of texts" (Lancaster, "Tracking" 194). With this added distance between linguistics and composition in the late twentieth century, rhetorical genre studies in composition focused overwhelmingly on context, unlike genre studies developing simultaneously in applied linguistics (Aull, *First-Year University Writing* 37–39). Rhetorical genre studies encouraged analyzing textual patterns according to "what those patterns reveal about the context in which the genre is used" (Bawarshi, *Genre* 158), and composition researchers sought to "explore the dynamic relations between social contexts and the actions of individuals" within "activity systems," such as a college course (Deans 292).

The emphasis on activity systems stems from activity theory, an important theoretical influence for genre studies that emphasizes genre contexts and actions. Focused on how disciplinary and research activities motivate school genres, activity theory emphasizes that genres are residues of repetitive action:

> The various genres of student writing—essay, research paper, laboratory report, case study, thesis, dissertation—each have a history, which reflects the development of the genres of professional disciplinary practice: scholarly essay, research article, experimental article, case study, and so on. Moreover, traditions of writing instruction have grown up in various disciplines to prepare and select newcomers for their activity systems. (Russell, "Writing and Genre" 232)

Here David Russell underscores that disciplinary activity systems create idiosyncratic sociohistorical contexts that cannot be accounted for in composition courses that teach general, non-discipline-specific academic writing, a critique taken up in widely cited contemporary composition research (Downs and Wardle; Wardle). Russell cites Cheryl Geisler's study of students writing in the discipline of philosophy, in which "Experts don't merely know and apply rules, they constantly recreate and reinterpret them in dynamic social-historical conditions using writing and other semiotic means" (233). By contrast, undergraduate students in Geisler's study "wrote narratives closer to the genres of English classes, with which they were more familiar," and they were less successful (233). Geisler's study underscores my earlier point about communicative consciousness: without explicit guidance otherwise, the writing that students practice most frequently constitutes the writing and truth conditions they are most likely to recreate.

Based on the premise that academic discourse depends on specific and widely variant activity systems, some composition scholars assert that the label "academic discourse" (or universal educated discourse) is a category mistake (Downs and Wardle 556). Russell's articulation of this perspective is worth repeating at length here:

> Disciplinary discourses vary immensely, and even when activity systems appropriate identical discourse features, they do so for differing object(ive)s and thus often use the features differently. For example, pointing to the footnotes in a theoretical physics article and those in an article from *PMLA* would not be very helpful to a novice learning to write both genres, as compared with pointing out the very different object(ive)s of the two disciplines' activity systems, the very different material conditions of their work, the vast differences in their histories—differences which explain the profound and crucial differences in their uses of citation and documentation. ("Activity" 13)

In this description, individual disciplinary contexts are so considerable that they eclipse even similarities between parallel textual features. Such disciplinary differences have likewise been used to explain why instructors "know good writing when they see it" but cannot describe how to write it, because their standards for writing depend on their own disciplinary contexts (Lea and Street 163).

Consistent with social turn composition studies, these ideas reflect what has been called the "contextualist" orientation of rhetorical genre studies, in which individual texts and contexts are the most important points of entry and emphasis for genre analysis. These emphases contrast the "linguistic" focus of applied genre studies that approach patterned language across texts and contexts as essential for understanding the work of textual genres (Flowerdew; see also Crusius). To use examples also related to documentation and citation, applied linguists have shown that integral citation practices across academic disciplines display shared values: writers regardless of discipline are more likely to use neutral verbs rather than critical reporting verbs when citing other scholars (Hyland, *Disciplinary Discourses*; Thompson and Ye).

Composition's contextualist orientation has afforded invaluable insights about student writing and has helped move English composition studies away from reductive perceptions of genre (Bawarshi, "Genre Function" 351–57; Devitt, *Writing* 163–78). It has enabled composition research to shed much-needed light on the many factors influencing writing development and performance in a time when student writing is often assessed according to limited mechanical features (see, e.g., Deane). Crucially, context-rich studies have increased awareness about the challenges associated with students' ability to transfer what they have learned in previous classes to new ones. They have thereby made genre-based research and instruction more accurate and cautious (Wardle 776–78).

The contextualist paradigm in composition has also led to two influential conclusions about discourse that have left the field without a tradition or framework for language-level analysis. One conclusion is that discourse is reflective but not constitutive of genres. Applications of genre and activity theories over the past few decades intimate a relationship between discourse and genre wherein genre is primary and discourse follows. Twenty years ago, for instance, Russell described that genres are constructed "by recurring social actions that *give rise to* regularities in the discourse that mediates them" (Russell, "Writing" 226; emphasis mine). Recently in an essay in *Threshold Concepts in Writing Studies*, Bill Hart-Davidson explains, "Regularities of textual form most lay people experience as the structural characteristics of genres *emerge from* these repeated instances of action and are reinforced by institutional power" (39; emphasis mine). As in most genre analysis in composition, these descriptions position the social actions of genres as the primary focus for study, leaving a conceptual gap in our understanding of the role of discourse in genre analysis.

Second and related, context-rich scholarship in composition has, if unwittingly, implied there is no real value in analyzing patterns of language across texts and contexts. Aside from exceptions, including scholarship on rhetorical grammar, style, discourse, and language-oriented genre studies,[2] social turn composition studies has been characterized by an "erasure" of systematic attention to language (Connors, "Erasure"; MacDonald, "Erasure"). Paul Butler argues that the consequential lack of language-level knowledge in composition has "deprived writers and teachers of an important reservoir of conscious knowledge" about language (12–13), such as knowledge of stylistic grammar (Ray) and lexical and grammatical realizations of stance (Aull and Lancaster).

This is not to say discourse is not theoretically emphasized in genre studies in composition, as noted in the introduction. Carolyn Miller's pivotal 1984 article, "Genre as Social Action," cast genres as semiotic systems, influenced by context as well as text (Devitt, "Written Language"; Gere et al.). Rhetorical genre theory emphasizes that recurring language use in genres helps structure "the way individuals conceptualize and experience [rhetorical situations]" (Bawarshi, "Genre Function" 339–40). Genres depend "heavily on the intertextuality of discourse" discussed by Bakhtin (Devitt, "Generalizing" 576), and genres in schools highlight students' apprenticeship and socialization through norms of discourse (C. Miller, "Genre as Social Action (1984)" 59). Amy Devitt writes extensively about the ideas underpinning rhetorical genre theory, which "began with rhetorical situation and expand[ed] it to encompass a semiotic situation and social context" ("Generalizing" 576). The concept of *rhetorical situations* built on Lloyd F. Bitzer's earlier work, which underscored that genres both create discourse and are created by them: rhetorical situations lead to a "form of discourse . . . [that] comes to have a power of its own" (Bitzer 13). These descriptions theoretically evoke the primacy of discourse or at least a mutually informative relationship between discourse and genre.

In practice, however, decades of genre-based research have "largely . . . set aside" language or form (Devitt, "Re-fusing" 27), and dominant methodological and epistemological orientations have influenced not only how questions about student writing get answered but also what questions get asked. Genre analysis in composition has largely focused on "the interactions of people with texts" in individual cases and contexts (Russell, "Rethinking" 226), rather than on how language-level choices repeat across texts and contexts and help determine individual and collective choices. A pedagogical result is the focus on macrolevel rhetorical principles noted above. A conceptual result is that genre analysis in composition gives little insight into the constitutive power of discourse. A methodological result is that analytic methods that identify language-level patterns across texts are rarely used in English composition research even though they can complement composition theory and instruction (Aull, "Linguistic Attention"; Gere et al.; Lancaster, "Do" 450).

Adding to What We Know

This book proposes a different approach on two counts. Most obviously, my use of linguistic analysis suggests that discourse patterns are an important focus for examining student writing across courses, levels, and assignments. This does not imply that student discourse is identical regardless of context but rather that school genres and levels are constituted by discourse patterns that offer valuable insight. As such, the book draws on composition research as well as research and methods common in applied linguistics, which presume, first, that genre analysis should highlight the interconnected dimensions of lexico-grammatical features and rhetorical context (Swales and Feak 53), and second, that approaches to student writing should include explicit attention to language-level features. The latter assumption builds on the fact that writers and readers make decisions based on language, but those decisions are not always conscious. For instance, research shows that discourse-level patterns related to cohesion and epistemic stance can influence instructor grades even without instructors' conscious awareness of them (Wodak and Meyer; Odell et al.; Lancaster, "Using"). Such is the discursive force of pedagogical forms theorized by Foucault: they tacitly but persistently shape what is understood to be true.

In addition to discourse patterns, I see analysis of microlevel linguistic features as complementing our knowledge of macrolevel rhetorical principles and student writing. My view and my own pedagogical approach emphasize both: microlevel discourse patterns that illuminate macrolevel principles, and vice versa. Furthermore, I share—and see as constructive—skepticism about aggregated and automated text analytics without attention to context. John Guillory wrote in *PMLA* a few years ago that "the more distant tests are from the scene of teaching, the more limited their informational value" (666). This is true for a great deal of contemporary testing, but it need not be true of contemporary text analytics. As detailed in the next section, this book offers a descriptive study of patterns across individual texts and within them. Each view—a distant look at patterns across texts, and a close look at individual uses of patterns—benefits from the other.[3] As a complement to research on individual texts and contexts, studies like this offer an additional view of student writing, one between the remote view of educational testing and the close view of context-rich composition research.

What We Don't Know: Microlevel Discourse Patterns in Student Writing

The analysis in this book offers a view that resides between an exclusively remote and an exclusively close view of student writing. The remote view, popular in educational measurement and assessment, focuses on text-level details, such as lexical sophistication, syntactic complexity, and sentence length. Often, this view stems from computational tools used in automated writing evaluation of timed writing tasks (see, e.g., Coffin and Hewings; Doolan; Condon; Deane; Crossley et al., "What"; McNamara et al.). A remote view has shown, for instance, that lexical sophistication (or the production of advanced and difficult words) is associated with student writing quality, and lexical and phrasal features are stronger predictors of writing quality scores than features such as syntactic complexity or cohesion (Kyle and Crossley; Crossley et al., "Development"). Such research has offered text-level insights but has also been critiqued for focusing on mechanical knowledge and failing to account for writing as a rhetorical act embedded in specific contexts and purposes (see, e.g., Deane; Herrington and Moran).

The close view, more common in composition studies, focuses on writer- and context-level details such as individual students' writing beliefs and strategies or writing assignments in particular courses. Often, this view stems from student interview responses, participant observation, and close reading of curricular artifacts (e.g., Downs and Wardle; Sullivan; Beaufort; Driscoll and Powell; Wardle; DeStigter). A close view shows, for example, that a class of students report improved self-awareness about writing after a writing-about-writing course (Downs and Wardle). Such research has offered context-level insights but has also been critiqued for eliding empirical methods and discourse-level analysis (see, e.g., Connors, "Erasure"; MacDonald, "Erasure"; Micciche; Devitt, "Re-fusing"; Barton and Stygall).

These disparate views underscore a notable consequence of the development of composition studies since the mid–twentieth century: without linguistic insights in composition research and teaching, language patterns in student writing have primarily been measured in assessments, rather than interpreted by compositionists. This book strives to begin filling the gap between the two by exploring microlevel discourse patterns that connect to macrolevel principles in student writing. In so doing, it strives to illuminate the "powerful interrelationships of rhetoric and language" (Gere et al. 612) and support a plurality of methods and concepts for guiding contemporary textual analysis (Elliot et al.).

Although the analysis in this book is uncommon in composition, it builds on extant concepts in the field. The book approaches school genres as social conditions that underpin knowledge, and discourse as textual conditions that illustrate and enact knowledge. The analysis strives to connect these theoretical ideas with empirical textual patterns. In this way, I treat discourse as both an object of analysis—the focus of corpus linguistic and close textual study—and as constitutive of knowledge—part of the reflection and creation of social, historical, and generic conditions through which statements become credible and accepted as truth. To return to Bourdieu and Gee, the book strives to examine interworkings of school discourse is a social language, created and enforced through grammatical and lexical patterns that reify the values, social practices, and communicative functions of those who police them.

Supporting Diversity in Higher Education

An approach that interrogates academic discourse expectations supports commitments to diversity long held in higher education and English studies. Clear construct representation—transparency about what is emphasized (and not emphasized) in writing assigned—is crucial for social justice and the advancement of opportunity in writing assessment, as discussed most recently by Mya Poe, Asao Inoue, and Norbert Elliot (Poe et al., *Writing*). In this book I show that such efforts are aided by examining student discourse patterns, thereby resisting the common presumption that students should (and will) unconsciously assimilate academic discourse. Put another way: in school genres, some genre users—those who assign and evaluate genre instantiations—have more power than others—those who are evaluated through them.[4] Those with the most power must especially interrogate that discursive reproduction.

Patterned discourse in student writing implicates both text-level forces, like recurring lexis and grammar, and context-level forces, like assignment expectations and student level. To this end, in the next chapter, I review common postsecondary writing assignments and their shared rhetorical aims, and in subsequent chapters, I analyze discourse patterns in successful (A-graded) writing across assignment genres and student levels. In terms of student level, I focus on two important, transitional periods in student writing, first-year writing in college composition courses, and upper-level writing in late-undergraduate- and early-graduate-level courses. Each is an important point of access in higher education.

In terms of assignment genres, I focus on the two most commonly documented genre families in higher education: persuasive argumentative writing and analytic explanatory writing. Persuasive argumentative writing is represented in first-year writing in argumentative essays, a school genre that serves as "the gatekeeping mechanism within individual courses as well as at critical stages of passage through secondary schools and into college" (Heath 105). Upper-level argumentative writing is represented in argumentative essays and critiques. Analytic explanatory writing is represented in first-year writing in annotated bibliographies and visual analyses and in upper-level writing in research papers and reports. (For concision, I hereafter refer to these genre families as argumentative writing and explanatory writing.)

Analyzing Student Discourse and School Genres: Two Views

Describing computational analytics used in authorship studies, Matthew L. Jockers writes that "a consistent problem" in authorship attribution is the possibility that factors such as genre "may influence or even overpower the latent authorial signal" (63). This is a good way to think of precisely the problem of interest in this book: the discourse patterns that, irrespective of the more idiosyncratic choices of individual student writers, significantly characterize school genres and student levels. This view of patterns across many texts complements and provides added insight to studies that analyze a few texts.

I emphasize this additive—versus competing—view because any analytic method privileges particular ways of knowing. Analysis of individual texts privileges individual texts over what they share across time or space. Macroanalysis across many texts privileges textual patterns over textual outliers. Benjamin Mangrum poses the latter point as a critique of macroanalysis, but it is more apt to view it as descriptive fact: analysis across texts privileges patterned choices, just as analysis of individual texts privileges individual choices. Since no single view is comprehensive, what we know about constitutive discourse patterns in academic writing can be informed by multiple views, close and distant. A plurality of ways of analyzing texts means a plurality of conclusions about them.

As a complement to more common, context-rich analysis of student writing, this book offers an analysis based on patterns that appear rewarded across student papers regardless of individual students or classroom contexts. To do so, I use computer-aided tools to uncover student discourse patterns across texts, and I use close analysis of individual texts to clarify the use and effect of those patterns. With this approach, I identify the most persistent and significant choices in successful writing: those that appear in at least 90% of the student texts in a given genre or level and those that appear often enough to be statistically highly unlikely to be due to chance ($p<.001$). These patterns point to discursive choices that successful students make despite varying student backgrounds, instructors, and assignment topics.

More specifically, I use corpus linguistic tools to expose genre-specific and level-specific lexical and grammatical patterns that repeat across hundreds of student papers. The tools are designed for "looking at how words behave in texts" (Scott) by parsing and sorting language according to patterns (Barlow).[5] To complement this distant view, I analyze each pattern in light of common uses within and across individual student texts: concordance, collocation, and cluster analysis help me identify lexical and syntactic uses of overall patterns, and I closely analyze example passages to highlight how individual students use the patterns in their writing. The close analysis also offers concrete examples that can be used in writing instruction and feedback; example passages analyzed in chapters 3 and 4 can be used to complement classroom activities outlined in the afterword. In sum, to gain a unique view of student discourse and school genres, I draw on computer-aided corpus linguistic tools and human-aided analysis, using distant reading and close reading in complementary ways.

Two Analytic Approaches: Keyword and Stance Word Frequency

I identify student discourse patterns using two approaches: *keyword analysis* and *word frequency analysis*. Keyword analysis identifies the lexical and grammatical choices that are key, or statistically significantly more frequent, in one corpus relative to another. In chapters 3 and 4, for instance, I use keyword analysis to identify the patterns that significantly characterize each genre family at the same level, for example, upper-level argumentative writing relative to upper-level explanatory writing, and vice versa. In chapter 5, keyword analysis helps identify those discourse patterns that significantly characterize each genre family, regardless of level, and each student level, regardless of genre.

One valuable aspect of keyword analysis, according to Paul Baker, is that it "highlight[s] the existence of types of (embedded) discourse or ideology" by "direct[ing] the researcher to important concepts in a text (in relation to other texts)" (3). This explanation stresses the descriptive versus prescriptive aim of keyword analysis, in this case, to expose those patterns repeatedly privileged in student writing. In particular, the keyword analyses in chapters 3 and 4 direct attention to discourse patterns and values embedded in genre-specific assignments, and the keyword analysis in chapter 5 highlights discourse patterns and values embedded in writing at the beginning and end of higher education.

Consider, for instance, two examples from the analysis in chapter 4. Keyword analysis shows that in their argumentative writing, upper-level students use possessive pronouns (*his*, *their*, *her*, *its*, *our*, *my*, in that order) significantly more often than they do in explanatory writing. Because no one pronoun is used overwhelmingly, this is a grammatical pattern realized in several different iterations. Together with recurring use of the genitive marker *'s* (e.g., *Butler'***s**, *Hume'***s**), these patterns highlight rhetorical characteristics rewarded in upper-level argumentative versus explanatory assignments: a more interactive style and more emphasis on human ideas and needs (cited scholars, people generally, and sometimes the writer and reader). By contrast, a key grammatical pattern in upper-level explanatory writing is the use of more noun phrases than pronouns—for example, *results from recent research*, *the final step in rehabilitation*. The repeated use of nouns in explanatory writing enacts a more impersonal style and an emphasis on research processes and outcomes. In turn, these patterns subtly and persistently create genre-specific stories about who and what makes knowledge. Judging by their unique salience in A-graded papers, these patterns show that upper-level students who use them are rewarded for doing so. Keyword analysis, the first analytic approach, is therefore "bottom up"—it begins with the texts (or, more specifically, what is uniquely frequent in each set of texts).

The second approach, word frequency analysis of stance words, is "top down"—it begins with existing research on academic writing. More specifically, the second approach begins with a predetermined set of language features and identifies the comparative frequencies of those features in different corpora. In this case, I examine stance words that in previous research correspond to student writing level. For instance, research in composition and applied linguistics shows that first-year writers tend to use stance words that intensify and generalize (e.g., *clearly* and *always*), whereas upper-level student writers and professional academic writers use these words less (Barton, "Evidentials"; Aull and Lancaster). The analysis in this book helps extend this research by exploring stance at different levels as well as in different assignment genres. I introduce stance words in more detail below before describing the stance analysis in the book.[6]

Stance words explicitly frame written ideas, guiding readers to perceive propositional (or referential) information in particular ways. For instance, if the propositional content "I heard a fly buzz when I died" instead reads "*Perhaps* I heard a fly buzz when I died," the hedge *perhaps* qualifies the proposition, opening dialogic space and leaving room for doubt. By contrast, the iteration "I *definitely* heard a fly buzz when I died" conveys the opposite. Using *definitely* boosts (or intensifies) the statement to show epistemic certainty about the fly buzzing, closing dialogic space by suggesting there is no room for an alternative conclusion. In addition to epistemic clues, stance words can provide textual clues. For example, the iteration "*However*, I heard a fly buzz when I died," includes the counter *however*, framing the proposition as a denial of or counter to something that preceded the proposition, such as that a dying person cannot hear flies. These examples show how writers can use stance words to indicate "where [they] stand in relation to readers and their [propositional] material" (Soliday 37).[7]

The distinction between stance words and propositional content often overlaps, but specifically analyzing stance words can be analytically and pedagogically useful, particularly because student writers may be unfamiliar with academic stance expectations and unaware of the cumulative rhetorical effects of stance patterns across a full text. For instance, research indicates that first-year, upper-level, and professional academic writers use generality words such as *all*, *everyone*, and *never* in similar rhetorical ways: to project collective ideas or beliefs and to emphasize the wide applicability of a statement. Yet first-year writers use them significantly more than the experienced writers and ultimately convey overly generalized arguments (Aull et al.).

The stance analysis in this book focuses on five types of stance words that clearly distinguish first-year and upper-level writing in previous research. Of these five, three—hedges, boosters, and generality words—are epistemic words, which indicate the level of certainty and generalizability of attendant statements. As in the earlier example, hedges such as *perhaps* or *possibly* open dialogic space by leaving room for exceptions. They allow writers to make statements without implying they are fully certain or proven, and they often contribute to civility in academic writing by downplaying critical or debatable statements. Boosters such as *definitely* and *clearly*, by contrast, increase the level of certainty about a statement. They indicate full epistemic commitment and close dialogic space. Finally, generality words such as *everyone*, *people*, and *never* indicate a statement applies beyond a specific context or example; they too close dialogic space, leaving no room for exceptions. Previous research shows that first-year writers use fewer hedges, more boosters, and more generality words than upper-level writers; upper-level writers use more hedges relative to boosters and craft more circumspect statements (Aull et al.).

The other two stance categories—counters and reformulation words—serve as textual clues: they help convey how information fits together or how particular statements relate to other statements. Specifically, counters such as *instead* or *however* explicitly indicate that a statement contrasts a previous one. Reformulation words, as the name indicates, draw attention to the reformulation of previous information to highlight elucidation, exemplification, counterexpectancy, or emphasis. Both show attention to an audience's need to understand how information connects across sentences and paragraphs. Previous research shows that first-year writers use fewer reformulation words and counters than their upper-level peers (Aull and Lancaster).

The analysis in this book aims to extend this earlier research by accounting for both genre and level with respect to how students explicitly craft stance in their writing. Further, the focus on stance words examines intra- and interpersonal aspects of student writing in a way that has been underrepresented in research to date, as discussed in chapters 3–5. As with the keyword patterns, all the stance word patterns are persistent, appearing in at least 90% of the texts in each student writing corpus analyzed. In contrast to the keyword pattern analysis, where I identify only the most frequent patterns, in the stance analysis I offer

Table 1. Epistemic Stance Words

STANCE WORD	EXAMPLE USES	RHETORICAL EFFECT
Hedges	*may be argued, most likely, to a certain extent, to a certain level, it is not clear / not indisputable that, it may be true / may prove true, this might suggest*	Opens dialogic space, leaves room for alternatives, downplays certainty and directness
Boosters	*certainly a case of, certainly a consideration, certainly a factor, has clear import, there is a clear connection between, clearly agree, clearly appear*	Closes dialogic space, leaves little to no room for alternatives, emphasizes certainty
Generality words	*never been the case, has always been, people today, anybody can see that, none of the examples, no one knows, nothing can be done, all cases show, never/always, society, the world, Americans, human beings, people*	Shows wide applicability, extrapolates across contexts, time, and/or groups

Table 2. Textual Stance Words

STANCE WORD	EXAMPLE USES	RHETORICAL EFFECT
Counters	*alternatively, although, at the same time, but, in/by contrast, conversely, however, on one / the other hand, nevertheless, rather, still, though, yet*	Signals contrast or counter to previous information
Reformulation words	Elucidation: *to be precise, put another way, put differently, i.e., that is, in other words, here I mean, to put it simply* Exemplification: *for example, for instance, an example of, to illustrate* Emphasis: *specifically, in particular, particularly, especially, namely* Counterexpectancy: (sometimes follow concessions marked by, e.g., *while, although, it is true, does account for*) *as a matter of fact, in fact, indeed*	Signals reformulation of information according to writer, to illustrate, elucidate, emphasize, or offer counterintuitive information

comparative frequencies for each pattern across the corpora. Two tables offer a synopsis of stance words and their rhetorical effects: table 1 notes epistemic clues, or those clues that relate to explicit words of caution, certainty, and generality, and table 2 describes textual clues, or those clues that draw explicit attention to the rhetorical relationship between ideas.[8]

A Preview of Key Ideas

Together, the analysis in the book strives to expand what we know about three important considerations for student writing: first, the nature of common writing assignments in higher education, second, student discourse across levels and genres, and third, implications for student discourse patterns. These are previewed below and discussed more in subsequent chapters.

The Nature of Writing Assignments in Higher Education

The treatment of writing assignments as *constructed response tasks* is consistent with contemporary genre theory in that it underscores that school writing tasks themselves shape students' responses (see, e.g., Bennett). The genre of writing assignments is therefore a key consideration for postsecondary writing and has been discussed in composition research vis-à-vis curriculum (Russell, "Activity"; Wardle), instruction (Bawarshi, *Genre*; C. Miller, "Genre as Social Action"), and assessment (Burstein et al.; Gere et al.; Beck and Jeffery). Students must succeed in these genres, which also reinforce particular disciplinary and transdisciplinary principles of academic writing (Thaiss and Zawacki).

Even assignments that can be considered part of the same genre are not identical. Genres are not rigid constructs but have fuzzy boundaries or borders (Medway), and, to a degree, all genres are "continually being 'remade' by different communities at different points of time, with new textual elements and traditions added, deleted, modified" (Haefner 131; see also Devitt, "Re-fusing"). Furthermore, though recurring features and standardization have been principle foci in genre analysis, recent scholarship underscores that we must also acknowledge variation in genre examples and uptake (Bastian; Devitt, "Genre"; Tardy).

Despite their mutable boundaries, however, genres persist and are useful to communities precisely because they are recognizable across texts. Genres share recognizable family resemblances that include prototypical moves and discourse meaningful for particular communities, such as academic fields (Grabe; J. Martin, "Universe"; C. Miller, "Genre as Social Action"; Nesi and Gardner; Swales, *Genre*). Thus, although "the differences among disciplines—and even among instructors within the same discipline and subdiscipline—in terms of the purposes and audiences . . . make it difficult to generalize" (Melzer W255), studying patterns in genre examples can shed light on writing expectations that are privileged, reinforced, and discoverable across individual student texts, including recurring discourse choices identified in this book. I specifically focus on genre families (sometimes called *macrogenres* or *umbrella genres*) as groups of genres with shared primary rhetorical aims, discussed in chapter 2.

Attention to discourse patterns can specifically enhance what we know about the connection between assignment tasks and how students write, a connection underexplored to date. Most research on writing assessment design focuses on the relation between student performance and task prompt or content. Composition research, for example, has examined the relation between assessment prompts and students' overall writing scores (Huot, "Literature"), and how the relation between tasks and scores relates to assessment validity (Yancey; Huot, *Rearticulating*). Applied linguistics assessment research has focused on the relation between student performance and writing task type or content, for instance, English-language learners' response to independent versus integrated tasks (Cumming et al.) or to unfamiliar versus more familiar topics (Tedick). Education research has examined the performance of particular student demographic groups vis-à-vis whether or not students have a choice of task topic (Gabrielson et al.).[9]

We know less about the relation between common student discourse patterns on the one hand, and writing task design on the other, although there are calls for this kind of work in both composition and applied linguistics (Gere et al.; Hamp-Lyons and Mathias). In addition, corpus analysts have indicated the need for "new indices [of patterned textual features] that take into consideration contextual factors such as the writing prompt" (Crossley et al., "What" 189) and have suggested we know little about the impact of different assignment details on writing tasks of the same genre (Aull, "Linguistic Attention" 5). This book strives to enhance what we know about postsecondary student writing by investigating discourse that emerges consistently within and across assignments at different student levels.

Student Discourse across Levels and Genres

Part of the reason discourse patterns remain tacit is that they accumulate across papers, paragraphs, and sentences in lexical and grammatical choices that may not seem notable when we read them one at a time. Successful student writers may sense choices that are successful, but many students may not; and successful or not, most students lack systematic understanding of those choices. The analysis in this book illuminates recurring patterns and rhetorical effects that may otherwise remain tacit. Consider some genre-specific grammatical patterns that build on the examples in the last section.

This study shows that first-year and upper-level writers are much more likely to add detail using dependent clauses in argumentative writing than in explanatory writing. These patterns help writers show explicit grammatical relationships between human subjects and their needs or ideas. This means, for example, that argumentative writing is more likely to include a sentence like *As preventing HIV becomes more possible, our efforts should include educational outreach*, which uses a dependent adverbial clause (*As preventing becomes . . .*) and a pronoun (*our*) to narrate a shared purpose at a particular moment in medical history. This also means that argumentative patterns share characteristics with interactive language use familiar to most students through spoken conversation and Web genres like online blogs (Biber; Biber and Egbert).

In explanatory writing, first-year and upper-level writers alike are more likely to add detail in noun phrases, creating a less personal, more informational style common in scientific writing (Klein) and academic writing more generally (Biber et al., "Speaking"). To continue the above example, explanatory writing is more likely to include a sentence such as *Educational outreach is an option for HIV prevention*, which foregrounds phenomena (*educational* ***outreach***, *HIV* ***prevention***) and does not emphasize human involvement the way the argumentative example does. These genre-specific rhetorical effects are constituted by patterned discourse across texts, and they intimate particular versions of what and who constructs knowledge in particular assignments.

Some patterns are clearly influenced by both genre and level. For instance, student use of epistemic words shows a potential developmental trajectory, regardless of genre, at least for successful student writers: in contrast with first-year writers, those at the upper level include fewer words that explicitly generalize their statements beyond a given example or context. Nevertheless, at both levels students show more use of generality in argumentative relative to explanatory writing.

Overall, too, the analysis of level-specific discourse points to the three sets of patterns noted in the introduction. These patterns appear uniquely valued in upper-level student writing, regardless of genre, and contribute to the rhetorical qualities of compression, civility, and cohesion that make academic writing both civil and challenging to read and write. In chapter 5, I outline these three qualities in detail and consider how they illuminate cognitive, interpersonal, and intrapersonal domains of writing as they are constituted in recurring discourse.

Implications for Student Discourse Patterns

This book highlights at least three motivations for a greater understanding of patterned discourse. One reason is pedagogical and specifically supports a range of learners in higher education. Discourse-level patterns offer textual anchors for macrolevel rhetorical principles. They provide concrete reference points for discussing reading and writing with students, especially those for whom academic discourse feels unfamiliar or impenetrable. Many instructors have writing goals for students, such as open-mindedness, audience awareness and flow, and reading goals, such as mindful reading (Carillo; Matsuda and Jeffery; Thaiss and Zawacki). These goals can be illuminated by more attention to discourse. In addition, since many students think instructor grades are entirely subjective—based on what each instructor wants—recurring discourse patterns help clarify shared, systematic expectations and values. Attention to discourse patterns along these lines can similarly facilitate connections across boundaries of postsecondary student learning. Some patterns and rhetorical effects I discuss in this book are genre- and level-specific, but others apply across levels, disciplines, and classrooms.

The second reason is conceptual. We know little about the constitutive power of discourse patterns in student writing in English composition studies. This is not for want of theoretical emphasis on discourse, and de-emphasizing discourse may emerge from productive dedication to context-rich genre analysis and resistance to narrowly formalistic approaches. But we have more to learn about habituated discourse that characterizes school genres and contexts. Because student writing is conceptualized according to how it is analyzed, such analysis helps expand our ideas about student writing.

The third reason is civic. We are surrounded by concerns about public discourse and calls for higher education to offer a response without sufficient knowledge about the discourse written in higher education. Discourse norms are not innocent or arbitrary, writes Anis Bawarshi, because using genres means "becoming socialized into producing not only certain kinds of texts" but also "ways of being and acting in the world, socially and rhetorically" (Bawarshi, "Genre Function" 78). Recurring discourse in student writing constructs particular ways of treating one's own and others' views, and these can remain largely tacit unless we make them explicit. In the remaining chapters, this book strives to offer new insights regarding social and rhetorical ways of being constituted by student discourse and school genres.

Notes

1. Some exceptions include composition scholarship emphasizing plagiarism, fallacies, and uncivil discourse, and curricula focused on civic learning and moral reasoning. See, e.g., V. Anderson; Cushman; Ervin; Friend; Matthews and Zimmerman; Stotsky; Tassoni and Thelin; Duffy, "Good Writer"; Scheffler; Crosswhite; D. Harrington.

2. See, e.g., Kolln and Hancock; Bacon; Micciche; Butler; Duncan and Vanguri; Ray; Barton and Stygall; Aull and Lancaster; Bazerman; Bazerman et al.; Berkenkotter and Huckin; Devitt, "Re-fusing."

3. Bernstein offers a memorable version of this idea in number 16 of his "Ninety-Five Theses": "Distant reading without reading is not reading. Close reading without toggling frames is myopia."

4. Frow uses a metaphor helpful for highlighting that genres create both rules and resources, but it especially applies to those in the position to recognize and choose among genre-specific choices: "Genre cues act rather like context sensitive drop-down menus in a software program, directing me to the layers and sublayers of information that respond to my particular and local purposes as a speaker, reader, or viewer" (1631).

5. The concordance software I use is *WordSmith Tools 6.0*, developed by Mike Scott. See the appendix for more details about keyword and stance analysis.

6. There is a rich pool of studies of stance words in academic writing that informs this discussion. See, e.g., Ädel; Barton, "Contrastive and Non-contrastive Connectives"; Crismore; Crismore and Farnsworth; Hyland, "Persuasion";

Hyland, *Disciplinary Discourses*; Hyland, *Metadiscourse*; Kuhi and Behnam; Li and Wharton; Mur-Duenas; Silver; Vande Kopple, "Some"; Vande Kopple, "Metadiscourse"; Aull and Lancaster; Hardy and Römer; Aull et al.; Hinkel, "Hedging"; Lancaster, "Exploring"; Lancaster, "Do"; Hyland and Tse). An example of stance word research focused on disciplinary differences includes work by Hyland and Hyland and Tse, which shows, for instance, that professional academic writers in the humanities use stance words that qualify their claims more frequently than academic writers in the natural sciences, which Hyland attributes to the importance of showcasing diplomatic interpretive reasoning (Hyland, "Stance"; Hyland and Tse).

7. Following Aull and Lancaster, here I view stance as encompassing both epistemic (or *interactional*) features commonly associated with stance, like hedges and boosters, as well as what have been labeled as more textual (or *interactive*) features, like adversative/contrast connectors and code glosses (e.g., in Hyland's work). In contrast, Hyland's "Stance and Engagement" uses a slightly narrower sense of stance, specifically referring to writer-oriented strategies whereby writers construct "a textual 'voice' or community recognized personality" (176).

8. In this and other tables, examples appear in italics, with target words italicized and bolded where relevant. The stance words analyzed come from the following studies that compare first-year and upper-level student writing and compile stance words from several previous studies. The counters and reformulation words are based on "Linguistic Markers of Stance" by Aull and Lancaster. The hedge and booster features, minus *always* and *never* (treated in later studies and in this study as generality words), are based on *First-Year University Writing* (Aull). The generality words are based on "Generality in Student and Expert Epistemic Stance" (Aull et al.). These articles detail the process of refining the lists of target features; e.g., to analyze generality words and boosters, negated and qualified uses were removed; e.g., *almost everyone* and *hardly everyone* were removed from analysis of the generality word *everyone*, and *not very* was removed from analysis of the booster *very*; also removed are iterations not related to stance (e.g., *percent of all* from uses of *all*).

9. A few studies have examined more directly connections between corpus patterns and writing task design in first-year writing, e.g., see Beck and Jeffery; Puma; Aull, *First-Year University Writing*.

2

School Genres

Constructing Student Writing through Assignments

I have so far suggested that student writing is understood according to how it is analyzed and constructed by how it is assessed. Chapter 1 in particular addressed the first premise by reviewing theoretical understandings of school genres and underlining the value of added attention to discourse in genre analysis. This chapter addresses the second premise by reviewing postsecondary writing assignments and identifying their distinct and shared rhetorical goals.

As constructed response tasks, assignments directly shape the writing students produce—different assignments will mean different student writing and different conclusions about student writing—and they are classroom artifacts that shed light on values and rhetorical contexts of postsecondary writing (Swales, *Genre*). This chapter's overview helps contextualize the analysis in subsequent chapters, and, consistent with those chapters, focuses on curricular, summative (grade-bearing) assignments.[1] As far as I know, this is the first overview of writing assignments in higher education that addresses first-year and upper-level assignments and draws out genres and writing constructs (valued abilities or proficiencies) across them.

The first-year and upper-level assignments I review below are documented in composition and writing-across-the-curriculum (WAC) research and standardized testing materials. The first section focuses on first-year writing and includes writing tasks from the late nineteenth and early twentieth centuries. These help historicize first-year assignments as part of a corrective response to a newly diverse student body enrolling in higher education at the time, and the first overview is informed by over a century of first-year composition curricula. The upper-level assignments, reviewed in the second section, have only more recently become an explicit focus of writing research in the United States, but WAC research and curricula provide many modern-day assignment examples. The third section offers a synthesis of first-year and upper-level writing assignments according to overall genre families, example tasks, and primary goals. The purpose of this synthesis is twofold: to build on previous attempts that have found "little consensus on what counts as central types of student writing or on how listed categories ought to be defined" (Römer and O'Donnell 168) and to delineate succinctly the two genre families of argumentative and explanatory writing analyzed in chapters 3–5.

The focus on two genre families rather than two assignments means that the analysis in the book underscores overall rhetorical aims and writing constructs that may be emphasized in a range of more specific tasks. I also strive to identify assignment goals that may be uniquely fulfilled in particular disciplines but that simultaneously relate to shared academic expectations.[2] This may be of particular importance for English composition programs because they are tasked with preparing students to write in a range of fields, even as many composition instructors are trained in literature or rhetoric. Many composition instructors, in other words, have been socialized by thinking and writing in these fields and may "mistake the genres of English studies for genres-in-general" (Wardle 769; see also Smit). This chapter does not include an exhaustive overview or critique of student writing assignments but rather provides a descriptive context for subsequent analysis, which in turn offers discourse-level insights to add to what we know about common assignment genres.

First-Year School Genres

Composition historians tend to trace the establishment of compulsory writing courses in the United States to late-nineteenth-century Harvard writing examinations (see, e.g., Berlin, *Writing*; Connors, *Composition-*

Rhetoric; S. Miller; Brereton, "Closer Look"). Textbooks and exams from that time illustrate that by 1910, rhetoric assignments shifted from oral speeches to written themes or essays required to demonstrate college-level writing (Brereton, *Origins* 437). The following example from Harvard's 1888 final writing examination tells students, "Write a short essay on one of the following subjects":

1. Baker's attitude toward the American Colonies
2. Webster's style
3. One of Miss Austen's characters
4. Scott's boyhood
5. Scott's leading characteristic as a writer (Brereton, *Origins* 444)[3]

Each example requires that students demonstrate writing skills and literary or historical knowledge, and each foregrounds human subjects in that they explicitly emphasize the work, ideas, or biography of a person. In terms of their primary rhetorical aims, tasks (1), (2), (3), and especially (4) solicit an analysis. By contrast, task (5) solicits an evaluative, arguable claim. In this way, the 1888 Harvard assignment displays two characteristics also emphasized in twentieth-century assignments. One, it foregrounds either persuasive argument, in which students take and defend a single position, or analytic explanation, in which students explain a process, historical moment, or literary text without foregrounding their own evaluation. And two, it allows students to choose either one to fulfill the same writing task.

Similarly, James Morgan Hart's 1895 *Handbook of English Composition* includes an essay task that could be either argumentative or explanatory depending on the student's choice, though it is unified under one, experiential topic. Addressing "Camping in the Adirondacks," first-year students may:

6. Describe the prominent features of lakes and rivers, woods and mountains
7. Discuss the gain to body and mind from such a trip (Brereton, *Origins* 451)

In these examples, whereas task (6) solicits descriptive analysis, task (7) solicits an evaluative argument.

The experiential focus of (6) and (7) reflects the increased use of personalized essay tasks in the early years of the twentieth century. These tasks foregrounded "a rhetorical praxis far more personal, private, [and] intimate" that "privileged the personal and sentimental" (Connors, "Personal Writing Assignments" 169). Such "personal romantic" essay tasks focused on topics such as incidents from school life or character descriptions of friends, and they reflected a shift away from nineteenth-century tasks that foregrounded impersonal topoi and synthesizing tasks such as keeping a commonplace book. They hastened an epistemological shift toward individualism in higher education curricula (169–76), and personal essay assignments had "all but complete acceptance" in 1900 (177).

But instructors had mixed responses to personal essay assignments, and by 1920, "literature and literary analysis provided a way out of the world of personal writing that made [many teachers] uncomfortable" (Connors, "Personal Writing Assignments" 179). While previously composition and literature had been kept "rigorously separate" at many institutions, the two came firmly together in such assignments (179) and in the formation of many new English departments at the time. The commingling of composition and literature continues to be visible in the employment of literature graduate students and faculty members to teach first-year writing (Berlin, *Rhetoric*; Connors, *Composition-Rhetoric*; S. Miller).

Six other examples from the nineteenth and early twentieth centuries show the shifting foci of writing tasks (toward personal and then literary ones), and they also foreground either an argumentative writing construct or an explanatory one. In contrast with the seven tasks above, only some of the following tasks presume some shared experiences or knowledge on the part of students. Each one asks for a "theme," "essay," or "essay theme."

Argument

8. Prove the maxim "Trust not appearances." (Connors, *Composition-Rhetoric* 304 [from Daniel Joudan, *Union Grammar*, 1812])
9. Discuss the idea in the following sentence: "Words, like men, have nervous prostration from overwork: they lose for a time their efficiency, their vitality; they cannot do their work, and they need rest." (Brereton, *Origins* 444 [Harvard final examination, 1888])

10. Read slowly the following extract from G. H. Palmer's *Self-Cultivation in English* [a paragraph about "literary endowment immediately recognized and eagerly envied"]. Does Mr. Palmer mean that anyone can learn to write well? How? (Brereton, *Origins* 436 [John M. Matthews and Edith Rickert, *Writing in English*, 1919])

Explanation

11. Describe the different parts of a ball game. (Brereton, *Origins* 352 [Robert Grosvenor Valentine, *Technology Review*, 1901])
12. [Discuss] the manufacture of malleable iron. (Brereton, *Origins* 492 [Franklin William Scott and Jacob Zeitlin, *College Readings in English Prose*, 1914])
13. Describe the differences between high school and college. (Brereton, *Origins* 483 [Young and Young, *Freshman English: A Manual*, 1914])

Along with reflecting both argumentative and explanatory goals, these early writing tasks imply a general (non-discipline-specific) audience, and they concern topics like human behaviors, literacy, American culture, and literature. These parameters are evidenced in later composition tasks described below, but they also highlight some broad parallels between early-twentieth-century school essays, written in composition courses, and popular magazine essays, read in composition and for leisure. Both types of essays reinforced college literacy and an accessible, generalist essay style growing in popularity at the time. By then, any intended distinction between school themes and school essays had blurred (Nunes 297–99), and the generalist essay of the early twentieth century was becoming less personal, less flexible, and more informational (Stuckey-French 49–77).

These broad but interesting parallels merit a brief digression here. As is widely documented, in the early twentieth century, mass readership periodicals helped create and fulfill the demand for affordable, accessible essay reading. Such material appeared in so-called middlebrow sources like the *Saturday Evening Post* and *Ladies Home Journal*, as well as in more established family magazines like *Harpers* and the *Atlantic* that were coming to "envy and emulate" middlebrow texts around this time (Stuckey-French 73; see also Trollinger and Kaestle). In this process, mass readership magazines were an important part of the transition from contemplative essays for a small, genteel readership to informative, generalist essays for wide circulation. (Already in 1902, Gerald Lee lamented that magazine essays were read for facts rather than principles [279–306, 319–28].) Informative, generalist essays were well suited for early-twentieth-century composition classes with a mix of learners who did not share background knowledge or possess discipline-specific training. In 1907, mass readership magazines were circulating enough that William James hinted that they formed a "new educational power" that would replace college education. Instead, mass readership essays became central to college education, at least in English composition.

Mass readership magazine essays, full of the "useful" opinions of "friendly generalists" (Stuckey-French 38), aimed to make sense of modern life (53) for an audience that Gerald Lee described was being "civili[zed] in the bulk" (Lee 52; see also Ohmann). They did so, according to Lee, by "playing upon the power of generalization" to cultivate shared convictions (298). This same universalizing appears to be a criterion for selecting canonical essays for composition courses, according to Gordon Harvey and Lynn Z. Bloom. The appeal of such essays lies in their "broadenings" or "moments of psychological generalization" (Harvey 652–53) that "narrate the experiences of a particular life in ways that can be generalized" (Bloom 415). Early twentieth century essays, in magazines and composition reading, offered a shared view of "human behavior" and "how life tends to go" (Harvey 652; see also Good).

College education was a specific topic about which mass readership magazines offered generalized advice and information: as the American middle class grew and higher education expanded, magazines helped promote and "demystify" the college experience (Stuckey-French 72). In so doing, they contributed directly to what Tom Reynolds calls the "powerful mythology" of college literacy as essential for those seeking social and cultural mobility (163). Indeed, the magazines became an important force in school and mass literacy by encouraging reading and writing and also depicting "college education as a natural next literacy step for those aspiring to employment in middle class business or professional positions" (Reynolds 164). In other words, the genre of generalist essays and the development of college writing courses in which students wrote generalist, argumentative essays were not separate: mass readership magazines appealed to a newly literate middle class and enabled them to read essays and write responses (e.g., in letters to editors); they also fortified a narrative of college literacy as essential for those seeking social and economic mobility and provided coverage of details about college. They even specifically addressed writing in composition courses. In one example, Hamilton Mabie, writer and editor for the *Ladies Home Journal*, suggested in 1908 that the emerging generalist essay was mature and evenhanded, and he encouraged students writing school themes to use a relaxed and familiar style, treating a topic as an "old friend" (Stuckey-French 64). In another example, college composition programs were debated in *Harper's* in 1911 (Roemer et al. 379).

As literacy and higher education expanded in the twentieth century, compulsory composition courses continued to be added in response to the real and imagined writing needs of a newly diverse body of college students (Berlin, *Rhetoric*; Brereton "Closer Look"; Lunsford). These courses were often taught by literature graduate students in programs also growing at the time (Berlin, *Writing*; Connors, *Composition-Rhetoric*). Writing tasks soliciting essays about canonical literature or general societal concerns were preferred assignments for these circumstances: they were easy to use for teachers untrained in composition and for students without shared background knowledge beyond literature. These assignments continued to solicit either persuasive argument or analytic explanation, as evidenced in the following tasks dating from 1920 to 1962:

14. The Advantages of Owning a Home in a Recently Developed Section of (Your Town) (Connors, "Personal Writing Assignments" 179)
15. The Character of Macbeth (Connors, "Personal Writing Assignments" 178)
16. The Role of Enobarbus in Antony and Cleopatra
17. Steps of Honor (a discussion of honor, using Brutus as a point of departure)
18. Who Was at Fault: Adam or Eve?
19. People Like It (an essay on evil)
20. Is the American Automobile Too Large?
21. Has College Spirit Faded? (Kitzhaber 30)[4]

These include explanatory tasks focused on literature, such as (15) and (16), as well as argumentative tasks that address literature and general social values (e.g., tasks 17 and 18). The final two tasks (20–21) solicit argumentative essays about general cultural developments of the time.

In Robert J. Connors's estimation, by 1920 resistance toward personal writing assignments led to the predominance of three types of assignments popular throughout the twentieth century: responses to literature, the "impersonal modes" of exposition and argument, and research papers that relied on students' finding external sources for support ("Personal Writing Assignments" 178). Still, Connors sees the continued discomfort with all of these assignments throughout the twentieth century as a reflection of instructors' "resignation about how students asked to write on political or social or educational problems" inevitably wrote in "general," "intangible," and "vague" ways ("Personal Writing Assignments" 179).

Twenty-first-century composition research shows that first-year assignments continue to reflect the three tasks noted by Connors, though they are often labeled according to academic genres. They include explanatory tasks like annotated bibliographies and argumentative tasks like argumentative essays, and essayistic argumentative writing is still particularly common (Burstein et al.; DeStigter; Haefner; Heath; Hesse; Moore and Morton; S. Miller; Dryer; Aull, "Connecting"). Argumentative essay assignments, written to demonstrate secondary learning and written language proficiency, appear to be especially common as students transition into writing in higher education (Moore and Morton; Wilcox and Jeffery) and to determine placement in college composition courses (Gere et al.; Toth and Aull). The following example tasks include assessments used to demonstrate adequate preparation for college writing and to place into specific college writing courses. These tasks provide slightly longer descriptions, and each one asks students to write an essay.

22. Drawing on one or more [perspective in Robert Kolker's "Cheating Upwards"], write an essay in which you take a position on why students cheat. (Aull, *First-Year University Writing* 58; University of Michigan writing placement, 2013)
23. Write an essay for a classroom instructor in which you take a position on whether participation in organized school athletics should be required. (Accuplacer test for college writing placement, 2016)
24. Read David Glenn's article "Divided Attention" from the *Chronicle of Higher Education*. Summarize the author's argument and evaluate the

argument's persuasiveness. (Zanders and Wilson 85, citing the University of Utah's Writing Placement)

25. Some people believe that high school classes should not begin before 9:00 a.m. Do you agree or disagree? Write an essay clearly explaining your opinion. (CAHSPE [California High School Proficiency Examination], 12th grade, October 2008)
26. Write a unified, coherent essay about the increasing presence of intelligent machines. In your essay, be sure to: clearly state your own perspective on the issue and analyze the relationship between your perspective and at least one other perspective. ("Writing Sample Essays"; ACT, 11th/12th grade, 2018)
27. Should your school participate in the national 'Shut Down Your Screen Week'?" ("Argument/Opinion"; Common Core, 11th/12th grade, 2016)
28. Write an essay in which you explain how Dana Gioia builds an argument to persuade his audience that the decline of reading in America will have a negative effect on society. ("Essay"; SAT, 11th/12th grade, 2016)

These tasks range—some pose open-ended questions, such as (22), and some emphasize reading argumentative essays, such as (24) and (28). Task (28) solicits analytic explanation; since March of 2016, the new SAT includes this kind of task, in which students are asked to analyze how an author makes an argument (rather than offer their own agreement or disagreement). Most of the tasks solicit persuasive argument and imply bivalent positions, and all the tasks solicit essays.

Argumentative essay tasks also appear in college composition courses (Crossley et al., "What"), but composition writing assignments tend to reflect, across a semester or year, an amalgam of the tasks noted above: argumentative essays; rhetorical, visual, or literary analysis; research papers; and personal (often literacy) narratives (Wardle 773). Elizabeth Wardle's study, for instance, looks closely at two assignments, the explanatory "observation assignment" and the "argument assignment." I use Wardle's summaries below.

29. For the observation assignment, teachers ask students to observe such things as a career fair, a work of art on campus, or a person working in the student's chosen field of study.

30. "The Argument" is assigned as a genre whose purpose is to write the genre. One assignment states, for example, "[T]he purpose of this position paper is to write an argument." (774–76)

Wardle critiques these assignments from an activity theory perspective, suggesting that the nature of the tasks ignore the discipline-specific ways experienced writers observe or argue (776–77).

Finally, the first-year assignments analyzed in chapter 3 come from two composition courses (a two-semester sequence) at the University of South Florida. The assignments and institution are described in detail in the next chapter but are noted here as representative composition tasks. These assignments focus on a general "global or cultural issue" selected by the students, and they include both explanatory and argumentative writing.[5] The following list includes all assignments for the two courses, and tasks (31), (33), (34), and (36) are analyzed in chapter 3.

31. Annotated bibliography: Summary of sources and explanation of connection to topic
32. What they say essay: Reviewing a topic and arguing how it has changed
33. Argumentative essay: Crafting and supporting a written argument
34. Visual analysis: Identifying and analyzing the strategies at work in two images
35. Argumentative analysis: Analyzing two opposing views and arguing for solution
36. Argumentative essay: Composing a multimodal argument

Each course contains an early explanatory assignment; in course one, the explanatory task (31) includes a review of research, and in course two, the explanatory task (34) includes a visual analysis. The midterm assignments in each course, tasks (32) and (35), solicit both explanatory and argumentative writing—the first part is explanatory, whereas the second part is argumentative. Each course then includes an argumentative assignment at the end of the term that solicits students' defense of a persuasive position (tasks 33 and 36).

Constructs in First-Year Writing

These example assignments highlight four writing constructs that have emerged in first-year writing assignments over the past century.[6] Two constructs already noted include persuasive argumentative writing and analytic explanatory writing. Another is essayistic writing. The assignments corroborate that composition writing standards favor essayistic prose valued in English studies (Dryer 28). Dylan B. Dryer suggests that although the privileging of essayistic prose "will not surprise some, given U.S. composition's typical housing in departments of English literature," the unquestioned norm is problematic: a "lack of self-consciousness about the uses, limitations, and site specificity of these conventions may be working against writers' ability to negotiate transitions to other local genres" (28). Jill Burstein, Norbert Elliot, and Hillary Molloy more unequivocally argue that the "predominant requirement of the genre of the essay remains a problematic barrier to students becoming effective writers across many genres" (Burstein et al. 134). The pervasive use of essays in school tasks can be cyclical, as first-year students draw on previous experiences as they navigate college-level courses, writing essays even if other genres are appropriate (Reiff and Bawarshi 323).

Although first-year explanatory and argumentative tasks both solicit essays, argumentative essays appear to be assigned—and also critiqued—the most.[7] Shirley Brice Heath argues that the argumentative essay in composition constructs writers "as solitary displayers of their knowledge" meant to "impel the reader to follow [their] thinking" (117) rather than to display "the multiplicity of voices and perspectives that lets readers see a mind at work" (118). Todd DeStigter suggests that writing research has focused on improving students' argumentative essays instead of questioning the rationale for their use, particularly after the popularity of Stephen Toulmin's approach to argument in the twentieth century. DeStigter more specifically asserts that the use of argumentative essays is premised on false assumptions about their connection to critical thinking and democracy (DeStigter 13; see also Haefner). This claim is echoed in recent scholarship suggesting that "the argument-based essay may be what Kenneth Burke called a 'cow path,' . . . a routine that has been retained because it has not been sufficiently questioned" (Aull and

Ross). Other compositionists question the relevance of the argumentative essay, advocating for more multimodal or discipline-specific genres, or those more common outside of first-year writing courses (Russell, "Activity"; Sullivan; Thaiss and Zawacki; Wysocki).

A fourth construct is generalist-cum-English writing: non-discipline-specific writing with hints of literary and rhetorical studies. First-year assignments tend to imply a general audience and draw attention to general topics rather than a discipline-specific lens or concern, as seen, for instance, in tasks (6)–(9), (11)–(13), and (29)–(30). Some tasks such as (10), (22), and (24) solicit a non-discipline-specific response to a general topic but focus on a piece of reading. These betray what Elizabeth Wardle describes as "a fundamental difficulty" (781) in first-year composition: students have not, and cannot yet, complete original research integral to most authentic academic writing tasks, which means they tend to write genres unique to composition itself (780–81). Some assignments invite literary analysis, such as (3)–(5) and (15), or rhetorical analysis, such as (28) and (34). As reflected in many of the assignment examples over time, like the other three constructs, this construct is at least a century old. It is worth underscoring that generalist writing is not the same as novice writing: generalist here refers not to the writer but to the audience. While some of these tasks may scaffold students' process of forming their ideas before the final assignment, many of them appear to assume that students can write authoritatively on the proposed topic; it is not clear whether they support students' need to "writ[e] their way *into* expertise" from a novice position (Sommers and Saltz 139).

Alternative approaches, including writing across the curriculum / writing in the disciplines (WID) and writing about writing (WAW), are still less common than this generalist approach but are growing (see, e.g., E. Martin; Russell, *Writing*; Thornburg; Walvoord; Thaiss and Porter). Recent research specifically brings together WAC and corpus linguistic analysis to identify linguistic and rhetorical demands across post-secondary courses (Hardy and Friginal; Hardy and Römer). An impetus for this work was the possible disconnect "between the tasks familiar to and assigned by [composition] instructors and the writing requirements across the curriculum" (Hardy and Friginal 119). Still, overall, most first-year assignments over time reflect the constructs of persuasive argumentative writing, analytic explanatory writing, essayistic prose, and generalist-cum-English writing.

Upper-Level School Genres

Whereas first-year composition is conventionally approached as a general introduction to college writing, upper-level writing has traditionally been approached as both discipline-specific and outside the main work of English composition. This means fewer studies that document the history of upper-level writing assignments, and historically, much more attention in English composition research on first-year than upper-level students. To a degree, this has changed, and there are multiple twenty-first century studies and resources designed to support student writing across the curriculum.

John C. Bean's *Engaging Ideas* aims to support instructors and students by offering alternatives to "the open-topic research paper." Open-topic assignments, Bean describes, are common but problematic because they do not offer clear specification of genre, audience, or purpose (91). Bean suggests that students confronting open-ended assignments will write "wandering" papers "rather than arguments," because the assignments do "not guide students toward formulating a problem, developing a thesis, or arguing within the conventions of a disciplinary genre" (91). Bean's first example that offers more sufficient guidance is used by a finance professor at Montana State University (90). The finance professor assigns "a series of short essays, each of which must support either the positive or the negative side of a thesis on a controversial question in finance"; for example:

> (A) The market is / is not efficient in strong-form, random-walk terms.
>
> (B) Bonds are / are not more risky investments than stocks. (90)

These examples are argumentative essay tasks in which students must defend an arguable position on general finance questions and concepts.

Bean suggests that the most common, traditional academic writing is "closed-form prose" characterized by "thesis-governed argumentation," and his descriptions repeat terms such as "argument" and "thesis." By this, Bean seems to mean that most academic writing is expository, follows a predictable organization, and coheres around a main idea, in contrast with "open form" belletristic prose that is creative and imaginative. Bean places writing assignments into two corresponding categories: the first and most common includes "thesis-governed academic writing"; the second includes "other kinds of assignments that let students write in alternative genres, often with a more personal voice and style" (Bean 91).

Though Bean's descriptions repeat the term "argument," his examples, like the first-year tasks, tend to fall into the categories of argumentative or explanatory writing. For instance, both types of tasks appear in Bean's second example assignment, which outlines four alternatives to the assignment, "Write an eight- to ten-page research paper on therapeutic touch (TT)" (92).

> (C) Research the professional literature on TT, looking especially for evidence-based studies. Then write a four- to five-page argument, addressed to the hospital governing board, supporting or attaching the board's decision to forbid the practice of TT.
>
> (D) Research the current professional literature on TT and write the "review of literature" section of [a] grant proposal.
>
> (E) Choose one [empirical study of TT]. Write a critical review of your selected article in which you (1) summarize the purpose, method, and results of the study . . . and (2) write a critical review of the article in which you analyze the extent to which it provides or doesn't provide a scientific basis for regarding [TT] as evidence-based medicine.
>
> (F) Write an eight- to ten-page exploratory research paper that describes chronologically your own search for a personal answer to [the question *should schools of nursing and major nursing organizations give their imprimatur to therapeutic touch?*]. The paper should start with a reflection on where you stood on this issue before you began your research, and why. . . . Then write a first-person, reflective narrative of your thinking process as you investigated your question. (92–94)

The first two examples above focus on one genre family: (C) is an argumentative task, whereas (D) is an explanatory task. Bean explains that (C) and (D) are "important real-world genres" and that (C) solicits a "civic argument" and "thesis," whereas (D), which is not described in terms of a thesis, is an academic genre that "invites inquiry" (94). To me, task (E) includes both explanatory and argumentative writing in a two-part paper; interestingly, Bean and faculty members responding to these options perceive (E) as the "most basic," teaching "the skills of summary and critical analysis needed for any of the more difficult options" (95). Finally, example (F) includes personal, reflective writing, which is not emphasized in this book but does appear in upper-level life science assignments sometimes called "empathy writing" (Lea and Street 162; Nesi and Gardner 42). Bean likens task (F) to a personal essay and suggests it "rewards uncertainty and inquiry" (93) more than tasks (C), (D), and (E).

Dan Melzer's recent large-scale survey of writing assignments explores a "panorama" of 2,100 assignment tasks from four hundred undergraduate courses across disciplines: one hundred courses in each of the following disciplines: natural and applied sciences; social sciences; business; and arts and humanities.[8] The two most common assignment genres that Melzer observes are the research paper and the short answer exam. Research papers focus on "becoming familiar, learning referencing techniques, gleaning information, summarizing information, and practicing scientific writing format" (W252). The examples he presents offer students a choice between argumentative or explanatory tasks, with more options constructing the latter. For instance, the following psychology research paper assignment offers a range of options for students to choose from:

> (G) A cross-cultural comparison on some topic of interest in psychology as well as another discipline (e.g., family structure, ceremonies and/or rituals . . .). Discuss how cross-cultural differences and similarities would be viewed and handled from the perspectives of a psychologist and a professional from the other field.
>
> (H) A report of the cross-cultural psychological observations you made in a place where you had exposure to another culture (e.g. a church, a theatre, a refugee center, an office) while being involved in an activity/job related to other disciplines (e.g. religion, art, social work, business administration).
>
> (I) A critique of your own major or minor field of study (if you are not a psychology major or minor) from the point of view of cross cultural psychology. You might discuss how inclusive and culturally sensitive the field of study is, citing specific research and theoretical examples.

> (J) An analysis of a movie, a piece of music, or some literature from another culture. Using our textbook information, explain how the concepts in the text are depicted in the piece you are analyzing and/or how the piece can be explained by some of the concepts in the text. (253–54)

In these examples, tasks (G), (H), and (J), emphasize analytic explanation, whereas (I) solicits a persuasive critique, an argumentative genre that Sunny Hyon describes as unfamiliar and challenging for many undergraduate students (87). Task (H) seems to parallel the "observation assignment" in Wardle's first-year assignments noted in the previous section. Based on the survey results, Melzer underscores that students are expected to engage a range of writing that depends on their courses, and he recommends "moving away from traditional, thesis-driven research papers and by teaching students to analyze and respond to multiple genres" (W259). He also concludes that writing-across-the-curriculum courses, which included more attention to writing and writing assignments than more traditional disciplinary courses, "certainly had a positive influence" on instructors (W258) and were a "powerful antidote" (W259) to limited uses of writing he observed in many upper-level courses.

Another survey study, conducted by Burstein, Elliot, and Molloy, solicited two kinds of information about writing assignments: first, common writing tasks in school and workplace settings, and second, perceived preparedness of students for writing tasks in those settings. Their conclusions are based on feedback from approximately seven hundred workplace, college, and K–12 educators and professionals. The study indicates that the following tasks were among those required significantly more often in college than in K–12 education or the workplace (though "business letters" were often required in the workplace):

> (K) abstract
> (L) academic e-mail
> (M) cover letter
> (N) research proposal (123)

In the study, these task descriptions do not include a great deal of detail, but (K) and (L) seem conventionally explanatory, whereas (M) may include a persuasive argument. Proposal tasks like (N) are also noted in

Bean's study ([D] grant proposals) and are likewise noted below as a common business course assignment. Such proposal tasks arguably include explanatory writing expectations, for example, a review of relevant research, as well as argumentative writing expectations, for example, a discussion of the value of the proposed research or idea. Burstein et al. point out that, along with annotated bibliographies, research proposals were among the "prevalent writing genres that faculty indicated that students were *least prepared* to undertake" (128; emphasis theirs).

Burstein et al.'s survey study also notes that the following tasks are among those required significantly more often in the workplace than in college:

(O) executive summary
(P) performance review
(Q) memo (125)

In these workplace genres, (O) and (Q) emphasize explanatory writing, whereas (P) solicits an evaluative argument. Task (P) is also listed in the archive of University of Maryland writing assignments reviewed next.

The University of Maryland English department's assignment archive offers another writing-across-the-curriculum resource ("Writing Assignments"). Aimed at supporting faculty members, this archive offers a list of thirty-five writing tasks accompanied by a brief description that includes the purpose and associated disciplines for each task.[9] Several assignments in the list are formative tasks, including annotations, group-project reports, note-taking, and reflective papers. The summative, grade-bearing assignments (the focus of this book) include both argumentative and explanatory tasks. For instance, explanatory tasks (R) through (X) below encourage students to "integrate and analyze" material, or to "identify and synthesize the main threads" while "reserving judgment." The language in these tasks seems to anticipate a preference for assigning argument; it notes, "it is often useful for students to detail the parameters of a discussion and to assess what is at stake from various perspectives" other than their own ("Writing Assignments"):

(R) analysis of a book review
(S) annotated bibliography
(T) book or article review

(U) review of the literature
(V) case study
(W) "translation" paper [i.e., a translation of a specialized text for a lay audience]
(X) professional article ("Writing Assignments")

Other tasks construct argumentative writing, including examples (Y) through (AA) below. These, by contrast are "evaluative" and "compel students to draw conclusions and take a stand":

(Y) newspaper commentary
(Z) letter to the editor
(AA) Web site review ("Writing Assignments")

The Web site likewise notes "appropriate discipline(s)" for the tasks; for instance, the "analysis of book review" is listed as pertaining to all disciplines, whereas the "position paper" is listed as pertaining to disciplines in humanities, social science, and education.

Research focused on individual college programs also offers examples of upper-level assignments. Wei Zhu's study of writing assignments in undergraduate and graduate-level business courses at a large research university reflects several of the aforementioned tasks. Like the University of Maryland's archive, for instance, Zhu notes case analyses, article and book reports, research papers, and reflection papers (118). Additionally, like Burstein et al.'s survey, Zhu's study notes "research proposal" assignments; in Zhu's study, the "research proposal" and "research paper" assignments are similar and are explanatory. Zhu calls these "empirical research" assignments and describes that students "were asked to present the research topic and questions, review related research literature, describe research methodology, and if the students had carried out the research, report the findings and discuss the results" (119). Research proposals were assigned less often and with less weight than reports and business proposals, which was the second type of proposal assignment Zhu documents:

(BB) business proposal (118)

Business proposal assignments, also referred to as "business plans" and "marketing plans," appear to include both explanatory and argumentative writing, but in delineated sections. They expect students to "describe and analyze the business/marketing situation, identify the specific goals and/or objectives of the company or the marketing program, and present strategies to be adopted to achieve the proposed goals and/or objectives" (121).

Another study that details assignments in a university context is that of Mya Poe, Neal Lerner, and Jennifer Craig, whose analysis of science and engineering writing at the Massachusetts Institute of Technology (MIT) likewise indicates the use of the aforementioned tasks, though they note that the writing assignments they observed reflected the influence of both professional and school genres. On the one hand, some writing tasks "call for students to assume identities as scientists or engineers" as they respond to assignments largely modeled after professional genres (Poe et al., *Learning* 19). These "apprenticeship activities" include a "grant proposal" and "research article" (19) like (N) and (W) above. To the research article genre, Poe et al. connect the following course goal from an Introduction to Experimental Biology and Communication class: "Understand the seven components (title, abstract, introduction, methods, results, discussion/conclusion, tables/figures) of a laboratory research paper" (22). On the other hand, the authors note that, alongside professional goals, "the powerful influences of schooling were consistent factors," including "the mixed messages they might receive for the goals of the assignment, or the varied audiences for whom they are writing" (20–21). A key conclusion for Poe et al. was that "[s]tudents who could imagine the audience's needs for their writing and connect that writing to past texts and future texts tended to have more success" (48).

Zak Lancaster's case study of upper-level writing in economics at the University of Michigan showcases a two-part explanatory and argumentative task that parallels (E) and (BB) above. The assignment requires that students analyze and describe an antitrust case and then argue for remedies to it:

> (CC) Choose an antitrust case with interesting economic and policy implications and then analyze the economic effects of the courts' decisions, including how and why the structure, conduct, and performance of the relevant markets may have changed after the court ruling. Then, argue for alternative legal remedies. ("Exploring" 41)

This upper-level economics assignment explicitly delineates a section emphasizing analytic explanation, followed by one emphasizing persuasive argument.

Finally, the Educational Testing Service (ETS) GRE General Test, which students take to qualify for graduate-level education, includes two writing tasks. These are concisely referred to as "the Issue Task" and "the Argument Task." Rather counter-intuitively, the former is an argumentative task, in which students write a persuasive argument, whereas the latter is an explanatory task in which students analyze an argument. Both ask for responses to a statement or statements, which are italicized in the examples below:[10]

(DD) Issue Task: *As people rely more and more on technology to solve problems, the ability of humans to think for themselves will surely deteriorate.*
Discuss the extent to which you agree or disagree with the statement and explain your reasoning for the position you take. In developing and supporting your position, you should consider ways in which the statement might or might not hold true and explain how these considerations shape your position.

(EE) Argument Task: *In surveys Mason City residents rank water sports (swimming, boating and fishing) among their favorite recreational activities. The Mason River flowing through the city is rarely used for these pursuits, however, and the city park department devotes little of its budget to maintaining riverside recreational facilities. For years there have been complaints from residents about the quality of the river's water and the river's smell. In response, the state has recently announced plans to clean up Mason River. Use of the river for water sports is therefore sure to increase. The city government should for that reason devote more money in this year's budget to riverside recreational facilities.*
Write a response in which you examine the stated and unstated assumptions of the argument. Be sure to explain how the argument depends on the assumptions and what the implications are if the assumptions prove unwarranted. ("Overview")

The GRE Web site further distinguishes these tasks by including the following description of the argument task: "You are not being asked to discuss whether the statements in the argument are true or accurate. You are not being asked to agree or disagree with the position stated. You are not being asked to express your own views on the subject being discussed (as you were in the Issue task)" ("Overview").

Constructs in Upper-Level Writing

As in first-year tasks, two upper-level constructs include argumentative writing and explanatory writing. Often, these appear in separate assignments, but they also appear in single assignments that specify students should practice both in separate sections. In addition, three constructs emphasized in upper-level writing are not emphasized in first-year assignments. One, unsurprisingly, is disciplinary specificity. Upper-level assignments tend to address discipline-specific concerns that require discipline-specific knowledge, whether or not upper-level writers are writing for a specialized audience.

Another upper-level construct is genre variability. Upper-level assignments show a greater range of genres and fewer essays. Some upper-level genres, including proposals, critiques, and case studies, do not appear in first-year examples. A third upper-level construct is the use of original research in genres such as case studies and grant proposals. In undergraduate courses, assignments including original research are relatively rare but sometimes assigned, and they increase in graduate-level courses (Römer and O'Donnell 173; Melzer W252).

School Genres in Higher Education

Even as research discussed in this chapter calls for detailed assignment descriptions for students, it can be challenging and rare for instructors to clarify parallels and distinctions between their own and other postsecondary writing assignments. Identifying overall genre families like persuasive argument and analytic explanation offers one way to highlight rhetorical aims across a range of assignments, both to make those aims more explicit and to highlight expectations that do and do not transfer across them.

To this end, two tables below bring together examples and genre families noted in this chapter, building as well on assignment descriptions by Ute Römer and Matthew Brook O'Donnell; and Hilary Nesi and Sheena Gardner. The tables are not exhaustive, but they synthesize common assignments according to genre family, genre, macrolevel purposes and characteristics, and example tasks. Table 3 addresses persuasive argumentative writing, whereas table 4 addresses analytic explanatory writing.

The genre family labels used here—persuasive argumentative writing and analytic explanatory writing—are clearly not as common as terms such as *argumentative essay* or *research paper*, but perhaps they would help foreground key expectations in assignment descriptions. "A discourse community's nomenclature for genres is an important source of insight," John M. Swales suggests in *Genre Analysis* (54). If students confront the range of assignment tasks noted in this chapter, they may reasonably be flummoxed by a label like *research paper*, which they may associate with inapplicable, prior discursive practices such as those from secondary school. Likewise, if instructors expect students to review existing research and propose an intervention to it, a description that indicates the assignment includes both explanatory and argumentative writing may be more clear than a label such as *argumentative essay*.

The ability of instructors and students to identify genre families, in other words, may highlight an assignment's principle rhetorical aims and

Table 3. Argumentative Writing in Higher Education

	SCHOOL GENRE FAMILY: PERSUASIVE ARGUMENTATIVE WRITING	
	ARGUMENTATIVE ESSAY	CRITIQUE/EVALUATION
Rhetorical Purpose	Demonstrates and develops ability to construct individual, persuasive argument on a topic supported with evidence/examples	Demonstrates and develops ability to construct individual, supported, persuasive critique of existing source or view
Rhetorical Characteristics	Text driven by arguable claim intended to persuade Arguments supported by evidence from source(s) described in light of the persuasive argument Aims to generate new idea or view adopted by audience	Text driven by argument aiming to persuade audience of particular response, evaluation and/or solution Arguments supported by evidence from source(s) critiqued Aims to generate new response/ evaluation
Genre Network / Example Tasks	Argumentative essay, editorial, position paper, promotional section of proposal	Evaluation of business practices, study, or problem, book review, article review, Web site review, performance review

Table 4. Explanatory Writing in Higher Education

	SCHOOL GENRE FAMILY: ANALYTIC EXPLANATORY WRITING			
	Rhetorical analysis	Research review	Report	Research paper
Rhetorical Purpose	Demonstrates and develops understanding and analysis of visual, audio, and/or textual objects and ability to describe them and their significance	Demonstrates and develops understanding and analysis of existing studies and perspectives and ability to describe them and their significance	Demonstrates and develops understanding of process or phenomenon and ability to describe its value, e.g., account of a problem/ issue/text, and/or how to carry out a procedure	Demonstrates and develops understanding of how to conduct and/or present original research in a field
Rhetorical Characteristics	Describes, analyzes visual, audio, and/or textual artifacts Description and analysis supported by examples from source(s) analyzed	Describes, analyzes sources Description and analysis supported by evidence/examples from source(s) analyzed	Explains process or phenomenon and its significance	Answers research question(s) Contains original data, or compiles existing data in new way Selection and description of data/sources supported by rationale and/or evidence Structured into sections (usually with subheadings, e.g., literature review, methods, results, discussion, conclusion)
Genre Network / Example Tasks	Visual analysis, rhetorical analysis	Annotated bibliography, literature review, comparison or synthesis of sources, review section of proposal	Research report, lab report, business report	Research paper, replication study

in turn mitigate the force of prior experiences that do not apply. Identifying genre families rather than individual tasks alone may furthermore help us support a flexible framework for assignment design—for designing tasks that fulfill instructor goals and, simultaneously, help students develop discursive identities that may or may not fit into existing academic or disciplinary genre categories (Poe et al., *Learning* 37). Genre families may also help students connect rhetorical aims between conventional academic assignments and increasingly common multimodal (auditory, visual, digital, etc.) tasks that students encounter in and beyond postsecondary courses (see, e.g., Wysocki; S. Harrington et al.). The next three chapters strive to elucidate further the rhetorical aims of explanatory and argumentative writing in light of patterned discourse.

Notes

1. This excludes more formative assessments, often used in the process of a course or larger assignment, such as "exercises" or "response papers" that are part of homework (Nesi and Gardner 36; Römer and O'Donnell 171). I use *task*, the term more often used in assessment research, and *assignment*, more often used by instructors, interchangeably in this chapter.

2. This goal is similar to the aim in systemic functional linguistics research on instructional *macrogenres*, such as narratives, evaluations, and explanations (Grabe; J. Martin, "Genre").

3. Further first-year examples tasks from the late nineteenth and early twentieth centuries can be found in Brereton, *Origins*, and in Brereton's more recent work on the Harvard entrance examination (Brereton, "Closer Look").

4. Tasks 16–21 appear in Kitzhaber's national survey (30). In the survey, approximately 75% of college students in the United States were placed into standard composition courses, wherein it was "fairly common practice" to require personal narrative writing at the start of the course (22). The first semester was commonly devoted to language study and the second to literature (though one-quarter focused the second course on rhetoric or logic). In addition to "a lot of impromptu writing" (25), weekly papers were common. Kitzhaber's description of weekly writing assignments also implies the primary goal of explanation versus argument: "Papers are customarily assigned at the rate of one a week, though written exercises of one kind or another may come more often. . . .

Topics generally are pointed toward the student's own experience and call for simple narrative or expository treatment" (19). Kitzhaber also documents more occasional examples, including narrative sketches, dramatic skits, or letters to hypothetical editors and members of congress (30).

5. See usflearn.instructure.com/courses/813386. The assignments are also described in detail in Aull, "Corpus."

6. Writing more broadly is a construct, but other more specific constructs in academic writing are also used to ensure that assignments have construct validity, meaning that a task reflects the behavior in the area being examined and measured. See, e.g., Poe; Slomp; Poe et al., *Writing*.

7. As early as 1842, G. Graham critiqued the use of freshman themes in a description that likens them to argumentative essays: "It has been argued that the *theme* is useful in a moral point of view, as it leads the young to reflect upon the nature and effects of right and wrong. . . . I do not believe that all the themes that were ever written have contributed to effect the least moral improvement in any one of the children who composed them" (13).

8. Melzer's main goal is to consider the assignments through the lenses of writing to learn and writing in the disciplines, whereas I apply his findings in order to identify common upper-level genres. Melzer's own classifications follow: up to 83% of them are *transactional writing*, within which most assignments (66%) are "informative rather than persuasive." Whereas 13% of the writing is "exploratory," "poetic writing and expressive writing are almost non-existent" (W245).

9. See more examples in the University of Maryland archive, "Writing Assignments across the Curriculum."

10. For more GRE general entrance exam tasks, see "Prepare."

3

Student Discourse in First-Year Genres

Assigning First-Year Writing

We can see in the composition curriculum of today the vestiges of its early development. Many colleges in the United States still approach composition courses as compulsory introductions to general academic writing. Most first-year assignments are designed and evaluated by instructors trained in English departments, and many reflect long-standing first-year writing constructs. These courses and assignments are often perceived as providing, if not remediation for missing writing preparation, then a foundation for writing in any field students pursue.

The feasibility of preparing composition students for writing in a range of fields is debatable, not least because composition carries its own disciplinary heritage visible in the assignments reviewed in chapter 2. As students write in first-year courses, they begin (consciously or not) to adopt the disciplinary ways of writing foregrounded in those courses, which "may facilitate their further studies within that discipline, but conversely, may disadvantage them in an unfamiliar disciplinary context" (North 449). Russell shows that unsuccessful undergraduates approached writing tasks "in terms of motives and goals more similar to genres in English classes," whereas successful graduate student writers succeeded "because they had appropriated the motives, goals, and genres" of their disciplines ("Rethinking" 233). To help mitigate this issue, some composition scholars encourage explicit instruction of academic discourse conventions (Bartholomae; Bizzell; Fahnestock and Secor; S. Mac-

Donald, *Professional Academic Writing*), and rhetorical genre scholars propose emphasizing genre analysis and awareness in composition rather than teaching particular genres (see, e.g., Devitt, *Writing*; Bawarshi, "Sites"; Bawarshi and Reiff). But in many cases discipline-specific and other norms in written discourse remain tacit to instructors themselves (Wilder and Wolfe; Lancaster, "Exploring").

Contemporary composition assignments furthermore reflect the tension between assignment tradition and innovation. Among others, Heath questions whether the "legacy" of the argumentative essay "is what we would choose for today's increasingly diverse student population" (107). Several studies advocate for more various and real-world assignment tasks (Burstein et al.; Bean; Melzer). Yet as shown in the previous chapter, many first-year assignments continue to solicit essays, often argumentative ones, and writing assignment descriptions that rely on terms such as *argumentative essay* may cue previous but inapplicable experiences for student writers; as with any assignment descriptions, these details cue particular choices and not others (Bawarshi, *Genre* 127). Many instructors, untrained in assignment design, remain unaware of the interpretive argument of different approaches to assessment (Elliot and Williamson; Kane; Poe; Aull "Corpus"; Aull "Tools") and reasonably rely on tradition as they design and describe writing assignments for students.

The above challenges related to composition assignment design—the expectation that composition courses will prepare students for many genres and disciplines, and institutionalized assignment norms—underscore the value of analysis that exposes expectations across assignments. This chapter offers a corpus linguistic and close textual analysis of first-year writing across the two common genre families delineated in chapter 2, persuasive argumentative and analytic explanatory writing, and, unique to many corpus-based studies, it is informed by assignment descriptions and rubrics.

First-Year Writing Context

The corpus of papers analyzed in this chapter was compiled in 2016 with support from a National Science Foundation (NSF) award ("Collaborative

Research"; see also Aull, "Corpus").[1] The essays were written by first-year composition students at the University of South Florida (USF), a large state institution serving a diverse student body.[2] Of the approximately 30,300 undergraduates and 9,700 graduate students enrolled at USF, 55% are identified as female, 45% as male, and the majority of students are identified as "white," "Hispanic / Latino/a," and "black or African American." Three-quarters of the students attend full-time, whereas the remaining attend part-time, often balancing work and school. Approximately 7% are categorized as international students, just above the national average (see "About USF" and *America's Best Value Colleges*, "University of South Florida").[3] In the 2019 *U.S. News and World Report* rankings, USF ranked number 124 according to *Best Colleges and National Universities* ("University of South Florida").

As in many colleges and universities in the United States, most USF students take composition (except those who transfer or receive exemption through AP credit), and the first-year composition courses at USF are housed in the English department. These courses, like the university, are characterized by a diverse body of students, and they are taught by a blend of full-time, graduate-student, and adjunct instructors, suggesting the USF composition program approximates many composition programs in the United States today (CCCC, "Statement").[4] The program enrolls approximately 4,500 undergraduate students each year in two standardized courses: Composition 1 and Composition 2.[5] At USF, most first-year students take Composition 1 and 2 in sequence, meaning that students in both courses can be considered first-year college writers but that the students in Composition 2 have slightly more experience. The first-year papers analyzed in this book are those that received A-graded papers in both courses and were therefore considered exemplary by course instructors across sections.

First-Year School Genres

As noted in chapter 2, all the composition assignments focus on a general global or cultural issue selected by the students, but two are argumentative and two are explanatory. The first writing assignment in Composition 1 is an annotated bibliography, or an analytic explanation of six recent research articles that address the issue selected by the student. The assignment description states, "Each entry will include an analysis of the article's rhetorical situation, succinct summary of the ideas contained in the source, and discussion of each article's historical context." The rubric categories of analysis and evidence indicate that the task should provide an "explanatory summary and analysis" of each source that shows adequate "focus on topic/issue" (Aull, "Corpus" 44–45).[6] This genre fits under the category of the *research review* genre described in chapter 2 (table 4), which has a primary rhetorical purpose of demonstrating understanding and analysis of existing studies and perspectives as well as the ability to describe them and their significance.

The final task in Composition 1 is an argumentative essay; it prioritizes students' defense of their own "evidence-based argument." The task is titled "Argumentative Essay: Joining the Conversation and Presenting My Argument," and the assignment description notes that students will "generate an arguable claim and write a 1,000–1,200 word academic essay to support that claim, based on providing background, including evidence, and explain[ing] and refut[ing]" counterclaims. While the annotated bibliography rubric does not mention an "arguable claim," the argumentative essay rubric emphasizes an "arguable claim" fifteen times, especially vis-à-vis how well it is developed and supported. The assignment shares qualities with argumentative tasks in which students are expected to develop their ability to construct an individual, persuasive argument on a topic and support it with evidence or examples, as described in chapter 2 (table 3).

Like the first composition course, Composition 2 includes an initial explanatory task and a final argumentative essay task. The first assignment is a rhetorical analysis of a visual argument. Students select a "stakeholder," or an "organization or individual with a vested interest," and then must "choose two specific images created by the organization (i.e. advertisements, PSAs, or static images used on a website, flyer, billboard, etc.), and analyze how these visual arguments reflect the organization's goals." Like the annotated bibliography rubric, the visual analysis rubric emphasizes explanatory writing; it does not mention argument or "arguable claims" and instead focuses on how well the project "explains the relationship between visual rhetoric in images and stakeholder's goals" (Aull, "Corpus" 44–45). This distinction highlights the difference between assignments that analyze visual arguments, versus those that produce their own visual arguments (George). Like the annotated bibliography assignment, the visual analysis assignment asks students to develop, demonstrate, and articulate their understanding of an object and its significance. It fits under the rhetorical analysis genres described in chapter 2 (table 4).

The final assignment in Composition 2 includes a multimodal argument with an argumentative essay. The following is the main description for the "formal essay" part of the assignment, which casts the assignment as an argumentative task:

> You will compose an argumentative essay of 1200–1400 words that (a) educates an audience of non-engaged stakeholders about the issue or topic; (b) engages the audience by convincing them that they should care about this issue or topic; and (c) empowers the audience to take action in some way. By the conclusion of the essay, the audience should feel both engaged with the topic and empowered to act. (Aull, "Corpus")

As in the Composition 1 course, the rubric for this task repeatedly emphasizes the students' "arguable claims" (noted twelve times), which should be persuasive and adequately supported with appropriate sources.

These three tasks—a review of research, a rhetorical analysis of visual texts, and an argumentative essay—appear common in composition assignments in the United States reviewed in chapter 2. The assignment details reflect the two genre families of argumentative writing and explanatory writing: the essay assignments solicit argumentative writing that foregrounds crafting and defending a persuasive position, and the annotated bibliography and visual analysis assignments solicit explanatory writing that foregrounds explicating the details and significance of objects of analysis. Because the writing analyzed is A-graded, the discourse patterns indicate what the instructors positively associate with each genre family.

Also notable is that the assignment sequence places research review and analysis tasks as precursors to a final, argumentative essay assignment. As in many composition courses, this sequence suggests argumentative writing is the summative rhetorical aim of first-year writing.

Table 5. First-Year Corpus Details

GENRE FAMILY	ARGUMENTATIVE WRITING		EXPLANATORY WRITING	
GENRE	ARGUMENTATIVE ESSAY	ARGUMENTATIVE ESSAY	ANNOTATED BIBLIOGRAPHY	VISUAL ANALYSIS
Number of Texts	101	230	76	215
Words per Text	~1,271	~1,248	~1,840	~1,436
Course and Sequence	Course 1, final project	Course 2, final project	Course 1, first project	Course 2, first project
Total Number of Texts	331		291	
Total Number of Words	414,247		393,077	
Reference Corpus for Comparative Analysis	Annotated Bibliography + Visual Analysis (291 texts)		Argumentative Essay + Argumentative Essay (331 texts)	

Table 5 notes the overall details about the first-year writing corpus analyzed in the next sections.[7]

First-Year Writing Analysis

To explore what distinguishes first-year explanatory and argumentative writing, I draw on the methods outlined in chapter 1, corpus linguistic analysis and close textual analysis of keyword and stance word patterns. The keyword analysis highlights the recurring lexical and grammatical choices first-year students make in argumentative and explanatory writing; the word frequency analysis highlights stance word patterns in each genre family. In the sections below, I discuss both the discourse patterns across texts as well as example passages that illustrate their use by individual students. All the keyword patterns I describe are persistent and significant: each one appears in at least 90% of the texts analyzed, and they appear with statistically significant frequency. All the stance word patterns I describe are likewise persistent, but I specify which patterns are and are not statistically significant.

Analysis I: What Keyword Patterns Distinguish First-Year Argumentative and Explanatory Writing?

Given the rhetorical aims of argumentative writing and explanatory writing, some distinctions discussed below seem straightforward. First-year argumentative writing, for instance, includes significantly more persuasive, modal verbs (*can*, *will*, *should*), whereas first-year explanatory writing uses more neutral, descriptive verbs (*shows*, *uses*, *makes*). Other distinctions I did not expect. For example, argumentative writing contains a wider range of grammatical patterns—several kinds of verbs, adverbs, prepositions, determiners, pronouns, and conjunctions marking dependent clauses—but is in many ways simpler. First-year argumentative writing contains simple, common nouns, which often emphasize people in large groups. It also contains dependent clauses, which tend to spell out detail. These findings corroborate those found in academic writing in England (Staples et al.). In this way, argumentative writing probably feels more familiar than explanatory writing to many first-year students, because dependent clauses are a common way of adding detail in conversational language use. By contrast, the first-year explanatory writing contains more syntactically dense noun phrases.

These overall patterns can be difficult to visualize without examples, so before considering the list of key discourse features in tables 6 and 7, consider brief paragraphs that exhibit several of the patterns. As is clear in later examples, these two passages are representative of first-year argumentative and explanatory writing in the study. I selected these and subsequent examples because they show several first-year, genre-specific patterns in a single passage.

The following passage from a first-year student's argumentative essay displays the grammatical variety highlighted in the argumentative discourse patterns. In the example, the first grammatical subject of each sentence is underlined to help show points of emphasis:

> Each and every day <u>the lives of these animals</u> are put in danger for the market of producers and consumers who demand these body parts. When <u>poachers</u> hunt the wild animals, a majority of the animals are left for dead because of the cruel attempts at accessing the body parts. <u>The poachers</u> use militarized weaponry to target and attack the animals, which allows them not to get caught.

In this passage, even the beginnings of the sentences reflect grammatical variety: the first sentence begins with an adverbial prepositional phrase, the second with a dependent clause, and the third with a noun phrase. This example also includes multiple types of verbs used to persuade, for instance, modal verbs like *can*, *will*, and *should* and infinitive verbs such as *to be*, *to help*, *can make*, and *cannot make*. The grammatical subjects highlight simple, common nouns, in this case, focused on animals and poachers. These subjects, combined with other argumentative patterns, facilitate an urgent narrative: infinitive verbs (*to target*, *[to] attack*) and lexical verbs (*demand*, *hunt*) convey actions and needs; and common nouns (*day*, *lives*, *parts*) convey the general, pervasive nature of the problem. Here and across first-year argumentative writing, causal relationships and implications are emphasized explicitly through subordinate clauses, in this case, beginning with *when* and *because*. Likewise, the use of *not* in the final dependent clause exhibits the common argumentative choice of explicitly showing negation and contrast.

By contrast, explanatory patterns show less grammatical variety but more syntactic density: first-year explanatory writing is characterized by more elements of compressed (or syntactically dense) noun and prepositional phrases. These create a more informational style. Consider the following short passage from a first-year visual analysis that includes most explanatory patterns:

> The United States Agency (USADA), a top organization, is against drug use in sports. They claim that using steroids and other medications lowers the values and honor of the true sport and has serious harmful effects on health (USADA). Therefore, the USADA makes a commitment to maintain the integrity of competition and protect the rights of professional athletes.

In this explanatory passage, several choices facilitate description of the USADA's stance on doping in sports. These include several components of complex noun phrases, including articles (*the*), nouns (e.g., *organization*, *honor*, *effects*, *integrity*, *rights*), and prepositional phrases (***in*** *sports*, ***on*** *health*, ***of*** *competition*, ***of*** *professional athletes*). Whereas the earlier argumentative passage focused on the relation between subjects in the passage (*poachers* and *animals*), this passage describes the USADA's stance through dependent clauses (*that using steroids and other medications*) and lexical reporting verbs (*claim*, *makes*). The final sentence contains

Table 6. Keyword Patterns in First-Year Argumentative Writing

KEYWORD PATTERNS	COMMON ITERATIONS AND COLLOCATIONS
Modal verbs	[noun or pronoun] **can/will/should/would** *[be/not/have]*
Infinitive verbs	*[to/can/not]* **help/make/get**
Infinitive **to be** verbs	*[to/can/should/not]* **be** *a*, **be** *the*, **be** *used*
Negation	*is* **not**, *do* **not**, *are* **not/n't**, **not** *only*, **not** *be*, **not** *have*
Can as modal verb	*people* **can** *be*, **can** *not*, **can** *have*, **can** *help*
For as preposition	[singular or plural noun] **for** *the future*, *responsible* **for**, *in order* **for**
Are as main verb	*they* **are**, *there* **are** *not*, *there* **are** *many*
Have as base verb and infinitive verb	*to* **have** *[a]*, *they* **have** *[been]*, *not* **have** *[to]*
Adverb (general)	**also/only/however/even**
After- or postdeterminer	**some/any/enough** *[of/people]*
Common nouns	*people* (~67% of common nouns), *media*
Subordinating conjunction	**because** *they are*, **because** *it is*, **when** *it comes to*
More as determiner or adverb*	[infinitive verb] **more** *than*, **more** *people*, **more** *likely*
Or as coordinating conjunction	*whether* **or** *not*, **or** *even*, *his* **or** *her*
These as determiner and pronoun	*[of]* **these** *animals*, **these** *are*, **these** *companies*
Adjective (general)	**other/social/human/new** *[and/the/health/people]*
But as countering conjunction	**but** *also*, **but** *the*, **but** *it*, **but** *they*
Degree adverb	*[it is]* **very/as/so/too**
Prepositional adverb in phrasal verb	*go* **on** / *stand* **up** / stand **out** / *end* **up**

* Keyword patterns of **more** in more detail: comparative after-determiner (42%), comparative degree adverb (41%), or comparative adverb (17%).

syntactically dense, embedded prepositional and noun phrases characteristic of first-year explanatory writing. Here, the noun phrases appear in parentheses with the embedded prepositional phrases in brackets: (*the integrity [of competition], the rights [of professional athletes]*).

The Distant View: Key Discourse across First-Year Texts

Now consider lists of all the key discourse patterns in each genre family. First, table 6 displays highly significant patterns in first-year argumentative writing relative to first-year explanatory writing, with the most significant keyword patterns appearing at the top.[8] The right-hand column lists the most frequent uses of each pattern, with additional detail provided parenthetically. These lists provide an overall view of the uses illustrated in example passages above and below, but they emphasize that these same choices persist in each genre family despite differences in individual student's writing or in specific course sections.

These discourse patterns shared across texts and contexts indicate that first-year argumentative writing shares qualities with relatively persuasive and conversational language use (see Staples et al.; Biber et al., "Speaking"), including adverbs and causative subordinating conjunctions characteristic of online blogging and discussion (Biber and Egbert). Several argumentative discourse patterns facilitate comparing and contrasting, including negation, conjunctions *but* and *or*, and *more* as a determiner or adverb. Usually more common in conversation than in academic writing, generic nouns are also frequent; the majority of the nouns refer to *people* without any modifiers (12.4% are modified by adjectives, e.g., *homeless people*, *American people*). In most first-year argumentative writing, the noun *people* collocates (or co-occurs) to the left of definitive or intensified verbs—for example, students write *people* ***are***, *people* ***will***, and *people* ***should***—and to the right of determiners *many* and *most*. These argumentative discourse patterns encourage general predictions and speculations about human behaviors.

Also of note is that argumentative discourse is characterized by more dependent clauses, which help draw explicit attention to relations between ideas and sentences. In particular, the use of *because*, the most frequent subordinating conjunction, draws attention to causal relationships, also a characteristic of interactive online language use (Biber and Egbert). Additionally, first-year argumentative writing is characterized by more phrasal verbs, which are associated with more informal language use and used increasingly in English today (Brown and Palmer). Recurring patterns, including phrasal verbs, modal verbs, subordinating clauses, and negation, highlight personal involvement and persuasion in first-year argumentative writing.

The explanatory discourse patterns in table 7 show the contrasting choices that are significantly more frequent in first-year explanatory writing. These patterns indicate that first-year explanatory writing shares qualities with more informational, less conversational language

Table 7. Keyword Patterns in First-Year Explanatory Writing

KEYWORD PATTERNS	COMMON ITERATIONS AND COLLOCATIONS
Articles	*the* (94% of articles): ***the*** *audience*, ***the*** *image*, ***the*** *article*, ***the*** *use*
Lexical verb, present tense	***shows/uses/makes/gives/states***
This as determiner	***this*** *article*, ***this*** *image*, ***this*** *is*, ***this*** *source*, ***this*** *study*
Is as main verb	*it* ***is***, *this* ***is***, *there* ***is*** *[a/the/an]*
Cardinal numbers	dates, percentages, number of years/images/organizations
Of as preposition	[singular or plural noun+of] *use* ***of***, *one* ***of***, *university* ***of*** *[the/a/this]*
Prepositions	[singular noun or past participle] ***from/about/through/into/like*** *[the/this]*
Also as adverb	*is* ***also***, *but* ***also***, *they* ***also***, *also* ***the***
Wh- determiners	***which/what*** *[the/is/they]*

use (see Biber and Gray). In particular, the patterns show that explanatory writing is characterized by several aspects of noun phrases (articles, determiners, prepositions) and lexical, present tense verbs.

These patterns show that explanatory writing is characterized by frequent noun phrases, which serve as the grammatical subjects of sentences (e.g. *this* ***study*** *says*, *this* ***article*** *shows*) and as the objects of prepositional phrases (e.g., *in this* ***article***, *in this* ***advertisement***). Frequent *in this* phrases tend to demarcate the specific scope of attendant claims by drawing attention to the sources of observations, and they also build cohesion by referring back to previously noted sources or views. The use of nouns and lexical verbs (e.g., *the article focuses on*, *these images show*) highlights descriptions of sources, studies, and other objects of analysis. Prepositional phrases aid description as well (e.g., *the nutritional quality [of meal offerings]*, *the effects [of doping] [on athletes]*, *consists [of two images]*). Frequent text connectives *also* and *and* add detail; these additive and coordinating connectives help students explicitly link descriptive details, for example, regarding origins, premises, or observations about the sources or objects they describe.[9]

Whereas these phrasal patterns suggest first-year explanatory writing shares qualities with relatively informational academic language use, fewer explanatory and more argumentative patterns suggest a wider range of features are welcome in argumentative writing and a more narrow set of patterns succeed in first-year explanatory writing. Also, both sets of patterns intimate the overlapping tendency to use *to be* as the main verb: *are* in argumentative writing, and *is* in explanatory writing. These keyword patterns reflect first-year students' regular use of *it is* and existential there (*there* **is**, *there* **are**), which facilitate general observations without a specific source or origin (Quirk et al.; see also Hinkel, "Simplicity").

In sum, the keyword analysis indicates that argumentative patterns help first-year writers foreground human behaviors, general observations, (dependent) clausal detail, and a more conversational style. Explanatory patterns help first-year writers foreground objects of analysis and offer detailed descriptions in noun and prepositional phrases. It is important to bear in mind that, as would be expected, first-year writing in both genre families contains a range of features, including explanatory and argumentative discourse. The keyword patterns, in other words, highlight recurring discourse that constitutes relative, overall rhetorical aims and effects. A close look at several examples in the next section illustrates how individual students use these patterns in their writing.

The Closer View: Key Discourse within First-Year Texts

The example passages below capture a range of writing by students in the first and second composition courses. They display choices made by still-developing first-year writers, but they also reflect the genre-specific patterns described in the last section. Beneath each passage, I discuss genre-specific patterns and also note rhetorical moves that emerged in the analysis. Throughout the examples, argumentative passages are listed by letter, and explanatory examples are indicated by number.

Argumentative Examples

In an argumentative essay titled "Beauty Does Not Equal a Size Zero," a first-year student in the first composition course uses several argumentative features; in the passage below, these choices help foreground persuasion and create a conversational style. As in the previous examples, initial grammatical subjects are underlined to help highlight points of emphasis:

> (A) As the subject of eating disorders continues to gain more awareness, people are starting to understand that preventative steps must be taken in order to combat this deadly disease. For instance, in the past Barbie dolls set unrealistic expectations for the appearance of women. Their dolls depicted women to have long thin legs, an unrealistically small waist and a seemingly impossible bust to hip ratio. However, nowadays Mattel is changing its Barbie doll to include women of many different shapes and sizes. There is solid evidence that mediums, like the media, have a much greater impact on the development of an eating disorder than internal factors do. It is for this reason the industry must be held accountable for mistakes. It is imperative that, in order to protect present and future generations of women, the media follows in [their] footsteps and takes action to right its wrongs.

In this passage, the student's grammatical subjects emphasize human actors (*people*, *their dolls*) as well as generalized, urgent observations (*it is imperative that*). Several argumentative patterns emphasize the writer's evaluation of a dramatic problem, for instance, adjectives *deadly* and *imperative*, adverbs *unrealistically* and *many*, and verbs that convey critique and necessity (*to gain*, *are starting*, *to combat*, *must be taken*, *must be held*).

This student's passage also follows a rhetorical move structure, or a stepwise organization of phrases and sentences, that emerged in the analysis. This rhetorical structure, which appeared in development (or body) paragraphs in both argumentative and explanatory writing, is facilitated by discourse-level clues and helps the writer move from general idea to more specific examples and back to a general link. The structure consists of four moves that usually appear in the following order: move (1) introduces the topic of a section or paragraph; move (2) offers specific examples and evidence; move (3) analyzes the evidence, offering an inference or interpretation; and move (4)—sometimes after several consecutive moves (2) and (3)—links back to the larger topic of the section or paragraph. In the case of example (A), move (1) is cued by a generic noun and present participle that draws attention to social or research trends: *people are starting to understand*. Move (2) offers specific examples or evidence, signaled by *for instance* (and addressed in the second, third, fourth, and fifth sentences). Move (3) offers analysis or interpretation of evidence; in example (A), this move is cued by *there is solid evidence*.

Fourth, move (4) links back to the main topic; above, this move is cued by wording focused on implications (*it is for this reason, it is imperative that*).

In the following passage, another first-year student in the first composition course likewise employs many argumentative discourse patterns. The passage appears in the student's conclusion to an argumentative essay titled "United States Lacks Proper Sex Education":

> (B) The research clearly shows that comprehensive sex education is more effective in preventing pregnancy and that abstinent only education may actually be contributing to high teen pregnancy rates. While the only way to be 100% certain that you will not get pregnant is through staying abstinent, many people choose to not stay abstinent. Abstinent only programs provide an education on how to have a positive healthy relationship and the emotional and physical pros of staying abstinent until marriage. Abstinent only programs encourage teens to not engage in sex; the program does not provide a thorough education on how to stay physically healthy, which has proven to effect the youth in America having a large correlation with teen pregnancies. On the other hand comprehensive sex education understands that not everyone will abstain from having sex and instead believes that the youth should be thoroughly taught on how and why they can prevent pregnancy and sexually transmitted diseases. Comprehensive sex education has proven to be effective and should be implemented nation wide.

This argumentative passage is fairly descriptive but contains several patterns that foreground persuasion. For instance, the first sentence places *The research* in the position of grammatical subject but uses the intensifying adverb *clearly* and lexical verb *shows* to frame dependent clauses that convey arguable claims: *that comprehensive sex education is more effective* and *that abstinent only education may actually be contributing to high teen pregnancy rates*. Nouns and pronouns—for example, common nouns *people* and *youth* and the second person pronoun *you*—emphasize general claims, human actors, and a conversational connection with readers. The passage also includes verbs, such as *understands* and *believes*, that emphasize opinions and beliefs (Hardy and Friginal 125).

The next example comes from another student's argumentative essay, this one written in the second composition course. The student includes this passage in the introduction to an essay titled "How Effective Is the Death Penalty?":

> (C) Imagine receiving a call that someone close to you was convicted and sentenced to death row; however, you know that this person did not commit the crime and that the law has made a mistake. Imagine when the sentence goes through and this loved one is executed, and years to come you find out that he/she was in fact innocent. This happened to the family of Cameron Todd Willingham, who was convicted of setting a fire that burned and killed his three children (Executed an Innocent). After years of further investigation more evidence has shown that Cameron Willingham was innocent and he did not commit arson. Unfortunately, this is one of many cases where the alleged offender who was executed was actually innocent, meaning the actual offender is still at large.

Here, this student writer uses several argumentative patterns that contribute to a conversational style and generalized, persuasive claims. These include adverbs (*however, Unfortunately, actually*), common nouns (such as *person*), and negation (*not true*). The use of the understood *you* as the grammatical subject in the first two sentences and repeated references to Cameron Todd Willingham and his family further facilitate reader-writer interaction and an emphasis on human actors.

Also written in the second composition course, another student's argumentative essay uses argumentative discourse to craft urgent, persuasive claims about animal testing. The following passage appears in an essay titled "Make the Choice to Make the Switch":

> (D) Although animal testing is a method that is helpful in engineering new products, it is inhumane, unnecessary, and needs to be stopped. Legally, there is no requirement in the United States for products to be tested on animals. Dr. Ron Hester, a professor at NYU with a doctorate in Chemistry explains, "Society demands that chemicals be tested. This requirement is exercised through legislation concerned with the safety of chemicals (through means of animals)" (Hester 4). This quote does a great job explaining the comfort that society gets from knowing that products that are released will not harm them.

This argumentative passage includes several patterns that contribute to the student's urgent argument about animal testing. The grammatical subjects address the general topic of animal testing as well as human subjects (e.g., *a professor* and *society*). The passage also contains *there is, it is* statements and evaluative adjectives, for example, ***there is** no requirement*, ***it is** inhumane*, and *does a **great** job*. With argumentative discourse such as modal and infinitive verbs (*needs to be stopped*) and negation (*no requirement, will not harm*), these patterns foreground the writer's claim and counter the alternative position that animal testing is a useful method when engineering new products. The writer's introduction to evidence in the third sentence includes key explanatory patterns, including an appositive noun phrase with descriptive prepositional phrases and a lexical verb (*Dr. Ron Hester, a professor at NYU with a doctorate in Chemistry, explains*). Overall, however, most of the textual space is devoted to developing the writer's arguable claim. This passage also follows the four rhetorical development moves noted above: move (1) introduces a trend (*animal testing, a method*); move (2) offers evidence (*Hester . . . explains*); move (3) offers an interpretation of the evidence (*This quote does a great job . . .*); and move (4) links back to the original, broader topic (*comfort that **society** gets*).

In a final example passage from an argumentative essay, another student writer in the second composition course makes a case for "Better Health" through the use of argumentative discourse patterns:

> (E) <u>The topic regarding whether individuals of food companies are responsible for high obesity rates</u> is very controversial. Generally, <u>both</u> are responsible for this issue, the restaurants that serve unhealthy, low cost food options, and the ones who make choices regarding food intake and physical exercise. <u>Individuals</u> need to be active and demand restaurants to serve healthy, low calorie food, which is affordable for everyone. On the other hand, <u>the big companies</u> need to be more concerned with the well being of the communities they operate in, in this case concerned with their effect on obesity. <u>The modern world</u> is facing a rapidly increasingly cheap, high-calories food, and with the sedentary lifestyle, it is not surprising that obesity has increased quickly in the last decades around the world.

In this passage, the student includes a concessive statement that highlights both sides of the issue discussed; this move seems encouraged by the assignment task, which asks students to consider the views of opposing stakeholders. In addition, the claim in the second sentence is hedged slightly by the stance word *generally*. Primarily, though, the passage emphasizes human actors and aims to make a persuasive case—the need for large food-production companies to provide healthier eating options—facilitated by several argumentative patterns. The second and third sentences offer directive statements using modal and infinitive verbs, stating what multiple stakeholders *need* to do. The final sentence makes a general claim about *The modern world* (and developments *around the world*) and uses several adverbs (*rapidly, increasingly, quickly*). The sentence also uses the unspecified grammatical subject *it* and negation to describe human actors generally (*it is* ***not*** *surprising that obesity has increased quickly*).

Explanatory Examples

The next example, this time showcasing explanatory discourse patterns, appears in a student's annotated bibliography. This passage was written by a student in the first composition course in an annotated bibliography titled "Single-Sex Schools":

> (1) During the last 10 years, <u>a lot of research</u> has been done to prove that [single-sex] education is better than [coeducational] education. <u>Much of this research</u> demonstrated how the brain works differently between boys and girls. Therefore, <u>each gender</u> has to have his/her educational system. In this article, <u>the author</u> goes against this idea by demonstrating how they are weak claims. <u>She</u> also says that educators who cite hormonal or brain research, as evidence of [single-sex] being better than [coeducational] schools, are often misusing or misconstruing these [studies]. <u>This article</u> looks over how things like hearing, vision and Nervous System are different in each gender. Moreover, <u>it</u> explains how they are not related to the idea that [single-sex] schools are better than [coeducational] schools. <u>The article</u> is going against the idea of choosing an educational system based on how the brain works. <u>It</u> illustrates how [single-sex] supporters use weak claims to convince people that [single-sex] schools are better than [coeducation].

In this example, explanatory patterns facilitate the student's description of an article and its contribution to debates about single-sex education. Noun phrases that feature articles, determiners, and embedded prepositional phrases place the emphasis on the article and the research it reports (e.g., *Much [of this research], the author, this/The article*). Lexical reporting verbs also help the writer foreground the article (e.g., *says, looks over, explains, illustrates*). The writer's use of prepositional phrases to modify verbs or the direct objects of verbs likewise adds detail to the description of related research (e.g., *works differently [between boys and girls], are different [in each gender], going against the idea [of choosing an educational system]*). This passage also provides a useful illustration of the difference between analytic reasoning, emphasized in this passage, and persuasive reasoning, emphasized in argumentative writing. This passage does convey some alignment with the article, at least in terms of its novelty; at the same time, the textual space is devoted to explaining the article in detail rather than advancing the writer's own arguable claim.

Lastly, explanatory example (1), which appears in a development paragraph, follows the rhetorical move structure noted above. First, move (1) introduces a topic reviewed in research with a general statement (***a lot of*** *research* . . .). Next, move (2) addresses more specific examples from that research and how the article in question addresses it (e.g., ***This article*** *looks over how things* ***like hearing*** . . .). Move (3), beginning in the second-to-last sentence, offers the student's inference from these examples (*This article is going against the idea of choosing* . . .). Finally, move (4) links back to the topic in the first sentence using similar nouns and the same comparative adjective (*single-sex, coeducational schools, better*).

Another student in the first composition course uses explanatory features in an annotated bibliography titled "The Effect of the Fast Food Revolution":

> (2) <u>This article</u> examines trends in the nutritional quality of fast food menus at eight different fast food menus at eight different fast food restaurants in the United States during the time period of 14 years. <u>Data relating to menu items and nutritional composition</u> were obtained by the official University of Minnesota Nutrition Coordinating center database which holds nutritional information in the United States, evaluated and given a score known as the healthy eating index. The higher the HEI score, the healthier <u>the meal options</u> a restaurant has to offer. <u>An interesting trend</u> was observed, the HEI scores which are updated

> each year continued to rise, showing that the nutritional quality of meal offerings has increased with time and hence, fast food restaurants are starting to respond to public demands for healthier meal options.

The grammatical subjects in this explanatory passage foreground the article and related research (e.g., ***article***, **Data**, *An interesting* ***trend***). So too do lexical verbs that modify research-related nouns (e.g., *this article* ***examines***, *database which* **holds** *nutritional information*). The passage also illustrates the explanatory pattern of adding detail through compressed prepositional phrases, which help describe the research in the article. For example, consider the string of phrases that modify *trends*, the direct object of the verb in the first sentence: *trends [in the nutritional quality][of fast food menus][at eight different fast food menus][at eight different fast food restaurants][in the United States][during the time period][of 14 years].* These prepositional phrases, which combine prepositions, articles, adjectives, and nouns, are one way academic writing provides compressed detail in syntactically compressed phrases (Biber and Gray).

Example (2) also contains several passive verb constructions, grammatically placing emphasis on research observations and outcomes rather than who or what caused them (see Boettger and Wulff; Conrad 318). For instance, sentences three and five contain passive verbs and the grammatical subjects *Data relating to menu items and nutritional composition* and *An interesting trend*, thereby foregrounding *data* and *trend* more than who obtained the data or observed the trend. The passage shares this characteristic with successful upper-level reports and research papers, which contain more passive constructions than upper-level argumentative essays or critiques (Hardy and Friginal 122). Finally, example (2) also follows the four development moves noted above: first, move (1) introduces a main topic reviewed in research (*trends in the nutritional quality of fast food restaurants*); next, move (2) addresses a more specific focus of that research (*Data relating to menu items and nutritional composition*); third, move (3) offers an interpretation of that example (*an* ***interesting*** *trend*); and finally, move (4) notes an outcome or link to the larger topic using an explicit transition and a noun used in the opening sentence (***hence***, *fast food* ***restaurants*** *are starting to respond*).

Another student in the first composition course uses explanatory features to unpack research on healthcare in the United States versus other countries. This passage comes from the student's annotated bibliography titled "Impact of Universal Access":

> (3) <u>The United States</u> remains one of few developed countries in the world that does not guarantee universal access to healthcare. <u>This</u> has been a longstanding conversation and is heavily debated in politics, medical journals, and scholarly articles. While <u>universal healthcare</u> has worked well in many countries around the world, the debate in America often centers around how to fund it and how it affects the healthcare workforce. <u>This</u> typically raises questions about: the fate of healthcare workers, such as doctors, if costs were fixed; students' desires of becoming a physician if it is no longer lucrative given the hundreds of thousands of dollars of student debt routinely incurred; tort reform implications on cost and accountability.

In this passage, the student's grammatical subjects focus on debates in the United States about universal healthcare. The use of a structure called "*unattended* this"—for example, *this has been* versus *this **issue** has been*—also appears in advanced academic writing across disciplines; professional academic writing includes unattended *this* 25–56% of the time, depending on the discipline (Swales, "Attended and Unattended 'This'" 10), and upper-level student writing contains unattended *this* between 19–37% of the time, depending on the discipline (Römer and Wulff 117). Explanatory patterns in example (3) include articles, nouns, and prepositions, and much of the detail in the passage appears in compressed noun phrases. These include, for instance, *the debate [in America]*, *one [of few developed countries][in the world]*, and *questions [about the fate][of healthcare workers]*.

The first-year author of explanatory example (4) wrote a visual analysis paper titled "Treatment for Posttraumatic Stress Disorder" in the second composition course, a passage of which appears below:

> (4) <u>The Department of Affairs</u> has a center for research and treatment of [Post Traumatic Stress Disorder (PTSD)] in veterans. <u>The organization</u> focuses on the different treatment options for veterans that are suffering from PTSD. <u>They</u> also keep up to date with the latest research in order to provide the best care possible for veterans. <u>The goal of this part of the VA</u> is to understand and treat PTSD. <u>The website</u> emphasizes that this organization has been the national center for

> PTSD for 25 years. The images throughout the website use visual and rhetorical appeals to convey their mission of assisting veterans that are suffering from PTSD. The primary message is that veterans need to be supported and the VA offers treatment options, as well as support systems, to help accomplish that goal.

As in other explanatory examples, this writer's grammatical subjects facilitate labeling and describing the object of analysis. Here the subjects specifically facilitate contextualizing and analyzing online images used on a PTSD research and treatment center Web site. In the passage, several prepositional phrases also facilitate compressed phrases to describe relevant nouns; for example, the first sentence describes *a center [for research and treatment][of PTSD][in veterans]*. Subsequent sentences include similarly compressed phrases that describe the goals, mission, and Web site of the center. The final two sentences begin to frame the analysis; the student uses a prepositional phrase to specify *images [throughout the website]* and the VA's *mission [of assisting veterans]* and uses attributive adjectives to describe the *visual and rhetorical appeals* and *primary message*. The writing also includes argumentative patterns, including infinitive verbs such as *The goal . . . is to understand and treat*, *veterans need to be supported*, and *to help accomplish*. But overall, the discourse patterns foreground a rhetorical aim of labeling and beginning to analyze an object of analysis.

Another first-year student in the second composition course wrote a visual analysis of materials from People for the Ethical Treatment of Animals (PETA) titled "Ceasing Animal Testing as We Know It," in which the student uses explanatory discourse features to delineate some conclusions in animal testing research:

> (5) Due to the tensions and pressures of ceasing animal use in scientific research, alternatives are beginning to be addressed in a new light. Natalie Burden, a member of the Innovation and Translation Group who holds a PhD in regulatory science and environmental safety, states that types of such approaches against animal testing are already in development and include methods, sequencing, and technologies, and computational modeling. This is relevant because it gives examples of alternatives that have the ability to influence society and cease the use of animals in research all together. PETA has strategi-

cally designed all of their campaigns to touch the hearts and minds of individuals in order to reflect change.

In this passage, the student's grammatical subjects focus on research, which helps frame an analysis of images used in PETA campaigns. The student's use of noun and prepositional phrases facilitates adding compressed detail. For instance, compressed noun phrases describe the cause (*tensions and pressures [of ceasing animal use][in scientific research], the use [of animals in research]*), an effect (*[in a new light]*), a source (*a member [of the Innovation and Translation Group]*), and what the student infers from the source (*the ability to influence society and cease the use [of animals][in research]*). The passive construction in the first sentence—*alternatives* ***are beginning to be addressed***—foregrounds the *alternatives* rather than human subjects or organizations addressing them. Also in example (5), we see the four rhetorical development moves noted above: move (1) introduces the topic by referencing research or social trends (*alternatives* to *animal use in scientific research . . . in a new light*); move (2) addresses a specific source for evidence (*Natalie Burden*); move (3) offers an interpretation (*This is* ***relevant***, *PETA has strategically designed*); and move (4) links back to the main topic of alternatives, or *change*.

Analysis II: What Stance Word Patterns Distinguish First-Year Explanatory and Argumentative Writing?

This section explores the degree to which first-year argumentative and explanatory writing are distinctive in their patterns of stance. As noted in detail in chapter 1, stance words frame information and guide readers toward particular perceptions of that information, and research shows that five types of stance words distinguish student writing by level. I briefly redefine these types below before turning to the analysis.

Hedges, *boosters*, and *generality words* are epistemic stance words: they indicate caution, certainty, and wide applicability, respectively. Hedges such as *perhaps* open dialogic space and withhold complete certainty, boosters such as *clearly* indicate full certainty and close dialogic space, and generality words such as *always* generalize across time or circumstances. *Counters* and *reformulation words* serve as textual clues that help convey explicit relationships between parts of a text. Counters such as *however* indicate that a statement denies or challenges a previous statement, and reformulation words such as *specifically* signal the restating or reframing of previously offered information. Below, I describe the overall stance word patterns and then turn to individual examples.

The Distant View: Stance across First-Year Texts

The analysis of stance words in first-year writing showed that four types of stance words are significantly more frequent in argumentative writing than in explanatory writing. Generality words represent the most significant difference; argumentative writing includes about 42.5% more generality words that explicitly apply statements across contexts, people, or time. Writers often use these words to show urgency or shared beliefs, for example, by suggesting that something increases *every year*, as in example (F) below, or is a great contribution *of our time*, as in example (G) below. Counters such as *but* and *however* are next; argumentative writing contains approximately 32% more counters than explanatory writing, and writers use these words to explicitly signal their move to contrast a previously noted idea. Boosters are about 29.5% more frequent in argumentative writing. Figure 1 displays comparative uses of each stance word in first-year genre families.

These stance word patterns reflect genre-specific trends with one exception. Hedges are used in strikingly similar frequencies: per 10,000 words, argumentative writing contains 56.3 hedges whereas explanatory writing contains 50.4, an insignificant difference. Furthermore, the proportion of hedges to boosters is similar in each genre family: boosters are significantly more frequent than hedges in both argumentative and explanatory writing, meaning that, regardless of genre, first-year writers tend to close rather than open dialogic space. In this way, both first-year genre families are distinct from published academic writing (regardless of discipline), which contains more hedges than boosters (Hyland, "Stance"; Aull, *First-Year University Writing*). A hedge-to-booster ratio can help capture the cumulative effect of epistemic certainty in a given text, and in this case, the ratio of hedges to boosters in explanatory writing—almost 1 to 2—is closer than that of argumentative writing, which is around 1 to 1.5.

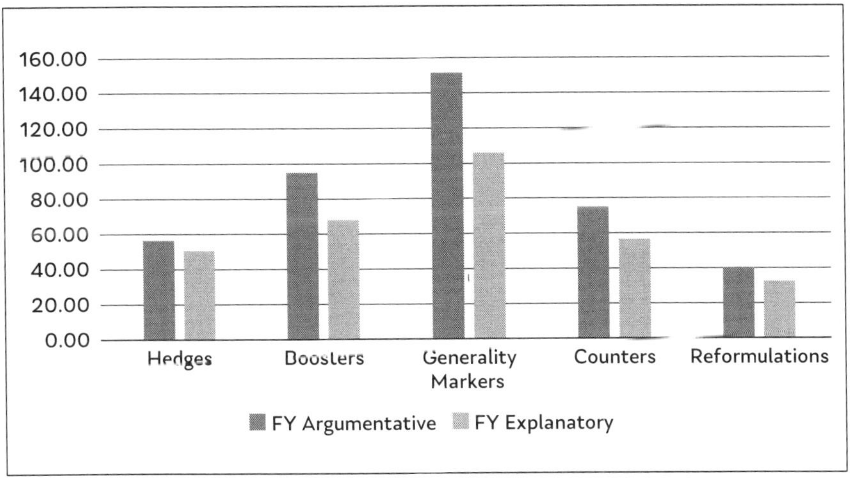

Figure 1. Stance Word Patterns in First-Year Writing, Instances per 10,000 Words

Taken together, generality words, counters, and boosters contribute to relatively strong and certain statements, and argumentative writing is characterized by a significantly higher use of each of these stance words. With fewer hedges, these patterns suggest first-year students perceive the need to exaggerate the certainty and generality of their statements in argumentative writing, as illustrated in examples below. Finally, argumentative writing also includes almost 24% more reformulation words, indicating students' perception that argumentative writing requires more explicit textual clues and reformulated information for readers.

Each genre family contains similar proportions of stance words: generality words are the most frequent, followed by counters, then boosters, then reformulation words, and then hedges. A final point is that the most frequently used stance words are identical regardless of genre family. In both genre families, the most frequent booster is *very*, the most frequent hedge is *likely*, the most frequent reformulation word is *such as*, the most frequent generality word is *people*, and the most frequent counter is *but*. This suggests first-year writers draw from a similar stance lexicon and also that differences are due to quantity rather than quality. Example passages below, in which stance words appear in bold, elucidate these patterns.

The Closer View: Stance within First-Year Texts

The example passages below include both argumentative and explanatory writing by students in the first and second composition courses. Beneath each passage, I discuss the use of stance words in the analysis. Throughout the examples, argumentative passages are listed by letter, and explanatory examples are indicated by number.

Argumentative Writing

Another student writing an argumentative essay in the first composition course chose to focus on the "Potential of Online Education." The student uses several stance words in the following example to emphasize urgency and persuasion:

> (F) In **a fast-paced world** with technology increasing so rapidly, it is important that the education system become comfortable with the modern age. Online education **can only get better** with the **vast** amount of technology being invented and improved **every year**. It is time to **seriously** consider the benefits of online education, and that it can be a powerful tool for future generations to make the most of.

In example (F), the student uses generality words (*a fast-paced* ***world***, ***every*** *year*) to emphasize the importance and wide applicability of the corresponding statements. In addition, boosters indicate the writer's full certainty—that online education *can* ***only*** *get better* and that it is time to *seriously* consider online education. Key argumentative patterns such as modal and infinitive verbs (*can be, to make the most of*) also facilitate making a case.

In the second composition course, a student writing an argumentative essay likewise employs several intensifiers to indicate urgent directives for readers. The essay, titled "Net Neutrality: Why We Need It Now," includes the following passage in the introduction:

> (G) The internet is an infinite avenue for open communication and the sharing of ways to connect and discover. That being said, the internet also creates a unique experience for each user, and **should not** be controlled by any one person, company, or industry. By having a free and open internet, users retain their voice and free speech by surfing

> online without restriction. One of the **best** explanations for the issue, theopeninter.net, states free and open internet is the **single greatest** technology of **our time**, and control **should not** be at the mercy of corporations.

In this example, several features emphasize the certainty and generalizability of claims, including *infinite avenue* and *without restriction*, as well as *single greatest technology of our time*. The passage also exhibits argumentative patterns discussed in the previous section, including modal verbs, infinitive verbs, and negation (***to connect*** *and* ***discover***, ***should not be*** *controlled*, ***should not be*** *at the mercy of corporations*).

Explanatory Writing

In explanatory writing, first-year students intensify and generalize less than in argumentative essays. For instance, in the following passage from an annotated bibliography titled "Vaccination Controversy," a student in the first composition course hedges several statements:

> (6) This evidence comes from a study in which a series of 12 patients had inflammatory bowel conditions and regressive developmental disorders, mostly autism. The inflammatory bowel **may** be caused by the vaccine, providing a **possible** biological mechanism. **However**, the authors **suggest** that this is **only** a coincidence. The authors reviewed evidence from several epidemiological studies that deal with the development of autism in order to prove their case. The studies suggested that it is **unlikely** that a vaccine given after birth would cause autism because neurological defects occur before birth.

In this passage, the student uses several hedges to downplay claims related to causal links between autism and vaccinations. The student then uses the counter *However* and the booster *only* to frame a more certain conclusion based on the article reviewed. Other language implies the writer's alignment with the article, for example, the student notes that the authors reviewed evidence from *several* studies to *prove* their conclusions. Still, in the subsequent sentence, the writer uses the hedge *unlikely*, which avoids implying full certainty about the relation between autism and vaccinations, and this passage overall contains a balance of opening and closing dialogic space.

Likewise, a first-year student in the second composition course, writing a visual analysis titled "Inspire their Minds," uses several hedges, as well as generality words, to describe contemporary issues related to technology:

> (7) **One could argue** that **most people** would recognize the idea that the twenty-first century is a time period where advancements in technology seem to be at their peak. In the same manner, this is a time period when social media has facilitated the ability to discuss issues of rights, **especially** those of minority groups such as women. The currency of these images and the way the issues they are discussing are so deeply intertwined to **society** improve their efficacy in carrying their message.

In example (7), the student's use of stance words frames the analysis of images advocating female participation in STEM education. This passage includes multiple hedge verbs, including one used to introduce a possible claim (*One could argue*) and one used to leave dialogic space open for an exception to a generalization about the twenty-first century (*a time period where advancements in technology* ***seem*** *to be at their peak*). The passage also contains a generalization about *society* as well as several explanatory patterns discussed in the previous section, including prepositional phrases, noun phrases, and many uses of the article *the* in noun phrases.[10]

Student Discourse in First-Year Genres

The analysis in this chapter shows several genre-specific patterns in first-year writing. Argumentative patterns facilitate making a conversational and persuasive case. Although first-year writers add detail through noun phrases in explanatory writing, in argumentative writing they more often add detail in less compressed, more explicit dependent clauses. In first-year argumentative writing, many statements address a general topic or concern rather than offer a response to an existing view or source, even when sources are incorporated as supportive evidence, whereas the opposite is true in explanatory writing.

In this way, first-year explanatory patterns delineate more circumspect claims, and they facilitate the goal of describing sources and others' views, rather than the argumentative objective of persuading readers. In generalized statements and in hedging and boosting patterns, first-year argumentative writing more often closes dialogic space; together, these patterns facilitate assertive claims. Argumentative writing also includes more explicit textual clues that signal countering statements and reformulations of previous information, and uses a wider range of grammatical and lexical patterns.

First-year explanatory patterns facilitate descriptive examinations focused on sources or objects. Several patterns contribute to detailed noun phrases and a more informational style, and these and other patterns foreground descriptions of sources. In terms of stance word patterns, explanatory writing displays a slightly closer balance of opening and closing dialogic space but still shows high levels of certainty overall. At the same time, the relatively lower use of most stance word categories suggests that in explanatory writing, first-year students do not explicitly frame and connect their statements as often as they do in argumentative writing. On the one hand, this means students are less likely to explicitly generalize or boost in explanatory writing; on the other hand, they are also less likely to offer cohesive connections for readers that explicitly signal reformulations or counters.

Thus, first-year writing—argumentative writing in particular—presents a kind of conundrum. First-year argumentative writing relies on dependent clauses, an option for adding detail that is relatively easy to follow, since dependent clauses are explicit about grammatical relationships and common in conversational language use. Such detail may be accessible for more writers and readers, because it is closer to what students have encountered in conversation and Web-based discussion, as well as to what they have written in their standardized secondary essays (Aull, *First-Year University Writing* 4). This type of writing also includes many patterns that intensify and generalize, closing dialogic space rather than leaving room for discussion or exceptions.

In conjunction with fewer keyword patterns than in argumentative writing, lower frequencies of most stance words in explanatory writing suggest that successful first-year explanatory writing requires a more narrow set of grammatical and lexical choices than successful first-year argumentative writing. In other words, the analysis indicates that first-year writers have fewer options for successful writing in explanatory assignments—but they also seem to practice opening dialogic space more often in these assignments. These considerations merit more attention in future research and instruction, but subsequent chapters strive to add to them.

As a start, these observations do add to previous research. Whereas first-year student writers may indeed use more "text-external" framing and "emphatic generality" than advanced academic writers (Aull, *First-Year University Writing* 71; Brown and Aull 394), they are still more apt to employ—and be rewarded for—these patterns in argumentative than in explanatory writing. These discourse patterns furthermore may approximate what first-year writers encounter in interactive spoken and written language use. Thus, the trope that academic writing is a conversation is true in a linguistic sense in first-year argumentative writing, which contains language features that emphasize the writer and reader and approximate spoken language qualities, including some exaggeration and generality. The same writing often emphatically asserts a single perspective. Even as these patterns do not clearly match the macrolevel rhetorical principles of cautious and open-minded writing noted in composition scholarship (D. Harrington; Stotsky; Duffy, "Good Writer") they could reasonably—if unconsciously—be part of first-year students' associations with argument and interactive discourse.

In that explanatory writing is characterized by a more informational style and a closer ratio between hedges and boosters, it is discursively closer to formal academic writing, which tends to be cautious (Hunston and Thompson; Hyland, "Stance"; Lancaster, "Interpersonal Stance"; Aull and Lancaster), indirect (Lancaster, "Do"), and syntactically compressed (Biber et al., "Speaking"; Biber and Gray). By extension, the analysis does not show a strong empirical relationship between first-year argumentative essays and many formal academic discourse practices. At the same time, first-year explanatory writing shows a more narrow range of successful options and includes patterns that are less interactive and explicit.

The analysis in this chapter poses important questions about the goal(s) of first-year writing assignments, because it suggests argumentative and explanatory discourse patterns in first-year writing constitute different sociocognitive habits. Argumentative patterns are, linguistically, more conversational and accessible. They ask students to practice a less dialogic, more interactive, and overtly persuasive style common in conversations and online writing for general audiences. Explanatory patterns are in some ways both more dialogic and less accessible. They contribute to the use of more qualified statements and fewer generalized claims and encourage a tendency toward more dense, less explicit detail. In this way, explanatory first-year patterns seem to approximate both positive and exclusive qualities of academic writing, in that they support writing that is more circumspect and harder to parse for unpracticed readers.

A possible inference is that this analysis confirms the value of assigning a range of genres. Another is that it validates the importance of explicit writing expectations that render transparent what instructors do and do not value and why. Above all, the analysis in this chapter suggests that my early observations about generalizations in first-year writing are not as straightforward as I thought, because they are coupled with discursive practices that students might reasonably associate with accessible, persuasive writing. These conclusions highlight the importance of continued efforts to understand how discourse choices construct distinctive ways of thinking and writing, further explored in the next two chapters.

Notes

1. Unlike the upper-level corpus analyzed in chapter 4, the first-year corpus I analyze is not freely available, highlighting the value of access to corpora of student writing.

2. See program details at www.usf.edu/arts-sciences/departments/english/writing-programs/index.aspx; for institutional details, see "About USF" and *America's Best Value Colleges*, "University of South Florida."

3. More specific geographic and racial demographic information follows: Students come from fifty states and more than 150 countries, and students are listed as 0.2% American Indian or Alaskan native, 6.2% Asian, 0.3% Pacific Islander, 10.8% black or African American, 20.1% Hispanic or Latino/a, 52.4% white, 3.6% two or more races, 1.4% unknown, and 5% are categorized as "nonresident aliens" (see "About USF").

4. See also the CCCC's "Bibliography of Resources on Labor in College Composition."

5. For more program details, see Moxley, "Big Data" and Aull, "Corpus." Since 2016 some curricular details have changed, including the order of assignments in the second composition course (Aull, "Corpus").

6. In this chapter, I draw on both the assignment descriptions and rubrics, though vis-à-vis the rubric descriptions, I especially focus on the categories of analysis and evidence because the categories of organization, format, and style are almost identical across the tasks. For more detail about these materials, see Aull, "Corpus."

7. With respect to "Total Number of Texts and Words" in table 5, here and in subsequent chapters, the number of words refers to the number of words in a corpus irrespective of whether or not the word is repeated. In corpus linguistics, this is referred to as *word tokens*. Here and in subsequent chapters, the total number of words refers to the word tokens in my version of the corpus that is not part-of-speech tagged.

8. See the appendix for a description of *keyness*.

9. These strategies appear to be rewarded in AP exam writing; for instance, writers who manipulate nominal groups to specify ideas and themes receive higher scores than writers who do not (Brown and Aull). In this study, similar rhetorical strategies appeared more often in explanatory assignment tasks.

10. Also interesting in the example is that in the final sentence, the student's syntax is unnecessarily complex and could arguably be simplified by adding detail in phrases rather than dependent clauses. In other words, the student intends the grammatical subject of the sentence to be the following, in which I have bracketed the prepositional phrase and underlined the relative clauses, which begin with implied *that*: *The currency [of these images] and the way* <u>*(that) the issues (that) they are discussing are so deeply intertwined to society*</u>. A modification of this grammatical subject using phrasal (vs. clausal) complexity might be the following: *the currency of these images and their entrenchment in society.*

4

Student Discourse in Upper-Level Genres

Assigning Upper-Level Writing

It is no real wonder that first-year writing dominates composition studies in the United States, given the major administrative, instructional, and assessment efforts it entails. Yet the millions of students each year who finish first-year courses must write at all levels and in most courses in higher education. Some institutions require both first-year and upper-level writing courses—Stanford University and the University of Michigan are two examples—though it is much more common that students are effectively on their own when completing upper-level writing assignments. Because faculty members lack time, training, or interest, or because they expect advanced students to be more prepared writers, upper-level writing tasks often take the guise of open-ended term paper assignments, turned in at the end of the term, on which instructors may or may not write feedback that students may or may not read (Bean 89–90). There are more specific assignments than this, of course; many examples are noted in chapter 2. But we have more to learn about writing assignments across upper-level courses (Römer and O'Donnell 168), and systematic analysis of both first-year and upper-level discourse remains relatively new in writing research in the United States.

The previous chapter explored first-year discourse patterns that construct genre-specific rhetorical effects, including argumentative patterns that facilitate a more conversational style, a focus on human actors, and more generalized claims and explanatory patterns that facilitate a more informational style, a focus on objects of study, and fewer epistemic and textual clues for readers. Whereas chapter 3 analyzed writing by students transitioning into undergraduate courses, this chapter analyzes writing by students transitioning out of undergraduate-level and into graduate-level writing.

Upper-Level Writing Context

The upper-level writing analyzed in this chapter was written by late-undergraduate- and early-graduate-level students at the University of Michigan (UM), a large, selective, moderately diverse institution. Approximately 28,312 undergraduate students and 15,339 graduate students are enrolled, and approximately 6.9% of the undergraduate students and 7.5% of the graduate students are categorized as international students. Demographic information provided by the university describes the students as 50% female and 50% male, and primarily "white," "Asian American," and "unknown" ("Undergraduate Admissions").[1] In the 2019 *U.S. News and World Report* rankings, UM was ranked 27 in undergraduate colleges according to *Best Colleges and National Universities* ("University of Michigan"). Graduate-level UM programs are also selective; almost all programs represented in this analysis rank among the top fifteen national programs, including psychology, education, engineering, political science, history, English, nursing, sociology, chemistry, computer science, and physics.[2] Given the selective nature of the undergraduate and graduate programs, successful upper-level writing at UM can be said to represent a very high standard of upper-level student writing.

The writing analyzed in this chapter represents part of the Michigan Corpus of Upper-Level Student Papers (MICUSP), the largest freely available corpus of late-undergraduate- and early-graduate-level student writing in English. Completed in 2010, the corpus consists of A-graded writing by over eight hundred students in their final year of undergraduate coursework or their first, second, or third year of graduate school. The corpus thus offers a unique resource for gaining insight into both upper-level curricular assignments and writing in response to them (Ädel and Römer 4).

Writing in MICUSP is categorized by discipline and discipline group. The four discipline groups are arts and humanities, social sciences, life sciences, and physical sciences. Arts and humanities disciplines include English, history and classical studies, linguistics, and philosophy. Social science disciplines include economics, education, political science, psychology, and sociology. Biological and health science (also called life science) disciplines include biology, natural resources and environment, and nursing. Physical sciences include civil and environmental engineering, industrial and operations engineering, mechanical engineering, and physics.

Upper-Level School Genres

As they compiled MICUSP, Ute Römer and Matthew O'Donnell noted the scarcity of available information about upper-level writing assignments and decided to use student papers to determine paper type categories (168). Römer and O'Donnell and their team identified seven paper types in upper-level writing: argumentative essays, creative writing, critiques/evaluations, proposals, reports, research papers, and response papers (170–71).

Four of these—argumentative essays, critiques, reports, and research papers—were by far the most common. Together, these four make up 90% of the writing in MICUSP, and each one also reflects all four discipline groups (whereas, for example, no proposals were submitted in the arts and humanities disciplines, and no creative writing was submitted in the physical science disciplines). Römer and O'Donnell describe upper-level argumentative essays as "thesis-driven." In them, students develop and demonstrate their ability to construct and support a persuasive argument. Likewise, upper-level "critiques/evaluations" must identify and defend an evaluation: they are "driven by an in-depth assessment" that is "positive and/or negative." In these papers, a student's assessment might gage effectiveness, validity, or usefulness and offer recommendations. Upper-level reports and research papers, conversely, are not driven by a thesis or evaluation. They are driven by research questions and description ("rather than critical assessment"); they may include a writer's opinion but are not driven by it (Römer and O'Donnell 170–71). In some cases, research papers additionally ask students to demonstrate their ability to describe or interpret original research or both.[3]

To analyze upper-level argumentative and explanatory writing, I compiled only the writing in these four common assignment genres: argumentative essays and critiques (hereafter essays and critiques) compose the upper-level genre family of argumentative writing, and reports and research papers make up the upper-level genre family of explanatory writing. Table 8 captures the overall details about the upper-level writing analyzed below.[4]

As the table shows, this corpus reflects some trends vis-à-vis student year, discipline, and the genres of writing assigned.[5] As student year increases, the proportion of reports and research papers increases, and the proportion of essays decreases, regardless of discipline. Over 60% of essays represented in this upper-level corpus were submitted by undergraduate students in their final year, whereas the remaining 40% were submitted by graduate students in their first, second, or third year. There is also disciplinary variation. The majority of upper-level essays (61%) were submitted by undergraduate students in arts and humanities and social sciences, and more students in English courses submitted essays than from any other discipline. By contrast, no essays were submitted by students in mechanical engineering or physics. Critiques were submitted in thirteen of the sixteen disciplines in the corpus, and mostly by students in philosophy and psychology.

Table 8. Upper-Level Corpus Details

GENRE FAMILY	ARGUMENTATIVE WRITING		EXPLANATORY WRITING	
GENRE	ARGUMENTATIVE ESSAY	CRITIQUE/ EVALUATION	RESEARCH PAPER	REPORT
Number of Texts	187	61	140	362
Words per Text	~3,929	~3,388	~4,350	~4,181
Texts by Final-Year Undergraduates	114 (61%)	34 (~55%)	74 (53%)	168 (~46%)
Number of Disciplines	14	13	14	16
Most Represented Discipline(s)	English	Philosophy, Psychology	Biology	Psychology
Total Number of Texts	248		502	
Total Number of Words	579, 917		1,329,155	
Reference Corpus for Comparative Analysis	Report + Research Paper		Argumentative Essay + Critique	

Some of the explanatory writing is slightly more universal: upper-level reports were submitted by students in all sixteen disciplines, and upper-level research papers were submitted by students in fourteen disciplines. Slightly fewer than half the upper level reports (46%) and a little more than half the upper-level research papers (53%) were written by undergraduate students, whereas the rest were submitted by graduate students. More students from psychology submitted reports than from any other discipline, whereas more students in biology submitted research papers than any other discipline. No students in English submitted research papers, providing an interesting contrast to the high number of essays submitted in English.

Upper-Level Writing Analysis

As in the first-year writing analysis, I draw on methods outlined in chapter 1 to analyze upper-level writing: corpus linguistic analysis and close textual analysis of keyword and stance word patterns. The keyword analysis identifies the unique lexical and grammatical choices that upper-level students make in each assignment genre, whereas the word frequency analysis identifies stance word patterns unique to each assignment genre. In the sections below, I discuss both the overall patterns across texts as well as several example passages that illustrate the use of those patterns by individual students. As in the previous chapter, all the keyword patterns I describe are highly significant and persistent; the stance word patterns analyzed are likewise persistent, and I specify which of the stance word patterns are significant in which genres.

Analysis I: What Keyword Patterns Distinguish Upper-Level Argumentative and Explanatory Writing?

Several of the argumentative and explanatory patterns overlap across first-year and upper-level writing, so the analysis in this chapter will be relatively easy to follow. Still, a list of textual patterns can be more difficult to imagine than a description; so first, I briefly summarize the patterns shown in tables 9 and 10, with attention to some parallels and distinctions between the two student levels. In the next section, I analyze several example passages from upper-level writing that illustrate students' use of these patterns.

A few interesting parallels emerge in first-year and upper-level argumentative writing. Two of these patterns facilitate comparing and contrasting: negation and the countering conjunction *but*. Also notable is that both first-year and upper-level argumentative writing include more dependent clauses than explanatory writing. Unlike in first-year writing, however, dependent clauses in upper-level writing do not tend to emphasize causal relations. Dependent clauses at the upper level are marked by *as* and *that*. Dependent clauses beginning with *that*, significantly more frequent in upper-level argumentative writing, offer more explicit information regarding grammatical relations and tend to characterize conversation versus writing (Biber and Gray 6; see also Biber et al., *Longman Grammar*).

Table 9. Keyword Patterns in Upper-Level Argumentative Writing

KEYWORD PATTERNS	COMMON ITERATIONS AND COLLOCATIONS
Lexical verb, present tense	***seems***, ***makes***, ***says***, ***becomes***, ***gives***
Genitive marker *'s*	singular proper nouns (59% of uses; e.g., *Hume's*), singular common nouns (29%; e.g., *woman's*)
Possessive pronouns	***his*** (32%), ***their, her*** (18%), ***its, our, my, your*** *[own/life/family, father, mother]*
Is as main verb	*it* ***is***, *there* ***is***, *this* ***is*** *[a/the/not]*
That as conjunction (81%) or determiner	***that*** *is, [the fact] is* ***that***
Negation	*it is* ***not***, *people do* ***not***
After- or postdeterminer	***such***, ***own***, ***same***, ***former***, ***latter*** *[a, time, an, way]*
But as countering conjunction	***but*** *the*, ***but*** *also*, ***but*** *it*
Adverbs (general)	***also***, ***only***, ***however***, ***even*** *[the/in/to/as]*
Third person singular pronoun *it*	***it*** *is* (31.6% of uses), ***it*** *seems*, ***it*** *was*, ***it*** *would*
Wh- determiners	***which***, ***what*** *[is/the/he/we]*
Infinitive verbs	*to/can* ***make***/***say***/***take***/***see***
As as conjunction	*just* ***as***, *much* ***as***
One as indefinite pronoun (48.6%) and cardinal number (45.2%)	***one's*** *own*, ***one*** *can*; *of* ***one***, ***one*** *of*, ***one*** *that*
Of *as preposition*	*idea* ***of***, *part* ***of***, *one* ***of***, *because* ***of*** *[the/a/his/their]*
Only as adverb (80%), adjective (20%)	***only*** *to*, ***only*** *in*, ***only*** *a*, ***only*** *one*
Adverb (of time)	*[and/is/would/can]* ***then***/***now***/***again***/***today*** *[the/it/is/we]*

Table 10. Keyword Patterns in Upper-Level Explanatory Writing

KEYWORD PATTERNS	COMMON ITERATIONS AND COLLOCATIONS
Cardinal numbers	figure and table numbers, citations, number of people/years in event or study
Lexical verb, past tense	**found/used/showed/included**
Past participle of lexical verb	*[was/were / were not]* **used/able/found**
Comparative adjectives	(usually modifies noun) ***higher/greater/lower/larger/better*** *[education, levels, understanding]*
Adjective (general)	(usually attributive) ***other, social, different, new, important*** *[effects/ideas]*
Common nouns	*people* (26.9%) / *data* (26.7%) / *species/media/dynamics*
For as preposition	***for*** *each/the/a/this*
Also as adverb	*is/but/are/can* ***also*** *be/the/have*
On as preposition (96.2%) and verb particle	*based/focus/research* ***on*** *the/a/their/this*
Coordinating conjunctions ***and*** (87%), ***or*** (11.6%), ***nor*** (0.4%)	between nouns (~76%, *ability* ***and*** *output, the time* ***and*** *money*) and/or before attributive adjectives (*education* ***and*** *other needs*)
More as comparative degree adverb (67.3%) and comparative determiner	*a/are/is* ***more*** *than /likely/of/important*

A similarity between first-year and upper-level explanatory writing is that both contain several patterns that contribute to compressed noun phrases (including adjectives, determiners, and nouns). These patterns facilitate detailed, compressed descriptions and can allow writers to omit explicit grammatical information such as the subjects (or agents) of a verb. At the same time, both upper-level explanatory and argumentative writing contain frequent prepositions, which suggests upper-level writing in both genre families is characterized by some patterns that contribute to phrasal density. I return to this point below and in chapter 5.

The Distant View: Key Discourse across Upper-Level Texts

In tables 9 and 10, I list the patterns (top to bottom) according to keyness, though all patterns I discuss are highly significant and appear in the majority of the texts in question. Table 9 shows those patterns that are significantly more frequent in upper-level argumentative writing than in explanatory writing. Table 10 displays the opposite discourse patterns:

those keyword patterns more prevalent in upper-level explanatory writing relative to argumentative writing.

The Closer View: Key Discourse within Upper-Level Texts

The student passages below illustrate how upper-level writers use key discourse patterns as they develop their ideas. As in chapter 3, I group these examples by genre family; first, argumentative examples are listed by letter, followed by explanatory examples listed by number. I selected these examples because they capture the range of student years and discipline groups in the upper-level corpus and showcase several patterns in a single passage. Along with key discourse patterns, upper-level writers use rhetorical moves that I note below the passages.

Argumentative Examples

The first argumentative example passage was written by a final-year undergraduate student studying English. The passage appears in the student's introductory paragraph, in an essay titled "Self-Destruction in *Kindred*":

> (A) <u>Self-mutilation and self-destruction</u> serve many roles in Octavia Butler's *Kindred*. <u>They</u> show the ties that Rufus, Dana, and Alice all have to one another. Although <u>Butler</u> uses three different characters who experience self-destruction and mutilation in different ways with a different meaning for each character, this theme of destruction contains an overarching message for the audience and society as a whole. As a human species, <u>we</u> are all related, with an average 0.03% difference in genetic makeup between the most seemingly different individuals (Kottak 1997). Thus, when <u>human beings</u> hurt each other, they are hurting themselves much like Dana is physically and emotionally hurt when she hurts her ancestor, Rufus. (ENG.G0.55.1)[6]

In this passage, the student uses several patterns that contribute to a conversational style, and her grammatical subjects emphasize literary characters, human beings generally, and destruction, a focal theme of the essay. Several patterns facilitate an emphasis on human ideas and needs, including the genitive marker and proper noun (*Butler's*), several pronouns (*her, we*), and the explicit reference to *human beings*. Other key argumentative patterns facilitate persuasion and extrapolation, including dependent clauses beginning with *that* and *when* (***that*** *. . . all have,* ***when*** *she hurts*), indefinite pronouns (***all*** *have,* ***one another***), and adverbs (*seemingly, physically, emotionally, most*). These patterns facilitate a thesis-driven paragraph that addresses human characters within and beyond the literary text the student analyzes.

Another example of upper-level argumentative writing in the humanities appears next, in a passage written by a first-year graduate student studying philosophy. The passage appears in an essay titled "Explanation and Understanding":

> (B) <u>All these examples</u> are meant to make an intuitive case for the idea of ideal understanding as having a pragmatic aspect in the sense of involving an ability to make use of knowledge about something. <u>The example with the cult leader</u> is supposed to show or suggest that we could understand something well in one respect—namely, that of being able to use our theories about things—while understanding it less well in another respect—namely, that of having as true beliefs as possible about the ways in which things depend on each other. <u>The idea</u> is in part that understanding is a concept that is represented by many different related things, namely the things needed to be able to make use of information in further theoretical reasoning or in successful practical deliberation and in action. If <u>this</u> is correct, then the intuitiveness of all the different theories considered above is explained. <u>They</u> all concern things that help us to make use of our knowledge of things. (PHI.G1.04.1)

In this passage, the student's writing foregrounds persuasive reasoning, a conversational emphasis on shared knowledge, and, ultimately, his proposed theory of understanding. Several argumentative patterns enact these rhetorical aims. The student's use of first person plural pronouns (***our*** *theories,* ***our*** *knowledge,* ***we*** *could*) foreground shared understanding and an emphasis on human ideas. Infinitive verbs (*an ability* ***to make*** *use of knowledge, supposed* ***to show***) delineate the student's claims and their value; his use of dependent clauses beginning with *that* (***that*** *understanding is,* ***that*** *help us*) clarify opinions. (By contrast, a more compressed, phrasal description of this concept would be *many related things* *represent the concept of understanding.*) In addition, the passage includes the four rhetorical development moves discussed in chapter 3, cued by corresponding discourse choices. First, the paragraph begins with move (1), which identifies a precise topic for the paragraph that follows prior evidence (***All** these examples*). Move (2) follows with a specific example (***The example** with the cult leader*), and move (3) offers analysis of that example (*The idea is . . .*). Finally, move (4) offers a link back to the overall idea (*all the different theories . . . explained*).

A first-year graduate student in biology shows some similar argumentative discourse patterns in the excerpt below. The passage appears in an argumentative essay called "The Evolution of Terrestriality: A Look at the Factors that Drove Tetrapods to Move onto Land":

> (C) <u>The origin of new species</u> depends on a complex combination of environmental conditions, ecological factors, and chance. <u>The environmental conditions of the Late Devonian</u> certainly made life difficult for aquatic organisms, as evidenced by the mass extinction event in the marine community (DiMichele and Cook, 1992; Johnson, et al., 1985; Long and Gordan, 2004); but had the opportunity for the colonization of land never been presented by the changes brought about by plants, the early aquatic tetrapods may have never survived long excursions in the terrestrial realm. <u>The chance coincidence of increasingly poor quality and decreasingly abundant aquatic habitats, an emerging high quality terrestrial ecosystem, and the acquiring of morphological adaptations by the first tetrapods</u> set the stage for one of the most important steps in the history of animal life. (BIO.G1.04.1)

This passage includes several dense noun phrases in grammatical subject positions; in this way, it reflects syntactic patterns that tend to appear in explanatory writing. The student's writing also contains several argumentative patterns that convey suspense and possibility, as the writer speculates about the origin and evolution of new species. Especially, patterns that intensify and indicate the large scope of the claims include adverbs (*certainly, early, never, increasingly, most*) and common nouns (*one of the most important* ***steps*** *in the* ***history*** *of* ***animal life***). This student also includes the four development moves, cued by discourse-level signals. Move (1) identifies a broad topic in the field (*origin of new species*); move (2) offers specific examples (*The environmental conditions*); move (3) offers and analysis of these examples (*The chance coincidence*); and move (4) shifts the paragraph to the larger takeaway for the interpretation offered (the factors that *set the stage for one of the most important steps in the history of animal life*).

A second-year graduate student in education likewise employs these moves and several argumentative patterns in her critique titled "Beyond Cognitive Skills to Enactment in Sociocultural Contexts":

> (D) In the field of education, much attention has been turned to the literacy achievement gap that exists between those students for whom there is a close match of home and school literacy, and those for whom this is not the case. In chapter 6 of *Cognitive Development and Learning* (Byrnes, 2001), the author gives only one paragraph to cultural differences in literacy; however, this is limited to differences in achievement according to ethnicity. It is also addressed in terms of quantitative differences rather than qualitative differences in literacy. This suggests a deficit model for minority literacy practices, which Byrnes discusses in chapter 12 as a "contextual view model" (pp. 323–4). While Byrnes does give limited discussion to different cultural contexts for literacy in chapter 12, he clearly does not foreground this in his discussion of beginning reading, instead drawing heavily on the connectionist model of Seidenberg and McClelland (1989). My criticisms of this model thus far are not to say that I don't see its importance for explaining the cognitive processes of reading; I do, but I want to expand it to include not only the four cognitive processors identified by Seidenberg and McClelland, but also critical sociocultural factors. Perhaps the answer is to situate the connectionist model within a sociocultural framework. (EDU.G2.03.1)

In this passage, the writer opens with a shared narrative of concerns in the field of education (*much attention has been turned to . . .*) before making an overtly persuasive case for including not only cognitive but also sociocultural factors in literacy studies. She uses several key argumentative patterns that facilitate persuasion, including infinitive verbs (*not **to say**, **to expand** it*), intensifying adverbs (*gives **only**, **clearly** does, drawing **heavily***), and the countering conjunction *but*. The passage displays a conversational style and foregrounds human ideas—Byrnes and others advocating a cognitive model, and the writer advocating a sociocultural framework—through argumentative patterns such as first person pronouns (***My** criticisms, **I** don't see, **I** do*) and third person pronouns (*he*). In addition, the writer uses the four development moves, cued by discourse-level patterns: move (1) notes a larger trend in the field (*much attention*), move (2) specifies examples (e.g., *the author gives . . . he clearly does not*), move (3) offers interpretation (*My criticisms . . .*), and move (4) links back to the larger takeaway from the interpretation offered (*Perhaps the answer . . .*).

In a somewhat divergent example below, a third-year graduate student studying natural resources uses argumentative discourse and an epistolary style in an argumentative essay titled "Policy Decision Memo":

> (E) Today, <u>Senators McCain and Lieberman</u> attached their climate change bill (S.1151) as an amendment (S.Amdt. 826) to the Energy Policy Act of 2005 (H.R.6). Contrary to your previous support of the McCain-Lieberman legislation, <u>I</u> recommend that tomorrow you vote against this amendment. Primarily, <u>your vote</u> will be a strong statement against their inclusion of subsidies to nuclear power utilities. <u>This</u> may prove to be the strongest platform that we can use to object to large government subsidies for nuclear power generators, and we can do so while remaining supportive of the main goal of McCain-Lieberman: reducing greenhouse gas emissions. <u>Voting against the amendment</u> is more symbolic than substantive, as Senators McCain and Lieberman have again not collected enough votes from moderate Republicans to give the bill a chance of passing. <u>The Climate Stewardship and Innovation Act of 2005</u> (S.Amdt. 86, S.1151) is a step ahead in the right direction on climate change. <u>It</u> would establish a cap and trade system to reduce greenhouse gas emissions in the United States, and potentially at the lowest cost. However, <u>the costs of doing so</u> are still large and uncertain, and therefore pose risks to this market and to the overall economy in the future. (NRE.G3.02.1)

In this passage, the student's writing approximates a professional letter or memo different from the essay form of previous examples, yet she employs similar argumentative discourse patterns. Several patterns emphasize conversational interaction and human ideas, including pronouns that directly address the reader (***your** vote*) and both the reader and writer (*we*). Other argumentative patterns contribute to general, persuasive claims, including common nouns (*the right* ***direction***, *a* ***chance***), infinitive and modal verbs (***to give***, ***to reduce***, ***would*** *establish*), adverbs (*Primarily*, *so*, *more*), and negation, all of which help the writer make her case and refute the alternative. The writer also utilizes two stance words discussed later in the chapter. Hedges *may* and *potentially* allow the writer to qualify speculative claims (***may*** *prove to be the strongest platform*, ***potentially*** *at the lowest cost*), and the counter *However* explicitly signals a contrast to the prior concessive statement about the Climate Stewardship and Innovation Act.

Explanatory Examples

Next, consider examples from upper-level explanatory writing. In these passages, upper-level students use explanatory discourse patterns that foreground comparisons and a more informational style. The first example passage, written by a final-year undergraduate student studying sociology, appears in a report titled "Sociological Perspectives on Organ Donation Against the Backdrop of Various Religions":

> (1) <u>Catholicism</u> seems more open to the idea of human tissue banking than Judaism because they do not require that the use be of immediate and specific benefit, as many Jews do (Campbell 1998: 296). <u>The Catholic Church</u> once viewed organ donation as mutilation, but now it can be seen as a charitable act (Rumsey 2003). Similarly within the Christian faith, <u>protestant beliefs</u> can range from very liberal to very conservative, especially with issues of body integrity. However, <u>it</u> is enough to say that most Christians agree that Jesus teaches his followers to love one another. Like many other religions, <u>altruistic acts</u> are celebrated and if something can be done to save someone's life, Christians often take on a role of personal responsibility, helping others when in need (Campbell 1998: 293). (SOC.G0.13.2)

This student uses several explanatory patterns that facilitate description, and the grammatical subjects tend to label religions and religious beliefs. Noun and prepositional phrases provide detail and comparison: *the idea [of human tissue banking], be [of immediate and specific benefit], seen [as a charitable act], range [from very liberal][to very conservative], beliefs . . . [with issues][of body integrity], a role [of personal responsibility]*. Explanatory patterns such as comparative adjectives and adverbs (*more open*, *as . . . do*, *similar, similarly*) additionally facilitate the rhetorical goal of synthesis, in this case between religious practices. Passive verb constructions include *can be seen* and *are celebrated*. These constructions place emphasis on aspects of religious beliefs; for instance, *are celebrated* emphasizes the grammatical subject *altruistic acts* rather than who celebrates them. The religious groups *Jews* and *Christians* occupy three grammatical subject positions, whereas the other subject positions foreground religions and beliefs.

These grammatical and lexical patterns foreground comparative explanation, even as the passage includes both argumentative and explanatory discourse (e.g., the use of the pronoun *it* in the clause *it is enough to say* is more characteristic of argumentative writing). In addition, the passage reflects the rhetorical development moves noted earlier, from topic to evidence to analysis to a link. Move (1), in the first clause, introduces the specific topic of the paragraph, facilitated by noun phrases and the comparative *more*; move (2), beginning in the second clause of sentence one, offers examples (connected by *similarly*); move (3) offers more specific analytic conclusions (*it is enough to say*); and move (4) links to the primary takeaway (that Christians may approach human tissue banking positively due to their view that saving a life is an altruistic act).

The next passage displays similar explanatory patterns, this time in a description of a medical intervention. The passage appears in a research paper titled "HIV Education Intervention" by a final-year undergraduate studying nursing:

> (2) <u>Objectives for this intervention</u> include the ability of every student, post-intervention, to list at least one way they could protect themselves from HIV. <u>All objectives</u> are listed in table 1. After designing an educational program on HIV <u>it</u> was presented to seven senior nursing students and one public health nursing instructor. <u>The students and instructor</u> critiqued the program and appropriate changes were made. <u>Arrangements</u> were made to implement the program to a group of 12 students at Ida High School in Monroe County. <u>The intervention</u> acts on the level of primary prevention. <u>Primary prevention efforts in public health</u> aim to inhibit development of disease before it starts. <u>The design of the intervention</u> is to take HIV-negative youth and provide them with the knowledge to protect themselves from infection and remain negative for their lives. (NUR.GO.13.1)

In this excerpt, the student's use of explanatory discourse patterns helps her foreground the steps and details of the research study she outlines. Dense noun and prepositional phrases delineate specific aspects of the research study (*Objectives [for this intervention], Primary prevention efforts [in public health], The design [of the intervention]*). Passive verb constructions foreground aspects of the research study rather than the human researchers behind them (e.g., <u>All objectives</u> ***are listed*** *in table 1*, <u>appropriate changes</u> ***were made***). Other key explanatory patterns also facilitate description of the research design, including the use of the preposition *for* (*for this intervention*) and common nouns (*group, students, prevention*). The final two sentences include infinitive verbs more common in argumentative writing; these help underscore the value of the intervention design (*to take . . . and provide . . . to protect . . . and remain*). This example also shows the use of nominalizations and noun phrases that add detail but also omit explicit grammatical information. For instance, the student writes, *The intervention acts on the level of primary prevention*, a sentence composed almost entirely of noun and prepositional phrases—nominalizations *intervention* and *prevention* and prepositional phrases *[on the level] [of primary prevention]*—with one lexical verb. These grammatical structures emphasize the *intervention* and *prevention* and omit explicit indication of the human subjects driving these processes.

In addition, the passage offers an example of the four rhetorical development moves in an explanatory paper: move (1) introduces *Objectives* of the intervention, move (2) specifies steps for achieving these objectives (*After designing, Arrangements were made*), move (3) offers analysis of how those steps will work (*efforts . . . aim to inhibit . . . before it starts*), and finally move (4) offers a link back to broad intervention objectives (preventative knowledge that will keep students disease-free *for their lives*).

The next explanatory passage comes from student writing in the humanities. The passage appears in a report titled "Clarissa Consumed" written by a first-year graduate student in English:

(3) <u>The meaning of Clarissa's slow and inevitable demise</u> has been explored in a variety of ways: as a saintly martyrdom; as a suicide; as resulting from a loss of self-respect; as a "political gesture." <u>Donalee Frega</u> attempts to confront the physical reality of that "lovely

skeleton" in her 1998 book, *Speaking in Hunger*, which examines Clarissa as anorexic. Clarissa's emaciation and her refusals or inability to eat bear similarity to the disease, so Frega brings the psychology of anorexia nervosa to bear upon Clarissa. She examines Clarissa's family dynamics as a possible cause, and suggests that Clarissa begins exhibiting food-controlling behavior at home around the family dinner table and continues it through her stay in the brothel and her final fast. In each setting, she claims, food represents a way for Clarissa to control her own body, and the people around her, by consenting or refusing to dine. (ENG.G1.01.1)

In example (3), the student uses several noun phrases in a review of a scholarly analysis. For instance, the first grammatical subject is a compressed noun phrase, which includes an embedded prepositional phrase and coordinated attributive adjectives (*The meaning of Clarissa's* ***slow and inevitable*** *demise*). Other explanatory patterns include passive constructions (*has been explored*), prepositional phrases (beginning with *in*, *of*, *as*, *to*, *through*, *for*, and *by*), and common nouns (*variety*, *ways*). These patterns help the student emphasize the literary text she analyzes and the scholar's interpretation she reviews. Several pronouns, proper nouns, and genitive markers emphasize human ideas and actions, but the patterns overall support the rhetorical aim of describing an object of study and showcasing interpretive reasoning, not foregrounding a persuasive thesis.

A second-year graduate student in linguistics uses similar explanatory patterns to delineate two theories in the introduction to a report titled "A CVX theory of Dutch Syllable Structure":

(4) The proposal that medial position syllabic rime is restricted to two slots maximally was demonstrated to be a tenable view in Borowsky (1989). In a departure from the more traditional viewpoint that onset clusters are constrained by principles of sonority, Dunamu (2002) proposes that complex onset clusters in English and Chinese are composed of one slot. Together, the two theories posit a CVX structure for syllable structure. The question remains as to whether this claim can be shown to hold for languages other than English and Chinese. This paper investigates the extent to which standard Dutch con be shown to conform to CVX theory. (LIN.G2.03.1)

This passage includes explanatory patterns that facilitate the student's explanation of traditional and innovative linguistic theories. Using compressed noun phrases, the student offers concise details about the theories, for instance, *a departure [from the more traditional viewpoint]* and *principles [of sonority]*. Likewise, the student's use of passive verb constructions (*was demonstrated, constrained by, can be shown*) foreground the linguistic proposal and ideas in question. Other keyword patterns that facilitate detailed synthesis include comparative adverbs and adjectives (*Together, more traditional viewpoint*). As in other explanatory passages, most of the discussion is devoted to elaborated description of a focus of study, which in this case provides a point of departure for the student's a test of CVX theory.[7]

A final explanatory example, also written in the social sciences, includes several explanatory patterns that facilitate the student's description and synthesis of research on heterosexuality and heteronormativity. Written by a third-year graduate student in psychology, the passage appears in a research paper titled "Development of the Heteronormative Attitudes and Beliefs Scale":

> (5) Rubin (1975), Rich (1980), and Jackson (1999), previously explored the obligatory . . . compulsory . . . (and) compulsive" pressures toward heterosexuality (all cited in Yep, p. 18). Yep builds on this work to elucidate the violence that heteronormativity inflicts on women (by requiring that they serve men in marriage and motherhood), men (by defining rigid expectations of hegemonic masculinity), sexual minorities (by defining them as "other" and thus not fully human), and individuals who experience multiple forms of prejudice and marginalization due to the intersections of racial, ethnic, gender, sexual, and other identities. Consistent with Yep's portrayal of heteronormative violence, Lind (2004) points out that sexual minorities living in poverty are especially disenfranchised; they have limited access to resources, and the social services that would otherwise be available to heterosexually-headed households are denied to them due to definitions of marriage and family in welfare law. (PSY.G3.06.1)

In this passage, the student devotes most textual space to explaining and comparing existing scholarship, especially through noun phrases. These include the list of syntactically dense phrases in the second sentence (*the violence that heteronormativity inflicts [on women][by requiring that they serve men][in marriage and motherhood]*), etc.), which ends with several coordinated attributive adjectives describing social identities in a prepositional phrase (*the intersections [of racial, ethnic, gender, sexual, and other identities]*). In the final clause in the passage, the writer uses a passive construction that places *the social services that would otherwise be available to heterosexually-headed households* in the grammatical subject position to emphasize the process and outcome (vs. the agents) of discrimination. In this passage, the writer both details research in compressed noun phrases and foregrounds human subjects involved in the research.

Analysis II: What Stance Word Patterns Distinguish Upper-Level Explanatory and Argumentative Writing?

This section turns to stance word patterns in upper-level explanatory and argumentative writing. As a brief reminder, three types of stance words provide epistemic clues. These help writers explicitly signal the level of certainty and applicability of their statements and include hedges (e.g., *likely*), boosters (e.g., *very*), and generality words (e.g., *always*). The final two types of stance words provide textual clues; counters (e.g., *but*) and reformulation words (e.g., *that is to say*) help writers explicitly convey cohesive relations between parts of a text.

The Distant View: Stance across Upper-Level Texts

Figure 2 displays comparative frequencies of each stance word in upper-level explanatory and argumentative writing.

This graphic representation helps highlight several notable stance word patterns in upper-level writing, including some that contrast with first-year stance word patterns. Most notable is that, regardless of genre, upper-level writing contains more hedges than boosters, whereas first-year writing contains more boosters than hedges, irrespective of genre. Also notable, in contrast with first-year patterns, is that no single stance category far exceeds the others. Reformulation words are used less than other words, but the other four types of stance words are all used between 75 and 100 times per 10,000 words. By contrast, in first-year

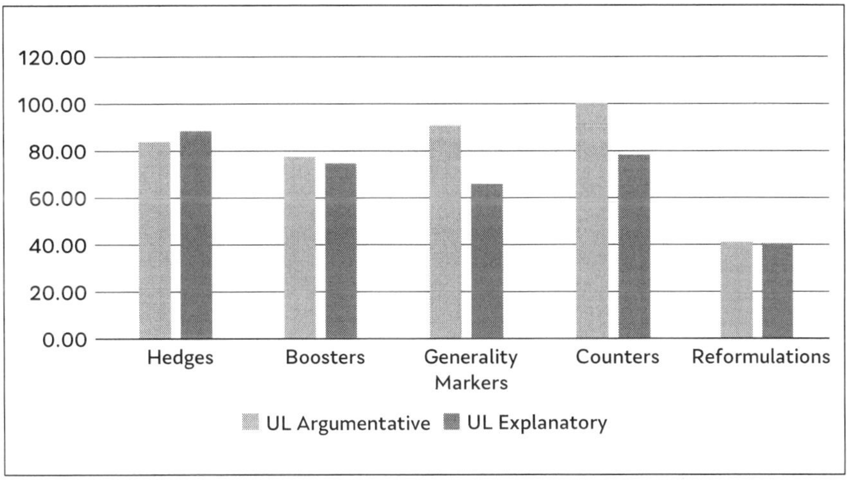

Figure 2. Stance Word Patterns in Upper-Level Writing, Instances per 10,000 Words

writing, generality words in both genres far exceeded other stance words (between 106 and 150 uses per 10,000 words).

In both assignment genres, upper-level discourse constitutes a close balance between opening dialogic space with hedges and closing dialogic space with boosters: argumentative writing contains 1.2 hedges to every booster, and explanatory writing contains 1.1 hedges to every booster. In addition, strikingly similar use of reformulation words—40.9 and 40.4 uses per 10,000 words—means that, regardless of genre, upper-level writing includes explicit cohesive ties related to reformulating information.

Whereas hedge and booster patterns create rhetorical balance in both genres, they also point to some genre-specific distinctions. Argumentative writing contains 4% more boosters, a moderately significant difference, whereas explanatory writing contains 6% more hedges, a highly significant difference. The use of more hedges and fewer boosters suggests that more explicitly qualified, circumspect statements are valued in explanatory writing relative to argumentative writing. More explicitly countered and generalized statements are valued in argumentative writing, which contains 37% more generality words and 27% more counters (both highly significant differences).[8]

A final overall note is that, as in the first-year analysis, the specific stance words used in each upper-level genre family are similar, suggesting that the primary difference is one of quantity rather than quality. In both upper-level genres, the most frequent hedges are *perhaps* and *likely*, the most frequent boosters are *must* and *very*, the most frequent generality words are *all* and *people*, the most frequent counters are *but* and *however*, and the most frequent reformulation words are *such as* and *for example*. Example passages below, in which stance words appear in bold, illustrate upper-level students' use of stance word patterns.

The Closer View: Stance within Upper-Level Texts

Argumentative Examples

In an argumentative essay titled "Economics of the Illicit-Drug Market," a final-year undergraduate student in economics includes several boosters to construct an overtly persuasive stance:

> (F) In an article published in the *New York Times* entitled "To More Inmates, Life Term Means Dying Behind Bars," Adam Liptak notes, "thousands of lifers are going into prisons each year, and in many states few are ever coming out, even in cases where judges and prosecutors did not intend to put them away forever." Keeping in mind that the estimated costs of incarcerating an offender for **merely** one year is between $30,000-$40,000, we can begin to comprehend the severity of the monetary crisis this situation presents. To further exacerbate the situation, **one must** also call to attention the reality that an aging population of prisoners **will undoubtedly** generate higher medical costs than a younger criminal population. (ECO.G0.03.1)

In this passage, the student writer uses Liptak's statement as a point of departure for a claim about *the severity* of the financial challenges presented by a growing and aging incarcerated population. The student's use of the booster *merely* amplifies his statement about the cost of even a short incarceration period. He further emphasizes and generalizes the scope of the claim with the help of the pronoun *one*, the emphatic modal verb *must*, the predictive modal verb *will*, and the adverb *undoubtedly*. Along with words that show urgency, such as *severity*, *crisis*, and *exacerbate*, this argumentative passage explicitly foregrounds persuasion, using stance words to create a sense of urgency. In addition, the writer's use of the pronoun *we* creates a conversational emphasis on shared concerns with the reader.

In another example, this one from an argumentative essay by a first-year graduate student in classics, the writer likewise uses stance words to clarify a specific position. The passage appears in an essay titled "The Bellum Hispaniense as a Face of Battle Narrative":

> (G) The anonymous Bellum Hispaniense from the Caesarian corpus is the closest thing we have to the soldier's eye view from a military campaign in Antiquity. (3) The author was a junior officer, **perhaps** a cavalry commander (praefectus equitum), (4) who gives us his account of the last action of Caesar's civil war, not from the 'eye of command', **but from** the perspective of a more common participant. The narrative, therefore, is not an over-arching analysis of Caesar's entire campaign, **but rather** an account based on the author's own experience of the war. **Yet, despite** the influence of John Keegan's The Face of Battle in Roman military studies and the diffusion of socio-cultural approaches to the Roman army, the author is **still** criticized for failing to provide a broad strategic analysis of Caesar's campaign: "As a military commentator he lacks a sense of proportion", focusing instead on minor engagements, war atrocities, and desertions. **In other words**: "trivialities displace the solid information the reader would like on strategy, or even on tactics". (6) It is proposed here **instead** to consider the author as war-participant, not a "war commentator", and to explore his "trivialities" for insights into a low-level Roman officer's experience of war and the workings of the late Republican army. (CLS.G1.04.1)

In this example, the writer uses several stance words that open and close dialogic space and explicitly position his claims in contrast with existing views. First, he uses a hedge (*perhaps*) in the second sentence to qualify a speculative claim that cannot be supported. After that, the writer begins to close dialogic space around a single claim. The second sentence includes negation and the countering conjunction *but* to begin outlining what he claims and does not claim (*not from . . . but from*). Several more counters appear in the sentences that follow, including *but rather*; *Yet, despite*; and *still*. Likewise, the counter *instead* explicitly signals the writer's own thesis at the end of the passage. Finally, several key argumentative words discussed in the previous section also appear; the opening sentence, for example, includes *is* as the main verb in a statement about superlative quality (*is the closest thing we have*). This and other statements at the start of the passage are interesting because they focus on an object of analysis, a common focus in explanatory writing. Yet the lexical and grammatical patterns throughout the passage—the stance word patterns as well as the use of *it is*, a superlative adjective (*closest*), and the pronoun *we*—convey singular emphasis and a conversational style. These patterns begin to intimate a persuasive style even before the overt claim that begins *It is proposed here instead.*

Explanatory Examples

Explanatory passages, in contrast, show less explicit contrast. In the passage below from a research paper written by a second-year graduate student studying natural resources, we can see less contrast but also the characteristic upper-level rhetorical balance between the opening and closing of dialogic space. The research paper is titled "Impact on Atmospheric Carbon Dioxide Levels: Sequestration vs. Reduced Emissions":

> (6) In my analysis, I assumed that sequestration is equivalent to fixation (as it represents the earth's ability to sequester carbon in vegetation). **However**, one **could** also consider man-made carbon sequestration and storage (CCS) techniques in devising a practical, comprehensive strategy to reduce GHG concentrations (for instance, the possibility of trapping emissions from coal-fired power plants and burying them underground). I also applied learnings from my literature review to assess which levers could in fact be altered and by how much. The results of the scenario modeling show that **the most** effective lever in altering atmospheric carbon dioxide levels is emissions: the range in carbon dioxide concentrations that result from halving or doubling emissions is the highest, at 1,229.9 ppm in year 2200 or 2,072.5 ppm maximum. (NRE.G2.07.1)

In this explanatory passage, the writer describes her analysis, foregrounding her own involvement with the first person pronoun *I*. The second sentence begins with the counter *However* to explicitly introduce an alternative consideration, and the hedge *could* opens dialogic space for this alternative. The final sentence contains a booster to foreground the writer's conclusion about *the most effective* focus for altering carbon dioxide concentrations. This sequence of hedging and then boosting creates what Lancaster describes as a rhetorical balance of expansion and contraction ("Interpersonal Stance" 6). In other words, the writer's use of both hedging and boosting allows her not only to address alternatives but also to foreground one approach. Finally, the grammatical subject in the last sentence foregrounds analysis findings (*The results of the scenario modeling*) rather than human subjects who carried out the analysis.

A final explanatory example below appears in a report titled "Seeking Hope at Home," written by a final-year undergraduate student studying political science" Here too the writer uses both hedging and boosting discourse:

> (7) **To an extent**, the 1948 Supreme Court case of Shelley v. Kraemer was an exception for its strong, unanimous opinion. **Though** it came under fire for its reasoning, the opinion was **still** regarded as a clear indictment of discriminatory housing policies and emboldened blacks as the Civil Rights Era dawned. For the first time, it provided fair housing advocates a legal foundation upon which they could galvanize change, prompting them to push harder for reform than ever before. The Shelley decision **did not** end a movement **but rather** sparked one by infusing energy and confidence into fair housing advocates who suddenly enjoyed the backing of Constitutional law. (POL.G0.29.1)

This passage opens with a hedged phrase, *To an extent*, followed by a statement about the exceptionality of *Shelley v. Kraemer.* The subsequent sentences include counters, which help the writer explicitly acknowledge and then offset critiques of the opinion from the case. This concession-counter move is facilitated by a passive construction (*was . . . **regarded***), which makes the Supreme Court case the grammatical subject and focus of the statement. The use of generalized, temporal phrases in the third sentence highlights the novelty of the decision (*For the first time, than ever before*). The counter in the final sentence helps emphasize the author's interpretation of the effect of the Shelley decision, by first suggesting what it *did not* do in contrast to what it did do. In addition, the passage displays the explanatory pattern of detailed phrases but implicit grammatical relations. For instance, in the first sentence, several prepositional and noun phrases convey specific details, but the sentence does not explicitly address who or what made the case opinion an exception. In this way, the sentence conveys compressed detail without explicitly clarifying grammatical relations. Finally, the use of negation and the countering conjunction *but* reflects key argumentative patterns discussed in the last section. This example highlights that distinctions between the genre families are based not on individual uses but on quantity, or cumulative rhetorical effects—the countering conjunction *but*, for example, is used similarly in upper-level argumentative and explanatory writing but is used significantly more in argumentative writing.

Student Discourse in Upper-Level Genres

The analysis in this chapter highlights patterns that construct distinct sociocognitive habits in different upper-level assignment genres. Upper-level argumentative writing includes a wider range of grammatical patterns—various verbs, pronouns, conjunctions, adverbs, and determiners. Recurring pronouns and genitive markers foreground human ideas and needs, and repetition of dependent clauses beginning with *that* underlines opinions and explicit grammatical relations. Recurring counters, adverbs, and negation in argumentative writing help upper-level writers make a persuasive case for particular ideas.

Upper-level explanatory writing exhibits a more narrow range of grammatical patterns and contains more noun and prepositional phrases. Upper-level explanatory writing is also characterized by a smaller set of verbs but more past participles used in passive constructions. Recurring noun phrases offer concise, compressed detail, though these also sometimes appear in upper-level argumentative writing. In upper-level explanatory writing, passive constructions facilitate an emphasis on research processes and outcomes, drawing less attention to the human agents driving those processes.

These genre-specific discourse patterns and rhetorical effects, in turn, help construct knowledge in particular ways. In argumentative writing, lexical and grammatical patterns facilitate a conversational style and making a case, and they foreground human ideas, including those of the writer and reader, in the construction of knowledge. Because they include some lexical and grammatical characteristics of interactive conversation and writing, they may be more accessible to a wider range of general and academic readers. The recurring lexical and grammatical choices in upper-level explanatory writing facilitate a more informational style. These patterns foreground research processes and outcomes in the construction of knowledge, and they make the writing denser and less explicit than upper-level argumentative writing.

Some upper-level patterns constitute similar sociocognitive practices, regardless of the writing assignment. Across both explanatory and argumentative writing, upper-level stance word patterns create a rhetorical balance of opening and closing dialogic space, and they draw explicit attention to reformulations for readers. These patterns intimate that, regardless of genre, making knowledge in upper-level writing includes acknowledging other views and offering new ideas as writers and readers coconstruct understanding. Also irrespective of assignment genre, upper-level patterns include some noun phrases, suggesting that successful upper-level writers are likely to use some dense phrases to add detail in their writing.

By exposing genre-specific discourse patterns in successful upper-level writing, the analysis in this chapter offers example connections between genre-specific expectations and specific microlevel discourse choices. It suggests successful upper-level writers are highly likely to add detail in dependent clauses and emphasize human ideas and needs in their argumentative writing but, in contrast, are strongly inclined to emphasize research processes and outcomes in their explanatory writing. The final chapter offers additional detail about genre-specific discourse regardless of student level, and level-specific discourse regardless of school genre. It also considers implications for discourse patterns in upper-level writing that constitute both civility and exclusivity.

Notes

1. More specific geographic and racial demographic information follows: UM students come from fifty states and at least 122 countries, and the most represented countries besides the United States include China, India, and South Korea. The student body is approximately 65% white, 15% Asian American, 10% unknown, 6% Hispanic/Latino American, and 5% black or African American, 5% Hispanic, and 1% Native American (see "Undergraduate Admissions").

2. Graduate student demographic information is less consolidated but is available by year and program in "Ethnicity Reports."

3. It is worth noting that the research paper goal of conducting original research may seem to students to focus on demonstrating research skills rather than a clear rhetorical writing goal. In other words, whereas the rhetorical purpose of essays is to construct and support an argument, and the rhetorical purpose of reports is to give an account of an issue or text and its significance, the rhetorical purpose of research papers is to present original research (Römer and O'Donnell 171). My hope is that the analysis in this chapter and chapter 5 can further elucidate the rhetorical purpose of research papers in terms of written discourse practices.

4. The corpus I use contains only the written text of the main paper sections, without abstracts, bibliographies, or tables, made accessible for educational use through *The Grammar Lab* developed by Brown (www.thegrammarlab.com).

5. Similar trends emerge in undergraduate writing in England (Nesi and Gardner).

6. Examples from the upper-level corpus are cited using their MICUSP paper tag. Papers in MICUSP are identified by a tag that shows discipline, level, and paper number, for instance, paper PHI.G3.01.1 in was written in philosophy (PHI) by a third-year graduate student (G3) who is student number 1 in this discipline; and this is the first paper he submitted. Note as well that in MICUSP, students selected "female or male" when submitting their papers, and I use corresponding pronouns when discussing each specific paper analyzed. (The first-year writing corpus does not include this metalevel data, and so I do not use gender-specific pronouns in the analysis of first-year writing.)

7. In addition, this passage exhibits Swales's three introductory rhetorical moves that, like the development moves I have discussed, are cued by discourse. The passage first "establishes a territory" (*The proposal that. . . . In a departure*), then identifies a gap or "niche" (*The question remains . . .*), and finally "occupies the niche" by suggesting how the writing will address the gap (*This paper investigates . . .*) (*Genres* 141). I discuss these moves in the pedagogical applications for students in the afterword.

8. It is worth bearing in mind that, though academic writing includes genre-specific expectations, overall it uses fewer boosters and more hedges than non-academic writing, regardless of field or genre; newspaper and magazine writing, for instance, tends to intensify more and qualify less, and spoken conversation is the most general and certain of all of these broad registers (Hyland, *Metadiscourse*).

5

A New View of Student Writing

A look across chapters 3 and 4 already suggests that some genre-specific patterns appear consistent in both first-year and upper-level writing. Argumentative writing at both levels, for instance, includes more dependent clauses and uses of the countering conjunction *but*, which contribute to more grammatically explicit detail and a more overtly persuasive style. Explanatory writing at both levels includes more aspects of noun phrases, facilitating a more informational style. We can also see several distinctions. For instance, articles (especially *the*) form a significant pattern in first-year explanatory (vs. argumentative) writing, but they form neither a key explanatory nor a key argumentative pattern in upper-level writing, because articles are frequent in upper-level writing regardless of genre.

This chapter provides additional details by looking at discourse patterns that persist in each genre regardless of student level and those that recur in each student level regardless of genre. In other words, this chapter looks at those discourse patterns rewarded in argumentative or explanatory writing regardless of whether a student is beginning college or graduate school, as well as those discourse patterns rewarded in upper-level writing regardless of whether students study biology or English or write an argumentative essay or a research paper.

As in previous chapters, I analyze student writing according to keyword patterns and stance word patterns; all keyword patterns I discuss are highly significant, and I note the significance of each stance word pattern. Likewise, all the patterns I discuss appear in at least 90% of the texts analyzed. This ensures the identification of cases where, for instance, an extremely frequent pattern in argumentative writing at one student level does not appear significant across both levels. One distinction in this chapter is that I organize the lists of discourse patterns according to rhetorical effects rather than by frequency alone. By this I mean that I group the patterns according to rhetorical emphases they facilitate to concisely build on (but not repeat) discussions and examples from previous chapters.

In the second part of the chapter, I focus at length on the discourse patterns that distinguish upper-level writing from first-year writing. These patterns appear valued in students' writing development in higher education, regardless of whether they write explanatory or argumentative assignments. They constitute three rhetorical qualities of academic writing that I noted early in the book—compression, civility, and cohesion—that are both valuable and vexed. They help make academic writing diplomatic but also inaccessible compared with more common language use.

The chapter closes with a taxonomy for thinking about how these three patterned effects relate to cognitive, intrapersonal, and interpersonal domains of writing, bringing us back to the book's initial queries: What discourse patterns are repeatedly practiced and rewarded in school genres? What do these suggest about how students repeatedly construct knowledge, writers, and readers in higher education? In turn, what discourses and ways of being and relating in the world are worth keeping and worth changing?

Genre-Specific Student Discourse

In this first analysis, I look at those discourse patterns repeatedly valued in argumentative or explanatory writing regardless of whether student writers are near the beginning or end of higher education. We can more pointedly investigate these genre-specific patterns by dividing the corpora by genre only, as outlined in table 11.

Based on comparative analysis of these corpora, we can see argumentative and explanatory patterns across both student levels. Overall, the data confirm that several genre distinctions noted earlier hold: argumentative writing contains more conversational language and is more explicit about meaning relationships; explanatory writing is more compressed and informational and less explicit about grammatical relationships. Together, these patterns suggest that argumentative writing may be more accessible for more students because it is more interactive and explicit. By contrast, the greater detail and less generalized patterns of explanatory

Table 11. Genre-Specific Corpora

GENRE FAMILY	ARGUMENTATIVE WRITING		EXPLANATORY WRITING	
GENRE	UPPER-LEVEL ARGUMENTATIVE ESSAY + CRITIQUE/ EVALUATION	FIRST-YEAR ARGUMENTATIVE ESSAY	UPPER-LEVEL RESEARCH PAPER + REPORT	FIRST YEAR ANNOTATED BIBLIOGRAPHY + VISUAL ANALYSIS
Number of Texts	248	331	502	291
Total Number of Texts	579		793	
Total Number of Words	994,164		1,722,232	
Words per Text	~1,717		~2,172	
Reference for Comparative Analysis	Explanatory Writing (First-Year + Upper-Level)		Argumentative Writing (First-Year + Upper-Level)	

writing may make it particularly challenging for those students unaccustomed to these expectations. These patterns are detailed and organized by rhetorical effects in tables 12 and 13.

First, table 12 shows discourse patterns that persist across argumentative writing regardless of student level.[1] The most significant pattern in argumentative writing across student levels is the repeated use of possessive and third person plural pronouns. This pattern facilitates an emphasis on human ideas and behaviors in argumentative writing. Recall, for example, the emphasis on human behaviors and beliefs in example (B) from chapter 3: *On the other hand comprehensive sex education understands that not everyone will abstain from having sex and instead believes that the youth should be thoroughly taught on how and why they can prevent pregnancy and sexually transmitted diseases.*

Also in argumentative writing, a range of verb forms help student writers emphasize persuasion. These verbs include necessity and prediction modals, often in evaluations of evidence or proposals for particular actions—for example, the use of *should* in the previous example. Along with more generality words (such as *everyone* in the example), the frequent use of *it is* and indefinite pronouns in argumentative writing facilitate general reflections and observations, for example, in iterations such as *it is clear that* and *one can see how.*

In addition, students' use of frequent dependent clauses and phrasal verbs create a relatively conversational style. These patterns delineate explicit relations between the subjects and objects that students write

Table 12. Discourse Patterns in Argumentative Writing

RHETORICAL EFFECT	KEYWORD PATTERNS	COMMON ITERATIONS AND COLLOCATIONS
Emphasize human needs, ideas, behaviors	Possessive pronouns	***their*** (36.5%), *his* (23%), ***her*** (12.6%), ***its, our, your*** *[own/life/family, father, mother]*
	They (third person plural pronoun)	[singular noun, *that* as conjunction] ***they*** *are/have/can/were*
Add detail	*That* as conjunction (~82%) and determiner	[singular noun] ***that*** *the/they/are/there*
	As as conjunction (45.5%)	[singular noun, preposition] ***as*** *the/well/they/much*
	Subordinating conjunction	[singular noun, plural noun] *because, when, while, since [the, they, there, this]*
Make a case	*Be* base form	*can/should/would/will/not* ***be*** *the/able/used*
	Negation	*it is* ***not****, people do* ***not***
	Modal verbs	*[singular noun]* ***can/will/would/should*** *[not/have/also]*
	But as countering conjunction	[singular noun] *but [also/the/not]*
	Or as conjunction	[singular noun, plural noun, infinitive verb] ***or*** *not/the/even*
	Infinitive verbs	*to* ***make/say/take/see***
	To as infinitive marker (76.5%) and as preposition	**to** *make/have/help/take*

	Adverb particle in phrasal verb	[infinitive verb / lexical verb, present participle] ***out/back/down/off*** *[the/and/for]*
	Adverbs (general)	***also, only, however, even*** *[the/and/more/that]*
Offer general observations	*It* (third person singular pronoun)	***it*** *is* (31.6%), ***it*** *seems/was/would*
	Is as main verb	*it/there/this* ***is*** *not/the/that*
	Are as main verb	[plural common noun] ***are*** *not/the/more*
	One as indefinite pronoun	***one's*** *own*, ***one*** *can*
	After- or postdeterminer	[infinitive verb, present participle] ***some, any, enough*** *[other, people, sort, time]*
RHETORICAL EFFECT	STANCE WORD PATTERNS	COMMON ITERATIONS AND COLLOCATIONS
Close dialogic space and apply statements across contexts	Significantly more boosters (13.2% more)	*very/must/clearly/quite/really/extremely/sure*
	Significantly more generality words (53.3% more)	*likely, perhaps, almost, usually, generally, relatively*
		all, people, any, human, society
Explicitly counter	Significantly more counters (25.3% more)	*but, however, while, till, although, though*

Table 13. Discourse Patterns in Explanatory Writing

RHETORICAL EFFECT	KEYWORD PATTERNS	COMMON ITERATIONS AND COLLOCATIONS
Emphasize research processes, outcomes, and sources	Cardinal numbers	figure and table numbers, citations, number of people/years in event or study
	On as preposition (96.2%) and verb particle	[singular noun, past participle] *based/focus/research* **on** *the/a/their/this*
	Lexical verb, past tense	**found/used/showed/made** *[the/that/from]*
	Past participle of lexical verb	*[was/were / were not]* **used/able/found**
	This as determiner	[infinitive verb, *that* as conjunction] **this** *article, study, image, paper, was*
Add detail	Adjective (usually attributive)	***other, social, different, new, important*** *[effects/ideas]*
	Also as adverb	*is/but/are/can* **also** *be/the/have*
	The as article	**the** *same/first/most/United*
	Coordinating conjunction *and*	[singular noun, plural noun, proper noun] ***and*** *the, that, their, other*
RHETORICAL EFFECT	STANCE WORD PATTERNS	COMMON ITERATIONS AND COLLOCATIONS
Open dialogic space	Significantly more hedges (17.6% more)	*(more/the)* ***likely, perhaps, almost, possibility, usually***

about. For instance, argumentative example (A) in chapter 4 includes the following sentence in which generality words and subordinating conjunctions appear in bold: *Thus,* ***when human beings*** *hurt each other, they are hurting themselves much* ***like*** *Dana is physically and emotionally hurt* ***when*** *she hurts her ancestor, Rufus.* This example includes generalized claims about human beings and also includes dependent clauses that clarify meaning relations in the sentence—who hurts whom and under what circumstances humans hurt themselves. I return to generality words and other stance word patterns below.

Table 13 shows discourse patterns that persist across explanatory writing regardless of student level. Whereas argumentative discourse patterns generate grammatical variety, clausal detail, and emphasis on persuasion and human ideas and behaviors, explanatory patterns offer less grammatical variety and favor descriptions of research processes and sources. The patterns, including articles, determiners, adjectives, numbers, and prepositions, contribute to detailed, compressed noun phrases that tend to foreground research objects or outcomes. With passive verb constructions, these explanatory patterns facilitate emphasis on sources and studies rather than on the agents generating them. Cohesive and coordinating patterns, such as the use of *and* and *also*, facilitate adding detail in explanatory writing; conversely, negation and the countering conjunction *but* in argumentative writing foreground contrast and the singling out of one set of ideas.

Whereas detailed phrases in explanatory writing help writers add specific detail, they also allow writers to be less grammatically explicit. For instance, explanatory example (2) in chapter 4 includes the following sentence: <u>Arrangements</u> *were made to implement the program to a group of 12 students at Ida High School in Monroe County. . . .* The use of the passive construction in this sentence places the emphasis on the *arrangements* and omits explicit information about who made the arrangements.

Argumentative and explanatory writing also show distinct patterns in stance word use, noted in tables 12 and 13 and visually captured in figure 3. In argumentative writing, more boosters (e.g., *doubtless, clearly*) and more generality words (e.g., *every, always*)—along with fewer hedges (e.g., *possible, in some cases*)—constitute relatively certain and widely applicable claims. Along with counters, these patterns convey emphasis, urgency, and contrast. In explanatory writing, epistemic stance word

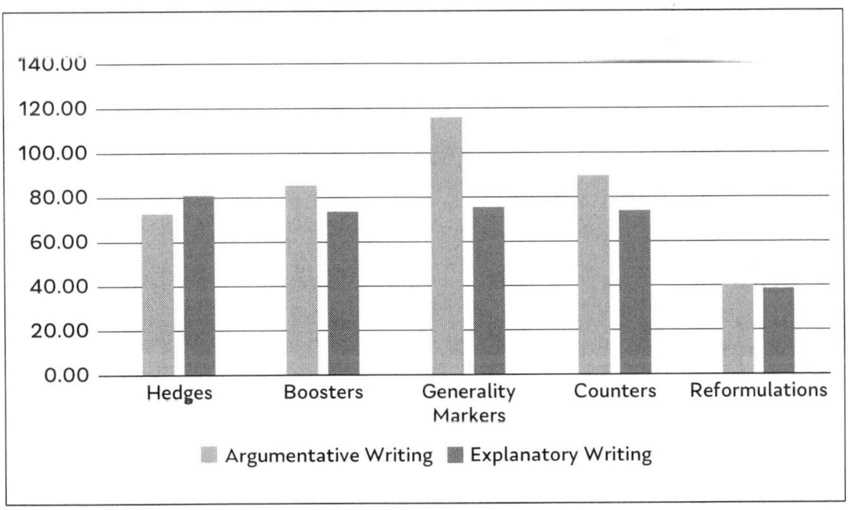

Figure 3. Stance Word Patterns by Assignment Genre, Instances per 10,000 Words

patterns—significantly more hedges, fewer boosters, and fewer generality words—form relatively less general, more cautious statements.

Interestingly, student writers use reformulation words comparably in both argumentative and explanatory writing. Reformulation words provide explicit textual clues for readers and foreground writers' ability to restate information. These patterns therefore suggest that across levels, instructors value discourse patterns that explicitly facilitate cohesion and reader engagement in both argumentative and explanatory writing assignments.

Together, keyword patterns and most stance word patterns suggest that argumentative and explanatory genres elicit distinct patterns in student writing, and these patterns construct knowledge, writers, and readers in particular ways. Argumentative writing patterns intimate that relatively certain and persuasive statements with an emphasis on human needs, ideas, and behaviors are part of making knowledge. Pronouns directly address human subjects, and stance word patterns also contribute to this version of knowledge construction by placing greater emphasis on the writers and readers of a given text. These argumentative patterns help writers reach and convince readers as part of participating in knowledge construction—for example, by using explicit clauses and a conversational style to engage readers, deploying boosters to amplify claims, and relying on counters and negation to refute competing positions. The wider variety of keyword patterns in argumentative writing also suggests that there are more lexical and grammatical choices rewarded in argumentative assignments than in explanatory assignments.

Explanatory writing patterns intimate that writers contribute to knowledge by offering more compressed, informational explanations about research sources and outcomes, without necessarily connecting these to more general observations. These patterns imply that these sources and processes themselves are part of constructing knowledge, independent of or in addition to human involvement. Relative to argumentative writing, stance word patterns in explanatory writing open more space for exceptions and alternatives, perhaps suggesting that such knowledge will continue to evolve through ongoing research. The fact that explanatory writing includes fewer unique patterns overall also suggests that a smaller range of lexical and grammatical choices are successful in explanatory writing.

Therefore, though argumentative and explanatory writing may have overlapping goals, such as demonstrating knowledge, and though some assignments may ask that students do both, genre-specific discourse patterns reveal compelling differences. They may also persist beneath many instructors' and students' conscious awareness. By implication, students less accustomed to one genre family may have few discursive strategies for fulfilling its rhetorical aims. Another implication is that unclear or identical assignment expectations for different genres are misleading—and a missed opportunity—in that they elide important rhetorical and linguistic distinctions. I take up this point in the afterword.

Level-Specific Student Discourse

In the final analysis below, I focus on level-specific discourse patterns, regardless of assignment genre. These we can explore by organizing the corpora by student level, as displayed in table 14.

Comparative analysis of keyword patterns and stance word patterns across these corpora identify patterns rewarded toward the beginning of curricular writing in higher education relative to those rewarded toward the end, and vice versa. In other words, this analysis does not identify all discourse patterns in successful first-year or upper-level writing, but rather those that recur at each level relative to the other. I discuss first-year patterns first but focus in particular on upper-level patterns, since these highlight discourse choices rewarded in student writing development over the course of higher education. The level-specific patterns include both explanatory and argumentative discourse, since writing at each level includes both. Thus in tables 15 and 16, I additionally note if

Table 14. Level-Specific Corpora

	First-Year		Upper-Level	
Genres	Argumentative Essay	Annotated Bibliography + Visual Analysis	Argumentative Essay + Critique/ Evaluation	Research Paper + Report
Number of Texts	331	291	248	502
Total Number of Texts	622		750	
Total Number of Words	807,324		1,909,072	
Words per Text	~1,298 words per text		~2,545 words per text	
Reference Corpus for Comparative Analysis	Upper-Level Writing (Argumentative + Explanatory)		First-Year Writing (Argumentative + Explanatory)	

Table 15. Discourse Patterns in First-Year Writing

RHETORICAL EFFECT	KEYWORD PATTERNS	COMMON ITERATIONS AND COLLOCATIONS
Make a case	*To* in infinitive verb form	*to* ***make/help/get/have***, *to* ***the/their/this***
	Infinitive verb FY argumentative pattern	***to help/make/get/take***
	Can as modal verb FY argumentative pattern	[singular noun / plural noun / pronoun *it*] ***can*** *not/help/also/make*
	Present participle, lexical verb	*using/making /trying/taking/getting*
	More as comparative degree adverb (~42%), comparative after- determiner (41%), and comparative adverb (~17%) FY argumentative pattern	[infinitive verb / present participle of lexical verb / singular noun] ***more*** *than/likely/ people*
	Modal verbs FY argumentative pattern	**can** (~33%) / **will** (19.5%) / **would** (~13%) / **should** (~12%) / **could/may/must** [*not / have/help/also*]
	Prepositional adverb as particle in phrasal verb FY argumentative pattern	[infinitive verb] ***out, down, back/off*** *[and/the/for]*
Offer general observations and emphasize human actors	Common nouns FY argumentative pattern	[determiners, infinitive verb] *people (64%)/media/data/statistics/species*
	It (third person singular pronoun)	[because/that] [singular noun] ***it*** *was/has/can*
	They (third person plural pronoun)	*that/because/what/and* ***they*** *are/have/can/will*
	Are as main verb FY argumentative pattern	[noun (*people*) / pronoun (*they*)] ***are*** *not/the/more/being*
	Is as main verb FY explanatory pattern	[noun/pronoun/*it*] ***is*** *the/not/that/also*
	Has (present perfect verb)	[singular noun / proper noun]/*it* ***has*** *been/become/the/not*

Focus on single source or object of study	Lexical verb, present tense FY explanatory pattern	[singular noun]/*it* ***shows*****/*****uses*****/*****makes*****/*****states***
	This as determiner FY explanatory pattern	[infinitive verb / singular noun]/*that* **this** *article/image/issue*
Add detail	*Also* as adverb FY explanatory pattern	[singular noun]/*is/but* ***also*** *the/has/uses*
	On as preposition (50.5%) and phrasal verb particle (49.5%)	[singular noun, plural noun (*impact*, *effects*)] ***on*** *the/their/how/this* [present participle of lexical verb / lexical verb (*focuses*)] ***on*** *the/their/how*
	By as preposition	[past participle of lexical verb / singular noun / plural noun] ***by*** *the/using/showing/making/their*
	That as conjunction (84%) and determiner FY argumentative pattern	[singular noun / plural noun / -s lexical verb] ***that*** *the/they/are*
RHETORICAL EFFECT	STANCE WORD PATTERNS	COMMON ITERATIONS AND COLLOCATIONS
Close dialogic space and apply claims across contexts	Significantly more boosters (17% more) Significantly more generality words (193% more)	Boosters: *must*, *very*, *really*, *clearly*, *fully* Higher booster use in first 10% of papers (2.79 per 10,000 words) and highest booster use in final 10% of papers (5.59 per 10,000 words); mid-paper 2.25 per 10,000 words Generality words: *people*, *all*, *society*, *human*, *any*, *the world*

Table 16. Discourse Patterns in Upper-Level Writing

RHETORICAL EFFECT	KEYWORD PATTERNS	COMMON COLLOCATIONS
Emphasize human needs and ideas	Genitive words UL argumentative pattern	Possessive use of common noun, e.g., ***women's/one's/children's/people's*** *[and, theory, life, own]*
Add detail	Adjective UL explanatory pattern	(usually attributive) ***other/social/different/important/new*** *[and/for/that/with]*
	Of as preposition UL argumentative pattern	*Number/one/part/use/because/amount* **of** *the/this/these/their*
	With as preposition	mostly follows nouns (and sometimes past participle of lexical verb), **with** *the/their/his/this/other*
	Comparative adjective UL explanatory pattern	usually in noun phrase or infinitive verb phrase; *higher/greater/lower/larger/better/further*
	Articles	*The* (94% of articles) *the same/first/most/other*
	In and *from* as prepositions	*In/from* follow nouns, participles, and infinitive verbs; often elaborates through description of attributes, purpose, or origin (***in*** *the/this/order/which*, **from** *the/this/their/his/her/each*)
	As as conjunction, preposition, adverb UL argumentative pattern	conjunction (~45% ***as*** *analyzed by*) [singular noun, plural noun] **as** *the/they/one/shown*, preposition (*such as, known as*), adverb (*seen as costly*)
	Which as determiner UL argumentative pattern	[singular noun, plural noun, proper noun], *in* ***which*** *the/are/was/they/would*

Emphasize processes and outcomes	Lexical verb, past tense UL explanatory pattern	*(and/they/that/who/which)* ***found/used/showed/made/became*** *(the/that)*
	Past participle of lexical verb UL explanatory pattern	used in passive constructions (47%) and perfect aspect (10%), as well as *used/based/found/given/shown [with/and/the/for/that]*
Explicitly compare and contrast	Adverbs (general) UL argumentative pattern	Sentence adverbs *(also/however/thus)*, specifiers *(even/both/especially)*
	After- or postdeterminer UL argumentative pattern	*same/such/own/former/latter [time/way/and/the]*
	But as countering coordinating conjunction UL argumentative pattern	[plural nouns / singular nouns / proper nouns] ***but*** *the/also/not*
RHETORICAL EFFECT	STANCE WORD PATTERNS	COMMON COLLOCATIONS
Open and close dialogic space	Significantly more hedges (39% more) Approximately even ratio hedges to boosters	Hedges: *perhaps, likely, almost* Lower booster use in first and final 10% of paper (1.83 per 10,000 words), lowest throughout middle of papers (1.46 per 10,000 words)
Explicitly counter and reformulate	Significantly more counters (23% more) Significantly more reformulation words (10% more)	Counters: *but, however, rather, thought* Reformulation words: *such as, for example, especially, in fact, specifically, in terms of, particularly*

the pattern was also significant in first-year or upper-level argumentative or explanatory writing.

The keyword patterns in first-year writing listed in table 15 enact a blend of strategies and effects. A range of verbs—infinitive, modal, and phrasal—facilitate making a case, and nouns and pronouns emphasize human actors. Common nouns such as *people*, as well as uses of *is* and *are* (especially *there are* and *it is*), support generalized observations. Patterns like the use of the determiner *this* focus attention on a single article or image, and some prepositional phrases and the adverb *also* add phrasal detail. The repeated use of two prepositions and the determiner *this* appear with noun phrases, which may indicate that successful first-year writers are beginning to approximate upper-level use of detailed phrases but have a smaller lexicon for this strategy. Several first-year discourse patterns contribute to a more persuasive and conversational style.

By contrast, upper-level writing contains less overtly persuasive and conversational patterns, displayed in table 16. Distinct from those of first-year writing, upper-level patterns place more emphasis on human needs and ideas than on human behaviors, and highlight research processes and outcomes over single objects of study. They also include more explicit cohesive ties, more hedges, fewer generality words, and a closer rhetorical balance between expanding and contracting dialogic space. Several of the upper-level patterns favor detailed noun phrases, including genitive markers, prepositions, determiners, and attributive adjectives. With passive constructions, these phrases contribute to an informational, dense style and often emphasize processes and conclusions without drawing explicit grammatical attention to the agents driving them.

Stance word patterns offer additional detail about how upper-level writers explicitly frame written material and guide readers, and they are noted in the tables and also represented in figure 4. This figure displays the comparative frequencies of each stance word in upper-level and first-year writing across genres.

On balance, first-year stance word patterns tend toward closed dialogic space and more generalized conclusions: first-year writing contains 1.5 boosters to every hedge and more generality words than any other stance word. Upper-level stance word patterns, by contrast, include sig-

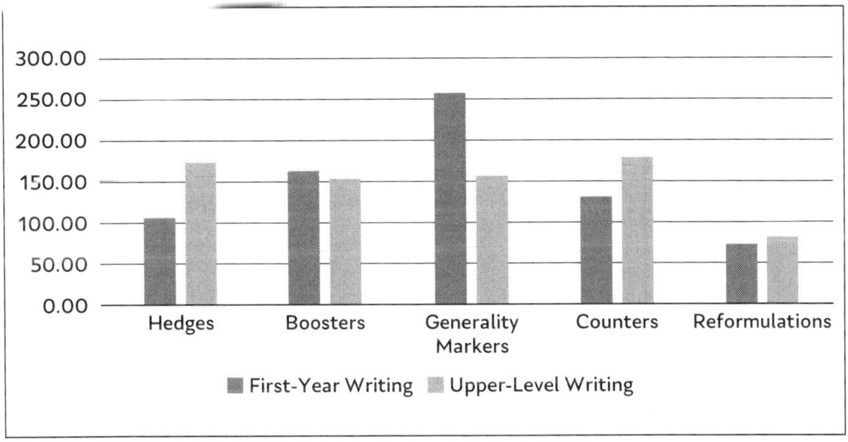

Figure 4. Stance Word Patterns by Student Level, Instances per 10,000 Words

nificantly fewer generality words. They also balance opening and closing dialogic space: upper-level writing contains 1.15 hedges for every booster, a ratio that approximates that of published academic writing in the Corpus of Contemporary American English, which contains 1.19 hedges to every booster (Aull, *First-Year University Writing* 96). Upper-level writers do use boosters to close dialogic space, particularly in paper introductions and conclusions, but less frequently than first-year students anywhere in their papers.[2] Upper-level stance word patterns also support more explicit textual cohesion: relative to first-year writing, upper-level writing contains significantly more counters and reformulation words.

Together, upper-level discourse patterns point to three rhetorical qualities that appear to be uniquely and repeatedly valued by the end of writing development in higher education: compression, civility, and cohesion. I have suggested these qualities are both vexed and valuable: compression makes academic writing inaccessible for unpracticed readers and writers; civility and cohesion make academic writing dialogically balanced and explicitly coherent for readers. I spell out these qualities and their implications below, drawing attention to both micro- and macrolevel choices.

In my descriptions, I strive to offer usable terminology for broad discussions about academic writing in higher education. I refer to a writer's *contribution* to avoid terms such as *argument* or *thesis* that may connote overtly persuasive contributions to the exclusion of analytic and descriptive ones. Upper-level writing is expected to contribute to knowledge—to demonstrate understanding, connect ideas, outline a way of seeing something, convince a reader—but these contributions can be either explanatory or argumentative, depending on the writing task. In my discussion, I also refer to a singular "writer" for grammatical ease, but this should be taken to stand in for both individual writers and collaborative groups of writers.

Compression: Concise Phrasal Detail

Upper-level writing is expected to provide detailed descriptions about the nature of its contribution. This detail is often presented in a concise and informational way, namely, through more syntactically dense noun phrases than are included in other language use (Biber; Biber et al., "Speaking"; Biber and Egbert). Douglas Biber and Bethany Gray show that most sentences in academic prose have optional phrasal modifiers, especially premodifiers like adjectives or nouns and postmodifiers like prepositional phrases (9), and upper-level patterns reflect these characteristics.

There are some additional ways that upper-level writers add detail, particularly in argumentative writing, and these strategies underscore that different grammatical choices create rather than reflect meaning. For example, in upper-level writing, phrasal detail often emphasizes processes without acknowledging the human actors driving them. Clausal detail, more common in argumentative upper-level writing, instead draws more explicit attention to grammatical relations between sentence subjects and objects. These different grammatical choices can tell different stories about what and who make knowledge. Regardless, however, more phrasal detail appears expected and rewarded in upper-level writing no matter the assignment.

Many prepositional phrases in upper-level writing include words and phrases that contribute to specification and precision, and this is consistent with patterns in published academic writing as well. Rita Simpson-Vlach and Nick C. Ellis's study of the most common phrases in published academic writing shows that the majority help writers increase precision. The two most common ways are through "specification of attributes," signaled by common phrases such as *an attempt to*, *are/was based on*, and *by virtue of*, and "identification and focus," signaled by phrases such as *[(as)] can be seen (in)*. Most of these phrases frame a subsequent noun (504). Similar phrases are common in upper-level writing, where the most common three-word phrases include *(in) such a way*, *based on the*, and *can be seen*.

Compressed, phrasal descriptions are notable in that they are unlike the lengthier and more explicit descriptions used in spoken conversation, online writing, and early undergraduate writing. They create concise detail and specification, but they also make upper-level writing uniquely challenging to parse relative to more common uses of language—they help make academic language exclusive. Since discourse patterns expected in student writing can be tacit, especially for novices and students who rarely receive A-level grades, this pattern of compressed noun phrases merits serious consideration: if we choose to privilege compressed, phrasal discourse, we should have good reasons why. With respect to this and other school discourse patterns, we should examine where intentional, relevant ways of thinking and writing end and where unquestioned discursive socialization begins.

Civility: Diplomatic Evidentiality

Upper-level writing is expected to make its contribution in thorough and diplomatic ways. This rhetorical quality underscores balance: balance between diplomacy, writers attention to others' contributions and potential concerns, and evidentiality, writers' attention to their own substantiated contribution. Upper-level patterns, regardless of genre, include a literal balance: almost equal hedging and boosting that leans toward hedging. These patterns constitute diplomatic evidentiality by both opening dialogic space to leave room for exceptions and reader concerns and closing dialogic space to highlight the writer's supported observations and particular contribution.

Research on academic writing shows that professional academic writers use stance words to convey more epistemic possibility than certainty and to be more indirect than direct in their criticisms (Hyland, "Stance"; Lancaster, "Do"; Swales, *Research*). Balancing hedges with some boosters helps upper-level students and professional academic writers position their own view as one among many (Aull and Lancaster 25), and common phrases in academic writing express more ability and possibility than evaluation and necessity (Simpson-Vlach and Ellis 506). Lancaster describes how a rhetorical balance of expanding and contracting dialogic space conveys the interpersonal positioning favored in academic writing ("Interpersonal Stance"). Concession-counter moves, which offer hedges or acknowledgment to alternative perspectives before countering them, are also valued in academic writing (Thompson). Along with directing critiques at ideas rather than people, these patterns help create a civil style in academic writing that discursively realizes several qualities long discussed in rhetoric and composition scholarship (Aull, "Civil Style").

Cohesion: Explicit Coherence

Upper-level writing is expected to provide explicit guidance about the connections between different parts of a text and to thereby guide readers through information and ideas. Textual clues help demonstrate a writer's ability and willingness to identify cohesive connections across various parts of a contribution. These clues mark larger and smaller rhetorical moves, for instance, between examples, paragraphs, and sections in a text.

Several keyword patterns and stance word patterns contribute to explicit cohesion. Reformulation words and counters provide explicit textual clues for readers and are significantly more frequent in upper-level writing. Sentence adverbs are the most common adverbs used by upper-level writers, and, in order of frequency, the most frequent sentence adverbs add information (*also*), counter previous information (*however*), show correlation (*thus*), and show specification and emphasis *(even, both, especially)*. Determiners such as *same, such, former,* and *latter* also draw explicit attention to how a subsequent idea or statement connects to a previous one. As we can see in table 15, first-year writing includes two patterns that contribute to explicit cohesion: *this* as a determiner and *also,* often in the phrase *but also.* But first-year writing does not (yet) have the same variety of explicit cohesive strategies visible in upper-level writing.

Rhetorical moves, cued by discourse, also help build cohesion. Research shows that academic articles across disciplines include three introductory moves that "create a research space" for the contribution of a given research article (Swales, *Genre* 141). These moves, discussed in detail in the second section of the afterword, are recognizable and cued by patterned language; they transition from broad to more specific ideas and together lead the reader to the novelty of a writer's contribution. In chapters 3 and 4, I introduced another move pattern that students use as they develop ideas in development (or "body") paragraphs. Move (1) introduces the topic of the section or paragraph, move (2) offers evidence or an example, move (3) analyzes the evidence, and move (4) offers a connection to an overarching idea in the text. All of these are cued by discourse-level patterns that help guide the reader through organized evidence and analysis (see chapters 3 and 4 and the afterword for details and examples).

A New Taxonomy: Making a Written Contribution through Macro- and Microlevel Choices

Throughout this book I suggest that patterned discourse offers insight for how we conceptualize student writing and assignments in higher education. A central tenet of this idea is that discourse patterns provide textual anchors for macrolevel rhetorical principles and therefore provide concrete reference points for discussing reading and writing with students. The taxonomy shown in figure 5 offers an example of how to expand current conceptualizations of student writing by connecting macrolevel writing expectations with microlevel discourse choices, specifically by linking strategies discussed in the last section with the cognitive, interpersonal, and intrapersonal domains of writing. Because genre influences all three of these, it exerts a continual influence captured on the left of the taxonomy.

Considering Patterned Discourse in Discussions about Discourse

This taxonomy offers example connections between macrolevel expectations and microlevel discourse patterns. In the cognitive domain, for instance, particular verbs and grammatical subjects offer concrete ways

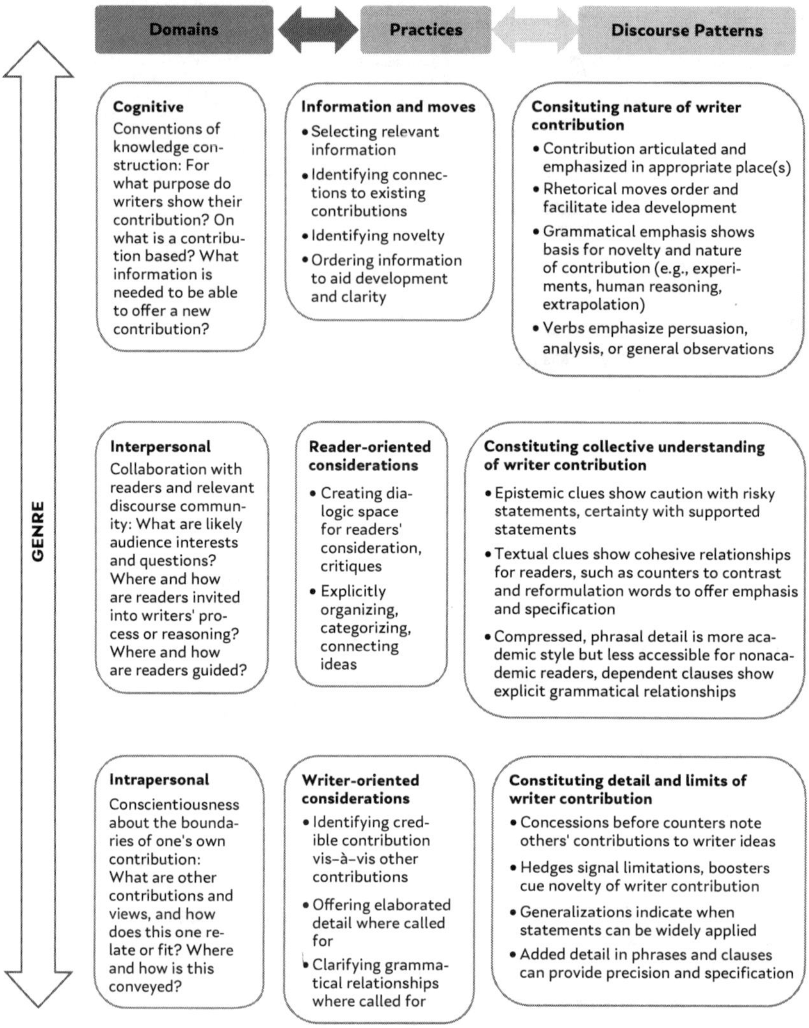

Figure 5. Taxonomy: Making a Written Contribution through Macro- and Microlevel Choices

to discuss genre "purpose." In the interpersonal domain, textual clues offer specific ways to discuss "flow" and "organization," and epistemic clues that open and close dialogic space offer concrete ways to discuss "audience" and the relationship between writers and readers. In the intrapersonal domain, concessions and counters offer concrete ways to discuss principles such as "open-mindedness" and "conviction."

The three values of compression, civility, and cohesion emerge as rhetorical qualities uniquely valued by the end of curricular writing in higher education. All three relate to how writers and readers construct knowledge and relate to one another. As such, all three relate to public and academic discussions about discourse: contemporary public discussions about civil and uncivil discourse and scholarly discussions about ethical student writing practices. I want to close by bringing these two discussions together and connecting them to the patterns analyzed in this book—to link discussions about discourse and writing to actual, patterned discourse and to underscore the value of such ties more broadly.

Concerns about contemporary discourse emphasize the urgent need for informed and open-minded exchange in a time lacking the "thoughtful public discussion and debate that we expect to produce positive change" (Rodin and Steinberg 1). Amid divisive political rhetoric and online echo chambers, such thoughtful exchange does not just require respectfulness, it requires debate: "frank discussions" that "look on civil language as an important linguistic tool" (Nilsen 68, 69; see also Crowley, *Toward a Civil Discourse*).

Higher education is tasked with modeling and enabling such debate. The Civic Learning and Democratic Engagement National Task Force labeled the early twenty-first century a "crucible moment" in which higher education must lead efforts to ensure that students become informed, civically engaged citizens (Civic Learning). The Association of American Colleges and Universities member Andrea Leskes wrote an addendum to the report specifically outlining civil discourse and "the crucial need for colleges and universities to commit strongly to its survival" (1). In her report, Leskes describes that civil discourse involves "a serious exchange of views" (3) and "embod[ies] open-mindedness" (4). All these calls underscore the need for informed, open-minded exchange, an objective also championed in the composition scholarship that addresses ethical practices for student writing.

The composition scholar David V. Harrington argued decades ago that "productive scholars in all fields of academic study generally believe in and practice a rather lofty standard of ethics in their writing" that includes "honest inquiry." Such inquiry entails "serious attempt[s] to get at the heart of a problem, to look at the many sides of a question, to take into account conflicting data . . . and to admit that what one is proving is 'probability' rather than 'absolute truth'" (182). This open-minded treatment of "many sides of a question," Harrington suggests, should be the focus of student writing instruction. More recently, James Crosswhite has described that student claims are "above all invitations to share a particular way of making sense of something" (62), which John Duffy echoes in his calls for student writing that fosters the "rhetorical virtue" of open-mindedness. When students must include varying perspectives in a paper, Duffy writes, they learn to inhabit "the perspective of The Other and to open themselves to the doubts and contradictions that attach to any worthwhile question" ("Good Writer" 238). Duffy also clarifies that such open-mindedness need not entail polite deference or silent forbearance: it includes "courage in confronting oppression" and addressing injustice ("Good Writer" 236). Upper-level writing across the curriculum also emphasizes open-mindedness. Chris Thaiss and Terry Myers Zawacki identify three characteristics of academic writing "regardless of differences among disciplines and individual teachers"; the first of these characteristics is that academic writing will show "clear evidence in writing that writer(s) have been persistent, open-minded, and disciplined in study" (5).

These calls for informed and open-minded exchange chiefly reflect the macrolevel principles associated with such exchange. But the analysis in this book, and in particular, the identification of the compression, civility, and cohesion of upper-level writing, provides some ways of thinking about these calls in terms of student discourse in school genres.

Discourse patterns that constitute civility show possibilities for balancing open-mindedness and conviction in "frank discussion" (Nilsen 68): stance word patterns that open dialogic space acknowledge possible concerns, limitations, and disagreements, alongside stance word patterns that close dialogic space to endorse substantiated ideas. Explicit moves and textual clues help create shared understanding of how writers are "making sense of something" (Crosswhite 62) and show writers' attention to readers' needs through the explicit organization and connection of ideas and sentences. These practices engage cognitive, interpersonal, and intrapersonal domains of writing, from the cognitive ability to select and parse information to the interpersonal ability to cue explicit relationships and rhetorical balance in a text to the intrapersonal ability to acknowledge the boundaries of any contribution as one among many.

Yet academic discourse patterns are also not democratic: compressed detail helps draw attention to how we look at "many sides of a question" (D. Harrington 182), but it is syntactically dense, taxing to read, and largely unique to academic writing. It is unlike what any student unaccustomed to advanced, written academic discourse is likely to find familiar. Writing is already an acquired skill—unlike spoken language, we do not learn it without explicit instruction—and tends to be enforced and vetted by people who already have a certain level of educational and social status, and who are far from their own early socialization into academic discourse. This leads to a few concluding remarks that I pose as a way to consider future directions for approaching student writing.

One finding in this book is that argumentative writing assignments may be more accessible and also more emphatic and generalized, particularly in early undergraduate writing. In other words, the writing assignments that invite students' most familiar, interactive language use are also the assignments that do not promote balanced dialogic space. An obvious response, already supported by research noted in chapter 1, is to assign a range of genres, not only slight modifications of traditional school genres, but more blended, public-facing, analytic explanatory as well as persuasive argumentative genres, so that students gain practice writing in a variety of ways.

But it seems to me that the tenacity of institutionalized discourses calls for more radical options, including exploring new genres and supporting students' ability to systematically analyze institutionalized discourses. First, we can revisit the writing we assign the most and consider new genres. Students, especially early undergraduate students, could benefit from more assignments that challenge them to attend methodically to others' views, such as by synthesizing views expressed on a topic in both academic and popular genres. Perhaps the students' own view could be just one view they analyze alongside others' views. Perhaps students could be given the option to write some of their assignments for a more academic audience or for a more general one. These options mean being open to writing and assignment tasks that may implicitly or explicitly read differently to us but may better support diverse writing goals and students in higher education.

More to the point—and a call that seems uniquely suited to the work of English studies—is to make students' patterned discourse in school genres the subject of continual, critical inquiry. This paradigm shift is aided by a few ontological orientations I strive to realize in this book. First is a willingness to consider that the lack of attention to discourse in English composition studies is based more on disciplinary history than on a lack of curiosity or theorizing about the constitutive role of patterned language. Second is a willingness to attend to microlevel patterns within and across written texts. Third is an openness to research in corpus linguistics and discourse analysis that can help direct said attention to patterns. And fourth is the commitment that analysis of academic discourse patterns should suggest not that these patterns are superior but that they are practiced and rewarded in school. Systematic, descriptive analysis of student writing means, in other words, recognizing the sobering and promising power of patterned discourse, which can remain tacit or be brought to light.

Overall, this endeavor means a commitment to seeing academic discourse as an acquired social language, and to believing that those of us who enforce and vet it should be as critical and transparent as possible. It means believing that if we investigate patterns repeatedly valued in higher education and find they do not support democratic, civil discourse, we should, in turn, challenge them. By including patterned discourse in these efforts, we can augment both our calls for a different kind of public discourse and our discussions about the role of student writing in these endeavors.

Notes

1. Because the tables are organized by rhetorical effects, discourse patterns are not noted in order of significance, though all patterns noted are highly sig-

nificant. See the appendix for additional tables organized by keyness and including common clusters.

2. The differences seem consistent with Barton's study of *Chronicle of Higher Education* essays versus first-year essays ("Evidentials"). Her analysis shows that expert writers use boosters and generalizations far less frequently than first-year students but that they use them to problematize ideas and facilitate argumentation, particularly in essay introductions and conclusions.

Afterword: Applications for Instructors and Students

This afterword offers considerations for instructor assignment design and activities for student analysis. The first section is written for instructors, particularly for use as they select and describe assignments with attention to discourse patterns. The second section is written for students, and it introduces discourse patterns related to stance, grammar, and rhetorical moves and then guides students through analysis of their own and others' writing with attention to these patterns.

For Instructors

This section offers guidance in three main areas: selecting and describing assignments, articulating expectations for successful student writing, and guiding students' awareness of their own and others' written discourse with sample assignments.

Choosing and Describing Assignments

This book identifies discourse patterns that are uniquely solicited by different assignment genres. By considering our assignment labels and descriptions in light of these patterns, we can make assignment goals more clear for both ourselves and our students. One place to start is with the genre families in this book, persuasive argumentative writing and analytic explanatory writing, which are expected in many different assignments but highlight distinct primary goals. Because each type of writing solicits particular discourse practices and rhetorical effects, a range of assignments in both genre families can help students gain varied writing practice.

As you design assignments for a course, you make decisions about which practices you want to emphasize and when. As you make those decisions, consider discourse patterns that students associate with argumentative and explanatory writing—both in terms of what you expect and do not expect in an assignment. I summarize some genre-specific considerations below before turning to questions of assignment design.

Argumentative Linguistic and Rhetorical Practices

Written Patterns

In argumentative writing assignments, successful student writers are more likely to practice a conversational style and offer relatively general and certain predictions or reflections. First-year college writers may especially think that argumentative writing should include certain and generalized claims. They may likewise assume that argumentative writing solicits their stance on a general topic rather than also or only a response to existing research on the topic. At the same time, first-year writers are also more likely to include explicit cohesive ties in argumentative writing than in explanatory writing, a habit that should serve them well in upper-level writing, regardless of genre.

In upper-level argumentative writing, students tend to connect research sources or analysis to general social concerns or needs. Upper-level writers are also more likely to add detail through both clausal and phrasal descriptions, as argumentative writing includes a greater range of grammatical options.

In both first-year and upper-level writing, successful student writers are more likely to display more epistemic certainty and generality and offer more explicit textual counters in response to argumentative assignments, as opposed to explanatory ones. Also at both levels, there are a wider range of successful lexical and grammatical choices in argumentative writing than in explanatory writing.

Example Assignments

Argumentative writing is assigned in argumentative essays, especially in early undergraduate coursework, though chapter 2 notes many scholars who critique the pervasive use of argumentative essays. Another assignment genre that solicits argumentative writing includes critiques or evaluations, such as an article or Web site review, as well as parts of proposal genres. Public and professional genres that use argumentative writing include editorials and performance reviews.

Explanatory
Linguistic and Rhetorical Practices

Written Patterns

In explanatory writing assignments, successful student writers are more likely to practice an informational style and offer descriptions and analysis of sources or objects. They also display less epistemic certainty and generality and offer fewer explicit counters.

Because argumentative essay writing is commonly assigned in secondary writing tasks, first-year students may be less familiar with explanatory writing and thus less practiced in phrasal descriptions and analysis-driven rather than thesis-driven writing. They may show less lexical variety in their explanatory writing as well as fewer explicit textual clues. In upper-level explanatory writing, successful writers are more likely to rely on detailed phrases for adding detail and use passive constructions to foreground research sources and outcomes.

In both first-year and upper-level writing, the smaller variety of keyword patterns in explanatory writing suggests there are fewer lexical and grammatical choices that succeed in explanatory writing relative to argumentative writing. This may be good news for students who are accustomed to explanatory writing but unhelpful for those who are not.

Example Assignments

Explanatory writing is assigned in annotated bibliographies and literature reviews, analyses, reports, and research papers. In particular, assignments that require students to synthesize sources in research reviews (such as annotated bibliographies and literature reviews) are common explanatory tasks across both first-year and upper-level writing. Public and professional genres that use explanatory writing include executive summaries and memos.

Articulating Assignment Expectations

Assignment descriptions that indicate both what students are expected to do and what they are not expected to do can help guide students' understanding of genre and assignment expectations. The following questions provide ways to think about whether to assign argumentative or explanatory writing, and how to make primary expectations clear for students. Trends I note in the framing of the questions come from my analysis of upper-level writing in chapters 4 and 5.

Audience, Purpose, Diplomacy

Advanced academic argumentative writing includes an overall balance between hedging and boosting, with slightly more boosters and more generalization. Advanced academic explanatory writing achieves an overall rhetorical balance and includes more hedges, and it tends to offer fewer statements that are generalized beyond a given context or example.

In this assignment, how general should observations or claims be? What is an example question or thesis that has an appropriate scope? What would be too broad? What would be too narrow?

In this assignment, how direct should writers be with criticisms? What is an example of an appropriate way to critique? What is an example of a critique that is too direct or indirect?

What kinds of questions and criticisms might be common for an audience or purpose like this one? Where and how do writers typically account for these?

Style, Detail, Cohesion

Argumentative writing tends to be more conversational—as academic writing goes— whereas explanatory writing favors a more informational style. Both usually include explicit reformulation, though argumentative writing includes more explicit counters.

Should students explicitly or implicitly engage their readers? Should students explicitly draw attention to themselves as writers? Why and when is this appropriate or inappropriate?

How densely informational should the writing be? How explicit should grammatical subjects be? Does phrasal or clausal detail characterize successful responses to this assignment?

What kind of textual cohesion is valued? Should students look for places to explicitly contrast? Do successful writers offer specification? Do they offer examples? How are these moves overtly indicated for readers?

What is an example piece of writing or a genre that approximates the style you expect? What is an example that approximates a style that is not welcome?

Evidence, Emphasis

Argumentative writing emphasizes human needs and ideas, whereas explanatory writing favors processes and outcomes.

Who and what are the leading actors in this assignment (e.g., students' opinions, existing opinions, original lab work, a text closely read?)

What disciplinary lens(es) do you use when you think about the assignment and your expectations? What kind of lens would *not* be useful for thinking about this assignment?

What kind of moves contribute to a successful response to this assignment? Should students offer evidence as well as analysis of that evidence? Under what circumstances, if any, should students offer evidence without commentary or interpretation?

What is the point of departure for arguments in the assignments? (E.g., Do students begin with a stance, or do they begin by reading existing views?)

How certain can the observations or claims be? What is an example conclusion that shows an appropriate level of certainty? What is an attempted contribution that would be too cautious? What is an example that appears overstated?

Helping Students Analyze Discourse in Their Own and Others' Writing

Assigning genre and discourse analysis can also help foster students' awareness of different discourse practices and rhetorical goals of writing. Below, I offer three sample assignments before turning to student-oriented materials, which offer students guidance for analyzing discourse their own and others' writing.

Example Analysis Assignments

Example Assignment: Self-Analysis

Students read a study of student writing, for example, Hardy and Römer (across fields in upper-level student writing in the United States); Nesi and Gardner (across levels and fields in undergraduate writing in England); Barton, "Evidentials" (across first-year and professional editorial essays); or Aull and Lancaster (across first-year, upper-level student writing and published academic writing in the United States).

In groups or individually, students analyze samples of their own writing at a certain level or discipline. In light of an aspect or two of their writing, students determine whether and how their own writing compares with the broader trends noted in the study they have read.

Based on the analysis, students answer, for example, How does your writing compare to writing of a given level or field? In what context(s) and how might you revise and why? What advice would you give a writer new to this level or field?

Example Assignment: Analyzing Trends and Variation

Students read a study of advanced writing, for example, of introductory moves (Swales, *Genre*), attitude (Barton, "Evidentials"), or stance words (Hyland, "Stance").

Students analyze the writing of these or other pieces in the light of the contribution they make (e.g., does Swales follow his own model?) or students find a counter example to the noted trends.

Students might answer questions like: How and when do writers show alignment with existing views or research? How and when do writers show the value or novelty of their ideas? What patterns and exceptions exist, and why? How and when are exceptions either allowed or valued?

Example Assignment: Writing Case Study

Students read a study of advanced writing that is relevant according to field, culture, genre of interest (e.g., those noted above, or from Hyland and Sancho Guinda).

Students read and analyze writing by on-campus writers across a few discipline groups (I have, for example, done anthropology, chemistry, religion, and journalism).

The writers offer a panel for the students titled "How to Write a _____ like a _____." (For example, in one case students read an NSF grant proposal written by a chemistry professor, who offered a ten- to fifteen-minute presentation on "How to Write a Grant Proposal like a Chemist.")

During the final weeks of the course, students design and carry out their own "How to Write a _____ like a _____" case study. These case studies focus on a local writer that the students select (on campus or off campus where possible and relevant) in a field and genre of their choice. Students analyze some of the writer's published writing, conduct a discourse-based interview with the writer, and then use their analysis and interview responses to suggest how the writer succeeded in the genre and field.

The final section below offers students an introduction to discourse patterns discussed in the book, followed by analysis activities. The goals for these are metacognitive: they aim to foster students' ability to recognize discourse patterns in the texts and genres they read, versus other assignments that focus on cultivating the ability to produce particular genres. To help scaffold these assignments, the analyses in previous chapters may be helpful; also useful are the sources listed at the end of the afterword that focus on written academic discourse (Ädel; Ädel and Römer; Aull, *First-Year University Writing*; Aull and Lancaster; Bacon; Barton, "Evidentials"; Biber and Gray; Biber et al., "Speaking"; Hardy and Friginal; Hardy and Römer; Hyland, *Metadiscourse* and "Stance"; Hyland and Guinda; Lancaster, "Interpersonal Stance"; Nesi and Gardner; Swales, *Genre*; Wingate).

For Students

This introduction explains how to analyze writing in terms of two main categories: stance word patterns and grammatical patterns. Each section includes analysis activities.

Analyzing Stance

Academic readers tend to be critical of overstated claims: they want precise, credible statements that can be supported. Without always realizing it, successful academic writers follow suit: they hedge their statements to avoid overstatement, such as by writing *it is **sometimes** true that*, rather than *it is **always** true that*. If, on the other hand, academic writers have good reason, they might do the opposite: they might boost a statement by writing *it is **certainly** the case that*, or they might generalize by writing *it is **always** the case that*. These may seem like small choices, but they add up.

Writers make these adjustments all the time, often in predictable patterns: we can, for instance, expect more hedged statements in academic writing and more generalized and boosted statements in magazine writing. Writers make some creative choices, but writing is rarely, if ever, entirely idiosyncratic. You may already pick up on some patterns in writing, but practice can make us even better at recognizing patterns of language that show us the conventions of different kinds of written texts.

Let's start by bringing to light some of your intuitions about language patterns. The two sentences below summarize the same research. One appears in an online argumentative essay, and one appears in an academic research article. Which is which?

> *Example 1.* Teens who use Facebook more often show more narcissistic tendencies while young adults who have a strong Facebook presence show more signs of other psychological disorders, including antisocial behaviors, mania, and aggressive tendencies.
>
> *Example 2.* Forget about radiation from cell phones: the real digital killer turns out to be Facebook.

The first sentence, as you probably guessed, comes from the academic article, whereas the second sentence comes from an online essay.[1] Now go a step further. How could you tell which was which? What clues in the sentences guided you?

Here are some clues you might have noticed in example 1:

> includes specific details about the impact of Facebook (*often show more narcissistic tendencies*)

details appear to come from a research study
describes the findings seemingly objectively and in third person
instead of using provocative words, uses words that make the statement more cautious and precise (not all teens, but instead *Teens who use Facebook*); also uses words that place behavior on a scale rather than as an extreme (*more often* and *more signs* instead of *the real digital killer*)

Conclusion: This sentence probably comes from a research-based academic paper. And here are some clues in example 2:

uses strong, intensified language (not just a *killer* but *the* ***real*** *. . . killer*)
addresses the reader directly by saying *(you) Forget about radiation*
presents only one perspective, without room for disagreement, in a definitive statement (*the real digital killer turns out to be Facebook*)

Conclusion: The sentence probably comes from an online argumentative essay.

All writing contains patterns, or clues, like these. They help make writing recognizable and successful for a given purpose and can help you decode successful writing if you know what to look for. Several of these clues are referred to as *stance words*, or words that provide explicit clues for readers in terms of epistemic and textual framing, discussed below. Some stance words are used more or less, depending on the genre of the writing. In particular, below I note how patterns of stance words are different in **argumentative writing assignments**, such as critiques or argumentative essays driven by a central thesis, than in **explanatory writing assignments**, such as reports or literature reviews driven by analysis and description.

Five types of stance clues are described below. The first three are epistemic, or truth-adjusting, clues—those words and phrases that explicitly show writers' caution, certainty, or generality. These are called *hedges*, *boosters*, and *generality words*.

Epistemic Clues: Discourse That Shows Caution, Certainty, and Generality

Words and phrases that qualify claims and show caution are called **hedges**. They include words like *perhaps*, *might*, *relatively*, *possible*, and *likely*. Writers use hedges to qualify a claim, or to make a claim without arguing that it is true in every case.

Words and phrases that do the opposite are called **boosters**. They include words like *clearly*, *without a doubt*, *only*, *definitely*, *must*, and *should*. These words intensify or show full certainty.

Academic writers often need to leave room for alternative perspectives, such as when making generalizations or when showing criticism. In these cases, hedges can be useful for displaying caution. In academic writing, research demonstrates that experienced writers use **hedges** to

show that a conclusion is based on reasoning rather than certain fact,
tone down risky claims,
acknowledge other research, and
account for a critical reader who may have an opposing view.[2]

At the same time, academic writers sometimes need to show conviction and emphasis. In these cases, **boosters** can be useful for intensifying a statement, such as when the writer has clear support or another good reason to emphasize a statement.

Thus, experienced academic writers use both **hedges** and **boosters**; together, they achieve a rhetorical balance of caution and conviction. The analysis in this book shows that, whereas early undergraduate writers use more boosters than hedges, successful upper-level writing (by late-undergraduate- and early-graduate-level students) shows a rhetorical balance between the two (with slightly more hedges) in both argumentative and explanatory writing assignments.

How Hedges and Boosters Change an Argument

Keeping in mind this information about hedges and boosters, consider the following sentences from A-graded, upper-level student writing. Both passages come from the concluding paragraphs of the student papers. In the examples, you will see ***hedges***, which show caution, italicized and bolded. Boosters, which indicate certainty, are underlined.

Passage (i) below comes from upper-level writing in response to an explanatory writing assignment. The passage is from a research paper titled "What Drives the Relationship between Education and Family? Evidence from China, 1982," written by a first-year graduate student in economics.

> (i) These analyses will be done for future study and will be based on a combined dataset of China Study (1964) and Chinese Household Income Project (1988, 1995). However, the three datasets are different in their specific universes and survey designs; moreover, although the time periods of the dataset covered 1982, in terms of China's intense transitions during 1980s, the ***possible*** results achieved from the above dataset ***may*** be unrepresentative and inconsistent with the situation in 1982. (ECO.G1.03.1)[3]

In passage (i), the writer explicitly calls attention to the limitations of a research study through the use of the hedges *possible* and *may*. By hedging the final statement in the passage, the writer avoids overstating the conclusions based on her study.

Passage (ii) below comes from upper-level writing in response to an argumentative assignment. The passage is from an argumentative essay written by a first-year graduate student in biology called "The Evolution of Terrestriality: A Look at the Factors that Drove Tetrapods to Move onto Land":

> (ii) The evolution of deciduousness in plants ***could*** have played a crucial role. Not only would mass senescing of leaves have enhanced the terrestrial ecosystem by enriching soil development (an evolutionary pull), it also ***likely*** caused anoxia in near-shore waters (Algeo and Scheckler, 1998; Clack, 2002b). As the plant matter decayed in the water, oxygen levels in the water would have decreased. This situation ***could have*** encouraged air breathing in some fish (Sayer and Davenport, 1991), which was a requisite step in the transition to life on land. <u>Certainly</u>, of course, the fish ***could have merely*** come up to the surface to breathe air and survived that way, but as Sayer and Davenport (1991) pointed out, many modern-day fish do leave anoxic waters. (BIO.G1.04.1)[4]

As you can see from the annotations, passage (i) contains mostly hedges, whereas passage (ii) includes hedges as well as boosters. Passage (ii) incorporates several hedges to show caution about inferences based on evolutionary biological evidence. Near the end of the passage, though, the writer uses a booster to acknowledge a potential counter which is in turn contradicted using the conjunction *but* in the final sentence. The analysis in this book shows successful upper-level writers often use hedges and boosters in this way: they hedge some of their conclusions to avoid committing to those that are not certain fact, and then they strategically boost the statements that they want to emphasize. This helps writers avoid overhedging and thus showing no certainty, but to also avoid overboosting and showing no caution.

Finally, **generality words** indicate that statements can be generalized, or applied beyond a specific context or example. For instance, consider the following argumentative essay written by a third-year graduate student in education titled "American Education: A Force for Democracy and Integration?" In the passage, generality words appear in bold:

> (iii) Schools continue their function as tools for integration to **society**. **Today's society** is more multi-cultural by nature, more willing to acknowledge the existence of other cultures, and frequently, if awkwardly, trying to fit them into a changing **society**. Similar to the attempt to inculcate democracy through education, however, we are improving in our efforts, but we have not yet reached the goal. Students now study black history and women's history, but for the most part, they do so in February and March, months dedicated to the study of those topics. (EDU.G3.03.3)

This passage includes three generalized references to *society* in order to indicate that the statements can be applied across students and contexts. In this case, these broad claims are part of the kind of argument the writer develops in this essay. Generality words can be used strategically in cases where writers have support or another good reason to emphasize a statement beyond a specific context or example. Broadly speaking, though, generality words are rarely used in academic writing relative to other kinds of writing, since academic writing tends to value more circumspect conclusions and statements limited to direct evidence.

Tables 17 and 18 offer several more examples of hedges, boosters, and generality words that you can use for reference in the activity below.

Analyzing Epistemic Clues in Your Writing

Now try annotating some of your own writing, marking these epistemic stance words using tables 17 and 18 for reference. Place a circle around hedged statements, a box around boosted statements, and brackets

Table 17. Example Epistemic Clues: Hedge Words

HEDGE WORDS	EXAMPLE USES	HEDGE PHRASES	EXAMPLE USES
may	*may be argued, may have similar results*	may not	*may not have intended, may not be clear, may not exist*
might	*might be a way forward, might be the result of*	most of the	*most of the cases, in most of the examples, most of the work focuses on*
often	*often has the effect, are often viewed as*	tend(s) to	*tend to assume, tends to increase*
possible	*it is possible that, makes it possible to*	in general	*for people in general, to people in general, society in general*
likely	*is likely to appear*	not necessarily	*does not necessarily mean*
perhaps	*perhaps there is a way, perhaps a place to begin, perhaps that is why*	not always	*has not always been, not always the case that*
almost	*almost all cases, almost entirely*	might not	*might not mean, might not clarify*
seem/s	*seem to make, seem to have been, it seems to me*	for the most part	*at least for the most part, for the most part was successful*
generally	*generally the assumption is, people generally*	in most cases	*was clear in most cases*
suggest/s	*I would suggest, evidence suggests that*	not really	*not really known, not really clear*
relatively	*relatively stable, relatively well*	not quite	*not quite the same as, not quite satisfactory*
probably	*(certain theorists) would probably respond*	not fully	*not fully determined, not fully clear*

around all generalized statements. Recall that this book shows that successful upper-level writing usually contains more hedges than boosters and try to strike an overall rhetorical balance. Within successful upper-level writing, argumentative writing tends to contain slightly more boosters than explanatory writing contains, but both kinds of writing achieve a balance overall of the two. There also tend to be significantly fewer generality words in explanatory than in argumentative writing.

As you look over your annotations, consider to what extent you have achieved a rhetorical balance by opening dialogic space (leaving relevant

Table 18. Example Epistemic Clues: Booster Words and Generality Words

BOOSTER WORDS	EXAMPLE USES	BOOSTER PHRASES	EXAMPLE USES
must	*must be emphasized, must be found*	the most	*the most important factor, the most obvious explanation, the most significant feature*
found	*have found that, found no differences*	of course	*and, of course, there are other considerations,*
very	*very important, very limited*	certainly not	*certainly not proven, certainly not the case that*
certainly	*certainly a case of, certainly a consideration, certainly a factor, certainly did not*	not possible	*not possible to test, is not possible for*
clear	*has clear import, clear connection between*	a lot	*a lot of people, a lot of research*
clearly	*clearly agree, clearly appear, clearly differed*	a great deal	*a great deal depends on, a great deal to say, we learn a great deal about*
GENERALITY WORDS	EXAMPLE USES	GENERALITY PHRASES	EXAMPLE USES
never	*never had a chance, never been the case*	people today	*people today*
always	*always means that, has always been*	the world	*the world we live in, the world today*
society	*society tells us that*	human beings	*we as human beings*

room for alternatives or exceptions) and closing dialogic space (showing full certainty and generality about supported or strategic statements). Then, consider your individual uses:

At what points of your paper do you use hedges? Would any additional hedges help avoid risky statements, such as those that are highly critical or that cannot be proven? Are any statements overhedged, with unnecessary qualification?

When do you boost your statements? Would any additional boosters help you emphasize claims you have supported with evidence?

When do you generalize, if ever? If generalizing is appropriate for the genre and audience for whom you write, where might you generalize strategically and effectively?

Textual Clues: Discourse That Shows Textual Connections

The other two stance categories analyzed in this book are textual clues, or those words and phrases that show cohesive connections in a text. **Counters** such as *nevertheless* or *however* explicitly signal a contrast or counter to previous information. **Reformulation words** like *in other words* explicitly indicate when writers reformulate previously offered or generally assumed information. With reformulation words such as *for instance*, writers signal they will offer an illustration. Reformulation words like *put another way* indicate writers will offer a restatement of information in order to clarify it. With reformulation words such as *in particular*, writers flag specification or emphasis; finally, with reformulation words like *in fact*, writers signal counterintuitive information.

Consider how these textual clues operate in two example passages. This first passage comes from an argumentative essay titled "Economics of the Illicit-Drug Market," written by a final-year undergraduate student in economics. The example includes underlined textual clues as well as the annotated epistemic clues discussed above:

> (iv) In particular, a major problem that must be called to the attention of policy makers, and the economists who advise on their behalf, is the observation and recognition of a nearly perfectly inelastic supply of drug offenders-dealers-at the street level. In other words, the supply of these offenders in the illicit drug market is not sensitive to the price of crime (punishment), but why should this be such a significant problem? (ECO.G0.03.1)

In example (iv), the writer uses the reformulation word *in particular* to indicate the sentence will offer a specific problem that needs to be addressed (a claim that is boosted by *must*). The next sentence restates the problem that needs to be addressed. The writer leads readers into this restatement with the reformulation word *In other words*.

The next example comes from a report in civil and environmental engineering titled "Worker Ergonomic Analysis," written by a first-year graduate student:

> (v) This activity received a score of 1 according to the Workplace Risk Factor Checklist developed by OSHA which is very low. Nevertheless,

> this <u>should not</u> be considered a safe activity since several other factors *can* negatively affect the worker. He is more prone to receiving burns in his body as well as damage to his vision. (CEE.G1.06.1)

In example (v), the writer notes a research outcome in the first sentence of the passage. The writer then explicitly counters what might be an expected response to this research outcome, by stating that it ***Nevertheless*** . . . *should not be considered* this way. The countering evidence is qualified with *can* to offer support for the recommendation without implying that a worker will necessarily receive burns or vision damage in all cases.

Table 19 offers more examples of counters and reformulation words you can use for reference in the activity below.

Analyzing Textual Clues in Your Writing

Now try annotating some of your own writing, using table 19 for reference. Consider using a single underline to mark counters and a double underline for reformulation words. The analysis in this book shows that successful upper-level writing includes more counters and reformulation words than first-year college writing. Within successful upper-level writing, writing in argumentative assignments uses more counters than writing in explanatory assignments, but both include reformulation words

Table 19. Example Textual Clues

TEXTUAL CLUES	EXAMPLES
Counters	*alternatively, although, at the same time, but, in/by contrast, conversely, however, on one / the other hand, nevertheless, rather, still, though, yet*
Reformulation words	Elucidation reformulation words: *to be precise, put another way, put differently, i.e., that is, in other words, here I mean, to put it simply* Exemplification reformulation words: *for example, for instance, an example of, to illustrate* Emphasis reformulation words: *specifically, in particular, particularly, especially, namely* Counterexpectancy reformulation words (sometimes follow concessions marked by words or phrases like *while, although, it is true, does account for*): *as a matter of fact, in fact, indeed*

equally. As you look over your annotations, consider to what extent you have offered explicit textual clues for your readers and to what extent these seem consistent with the genre and purpose of your writing. Then, consider your individual uses:

Where and why do you use counters? Would any additional counters or contrasts clarify information, particularly in argumentative writing? Are there places where a counter signals a contrast where a reformulation might be more useful?

Where and why do you reformulate? Would any additional reformulations provide clarification, examples, or emphasis?

Analyzing Grammar and Moves

The previous section focused on stance word patterns, or word and phrase patterns that writers use to show caution, certainty, and generality and to indicate cohesive connections across parts of a text. Successful upper-level students use these lexical patterns to provide explicit clues for readers according to the expectations of particular genres, audiences, and purposes. This section focuses on how these writers use grammatical patterns and moves in their writing for particular genres, audiences, and purposes as well.

By grammatical patterns, I refer to common functional uses of words and phrases. Just like lexical patterns, grammatical patterns can be different in different assignment genres. For instance, the analysis in this book shows that successful upper-level writing in argumentative assignments is characterized by the grammatical patterns and rhetorical effects noted in table 20 below.

These grammatical patterns help writers achieve rhetorical effects, including emphasizing human ideas and needs, adding detail, making a persuasive case, and achieving a rhetorical balance of hedging and boosting (with slightly more boosting than in explanatory writing). By contrast, successful upper-level writing in explanatory assignments is characterized by the grammatical patterns and rhetorical effects noted in table 21. These grammatical patterns in explanatory assignments help upper-level writers emphasize research processes and outcomes, add detail, explicitly reformulate information, and achieve a rhetorical balance between hedging and boosting (with more hedges than in argumentative writing). We will look at example uses of these patterns below.

Next, consider two types of moves—rhetorical steps achieved through sentences and paragraphs—in upper-level student writing. The first kind of move is introductory. This type was identified by John M. Swales, who noticed that across academic disciplines there were three moves that characterized introductions to academic research articles. These three rhetorical moves help "create a research space" by moving the reader from a more general topic to the specific contribution the writer(s) will make (Swales, *Genre*):

> Introductory move (I) "establishes a territory" by identifying existing research or views on a topic.
> Introductory move (II) identifies a gap or "niche" by showing a remaining question or problem in existing research.
> Introductory move (III) finally "occupies the niche" by suggesting how the writer will address said gap. (Swales, *Genre* 141)

The second category of move is that of development, and four moves of this type are discussed in chapters 3 and 4 of this book. These four development moves help students organize their evidence and analysis in a logical way, and they are often cued by discourse patterns noted in tables 20 and 21:

> Development move (1) introduces a particular idea or research trend that will be addressed in the paragraph(s) or section.
> Development move (2) offers and explains example(s) or evidence.
> Development move (3) offers an interpretation of said evidence.
> Development move (4) links the example(s) or analysis back to the original/ broader topic of the paragraph or section.

These development moves progress from general to specific and back to general, and a given paragraph or section may move back and forth between moves (2) and (3) before moving to the link in move (4).

Now consider two passages in light of both the grammatical patterns in tables 20 and 21, as well as the moves identified above. Example passage (vi) below comes from an introductory paragraph in an upper-level explanatory assignment. The passage includes Swales's three

Table 20. Grammatical Patterns in Upper-Level Argumentative Writing

RHETORICAL EFFECT	KEYWORD PATTERNS	COMMON USES
Emphasize human needs and ideas	Genitive markers	Possessive use of common noun, e.g., *women's/one's/children's/people's* [and, theory, life, own]
	Possessive pronouns	*his* (32%), *their, her* (18%), *its, our, my, your* [own/life/family, father, mother]
Add detail in dependent clauses	*That* as conjunction	***that*** *is*, [the fact] *is* ***that***
	As as conjunction	***as*** *analyzed by*, ***as*** *the/they/one/shown*
Make a case	*Only* as adverb (80%), adjective (20%)	***only*** *to*, ***only*** *in*, ***only*** *a*, ***only*** *one*
	Adverb of time	[and/is/would/can] **then/now/again/today** [the/it/is/we]
	Negation	*it is* ***not***; *people do* ***not***
	But as countering coordinating conjunction	[plural nouns / singular nouns / proper nouns] **but** *the/also/not*
RHETORICAL EFFECT	STANCE WORD PATTERNS	COMMON USES
Open and close dialogic space, boost slightly more	More boosters Approximately even ratio of hedges to boosters	*very, must, certain, known*
Explicitly counter and reformulate	More counters Similar reformulation words	Counters: *but, however, rather, thought* Reformulation words: *such as, for example, especially, in fact, specifically, in terms of, particularly*

introductory moves as well as several explanatory discourse patterns noted in table 21. This passage comes from a research paper titled "A CVX theory of Dutch Syllable Structure" that was written by a second-year graduate student in linguistics.[5] In the passage, the moves are labeled as they begin, and the first grammatical subject of each sentence is underlined to show points of emphasis:

> (vi) [Introductory move (I)] The proposal that medial position syllabic rime is restricted to two slots maximally was demonstrated to be a tenable view in Borowsky (1989). In a departure from the more

Table 21. Grammatical Patterns in Upper-Level Explanatory Writing

RHETORICAL EFFECT	KEYWORD PATTERNS	COMMON USES
Emphasize processes and outcomes	Passive verb constructions	Used in passive constructions (47%) and perfect aspect (10%), as well as *used/based/found/given/shown* [with/and/the/for/that]
	Past tense reporting verbs	[and/they/that/who/which] *found/used/showed/made/became* [the/that]
Add detail in phrases	Adjectives that modify nouns and show comparison	*other/social/different/important/new* [and/for/that/with] *higher/greater/lower/larger/better/further*
	Noun phrases with prepositional phrases	*In/from* follow nouns, participles, and infinitive verbs; often elaborates through description of attributes, purpose, or origin *(**in** the/this/order/which, **from** the/this/their/his/her/each)*
RHETORICAL EFFECT	STANCE WORD PATTERNS	COMMON USES
Open and close dialogic space, hedge more	More Hedges Approximately even ratio of hedges to boosters	Hedges: *perhaps, likely, almost*
	Similar Reformulation Word Use	Reformulation words: *such as, for example, especially, in fact, specifically, in terms of, particularly*

> **traditional viewpoint that onset clusters are constrained by principles of sonority, Dunamu (2002) proposes that complex onset clusters in English and Chinese are composed of one slot. Together, the two theories posit a CVX structure for syllable structure. [Introductory move (II)] The question remains as to whether this claim can be shown to hold for languages other than English and Chinese. [Introductory move (III)] This paper investigates the extent to which standard Dutch con be shown to conform to CVX theory. (LIN.G2.03.1)**

This introductory passage includes explanatory patterns that assist the student's description of linguistic theories. The student's use of noun and prepositional phrases offers detail, for example, *a departure [from the more traditional viewpoint], principles [of sonority]*. Likewise, the writer's use of passive constructions (*was demonstrated, are constrained by, can be shown*) allow him to foreground the linguistic proposal and ideas in question, rather than the human agents behind them. In keeping with the goals of analysis-driven explanation, most of the passage is devoted to elaborated description of a focus of study, which in this case provides a point of departure for the student's test of CVX theory.

This passage also exhibits Swales's three introductory rhetorical moves, signaled for readers with discourse-level clues. The passage first "establishes a territory" by indicating existing views: one view is signaled by *The* ***proposal*** *that* and the other by *In a departure from the more traditional* ***viewpoint***. Move (II) then identifies a gap or "niche" by beginning with *The question remains*. Finally, in move (III), the writer "occupies the niche" by suggesting how the writer's contribution will address the gap (*This paper investigates . . .*).

Now consider an argumentative example in passage (vii) below. The passage comes from a development (or body) paragraph of the same essay used in example (ii) above. It was written by a first-year graduate student in biology in an argumentative essay called "The Evolution of Terrestriality: A Look at the Factors that Drove Tetrapods to Move onto Land":

> (vii) [Development move (1)] The tectonic activity occurring in and around the Iapetus Sea at this time could have enhanced the effects of many various evolutionary pushes. As discussed previously, early tetrapod evolution appears to have been concentrated along the southern coast of Euramerica during the Late Devonian. [Development move (2)] During this time, Euramerica and Gondwana were converging, eventually forming Pangaea during the Permo-Carboniferous. This closing of the Iapetus Sea would have affected aquatic tetrapods living in this region in several ways. [Development move (3)] As the continents came together, the major direct effect would have been habitat loss, and this could happen in several ways. The convergence of continents would decrease the amount of coastlines and lower global sea level (Clack 2002b). The arrangement of the continents also led to a short period of global cooling and glaciation during the Famennian in Gondwana (Algeo and Scheckler, 1998; Johnson, et al, 1985; Van Der Voo, 1988). [Move (2)] The uptake of water by glaciers would have lowered sea level as well. For tetrapods living in coastal habitats,

> these compounding factors would have led to a great decline in available habitat. As the amount of habitat decreased, previously separated populations of animals would be brought together into more of a confined space. [Move (3)] In such a situation, the competition would be very intense. This recalls Ewer's (1955) emphasis on the importance of population pressure, as well as Goin and Goin's (1956) focus on competition, in tetrapod evolution. Clack (2002b) also noted that when previously separated populations are forced to share a common environment, the biodiversity would actually decrease, while distribution of the remaining species would increase. [Development move (4)] This intense competition would have been a strong evolutionary push for tetrapods to find another suitable habitat. (BIO.G1.04.1)

This essay passage contains several detailed noun phrases serving as grammatical subjects; in this way, it reflects syntactic patterns that appear in explanatory writing. The passage also contains several argumentative patterns that convey an emphasis on human ideas (*Ewer's . . . emphasis*, *Goin and Goin's*, *Clack*) and some that help make a case, including several modal verbs (e.g., *would have been*, *could happen*, *would decrease*). The passage also adds detail in dependent clauses marked by the conjunction *as*, for example, *As the continents came together* and *As the amount of habitat decreased*.

The passage also contains the four development moves. Move (1) identifies a topic in the paper (*tectonic activity*); move (2) offers specific examples and outcomes (*This closing*, *The uptake*); move (3) offers an analysis of these examples (*the major direct effect*, *this recalls*); and move (4) shifts the paragraph to the larger takeaway for the interpretation offered (*strong evolutionary push*), which alludes to the phrase *many various evolutionary pushes* in the opening sentence.

Analyzing Grammatical Patterns and Moves in Your Own Writing

Now consider your own writing. Begin by underlining the main subject of each sentence, like in the two examples above.

> In your writing, who are the leading actors? In other words, what do these grammatical subjects emphasize? Research? Human needs? Both?

What about other grammatical patterns: What kinds of verbs and nouns do you use? Do you tend to add detail in phrases or dependent clauses, or both?

Do these grammatical patterns seem consistent with the genre of the assignment and your instructor's expectations?

Now try labeling both introductory and development moves in your writing. Write in a bracketed roman numeral for each introductory move and a bracketed number for each development move.

What moves do you use, and in what order? How do you signal these moves for your readers?

Do the moves you make include all the necessary information? Are any moves left out or repetitive?

Does the order of your moves contribute to the logical build and development of your ideas? In other words, do you move from general ideas to specific ideas and back? Or do you go back and forth, which might confuse your readers?

Do these moves seem consistent with the genre of the assignment and your instructor's expectations?

Analyzing Stance Word Patterns, Grammatical Patterns, and Moves in Others' Writing

Now that you have analyzed patterns and moves in your own writing, select an example of reading from your course and annotate for these features. As you look over your annotations, consider between one and three patterns that seem especially notable. They might stand out, for example, because they seem similar to or different from the patterns in upper-level student writing outlined above. They might seem significant because they are particularly effective at achieving a rhetorical balance between opening and closing dialogic space. They might attract your attention because you see a rhetorical move described above or notice one not illustrated above.

First, select a text to analyze. For instance, you can select an article or essay you have read for this class or another class, or from the Michigan Corpus of Upper-Level Student Papers (MICUSP). If the text is long (e.g., 10,000 words or more), consider selecting one section on which to focus.

Next, annotate the text for several stance and grammatical patterns and introductory or development moves, or both.

Read your text and reread it, focusing on several of the features you annotated. Then, as part of responding to the questions below, consider what annotations are especially interesting to you. Select between one and three of these, according to how much evidence you have. (E.g., if you are focusing on moves or a pattern that is used a great deal, one is probably sufficient, but consider how multiple patterns work together in case two or three of them seem directly related.)

Then, based on your analysis, consider the rhetorical effects of the especially interesting patterns, for example, how the text presents a balanced or evidenced-based argument, what makes the text particularly cohesive, or what makes it appear to be argumentative or explanatory.

As you draw tentative conclusions, make sure to elucidate specific examples (do not only tell that the text contains certain features, but show how those features achieve a particular rhetorical effect). Also ensure that you have identified and contextualized the text you selected (e.g., where it was published, when, in what field) according to your instructor's expectations.

Summarize your analysis. List between one and three patterns that seem most interesting and explain **why**. Label and briefly describe each pattern for someone unfamiliar with them. Give example uses of these features in your analysis with the **rhetorical effect** of each of these features (or the rhetorical effect of the features together, if they appear to have a combined or overall effect). What recommendations might you offer a novice writer learning to write a text like the one you analyzed?

Further Reading

Ädel, Annelie. *Metadiscourse in L1 and L2 English*. John Benjamins Publishing, 2006.

Ädel, Annelie, and Ute Römer. "Research on Advanced Student Writing across Disciplines and Levels: Introducing the Michigan Corpus of Upper-Level Student Papers." *International Journal of Corpus Linguistics*, vol. 17, no. 1, 2012, pp. 3–34.

Aull, Laura Louise. *First-Year University Writing: A Corpus-Based Study with Implications for Pedagogy*. Palgrave Macmillan, 2015.

Aull, Laura Louise, and Zak Lancaster. "Linguistic Markers of Stance in Early and Advanced Academic Writing: A Corpus-Based Comparison." *Written Communication*, vol. 1, no. 33, 2014, pp. 151–83.

Bacon, Nora. "Style in Academic Writing." *The Centrality of Style*, edited by Mike Duncan and Star Medzerian Vanguri, WAC Clearinghouse / Parlor Press, 2013, pp. 173–90.

Barton, Ellen L. "Evidentials, Argumentation, and Epistemological Stance." *College English*, vol. 55, no. 7, 1993, pp. 745–69.

Biber, Douglas, and Bethany Gray. "Challenging Stereotypes About Academic Writing: Complexity, Elaboration, Explicitness." *Journal of English for Academic Purposes*, vol. 9, no. 1, 2010, pp. 2–20.

Biber, Douglas, et al. "Speaking and Writing in the University: A Multidimensional Comparison." *TESOL Quarterly*, vol. 36, no. 1, 2002, pp. 9–48.

Hardy, Jack A., and Eric Friginal. "Genre Variation in Student Writing: A Multi-Dimensional Analysis." *Journal of English for Academic Purposes*, vol. 22, 2016, pp. 119–31.

Hardy, Jack A., and Ute Römer. "Revealing Disciplinary Variation in Student Writing: A Multi-Dimensional Analysis of the Michigan Corpus of Upper-Level Student Papers (MICUSP)." *Corpora*, vol. 8, no. 2, 2013, pp. 183–207.

Hyland, Ken. *Metadiscourse: Exploring Interaction in Writing*. Continuum, 2005. Continuum Discourse Series.

———. "Stance and Engagement: A Model of Interaction in Academic Discourse." *Discourse Studies*, vol. 7, no. 2, 2005, pp. 173–92.

Lancaster, Zak. "Interpersonal Stance in L1 and L2 Students' Argumentative Writing in Economics: Implications for Faculty Development in WAC/WID Programs." *Across the Disciplines*, vol. 4, no. 8, 2011.

Swales, John M. *Genre Analysis: English in Academic and Research Settings*. Cambridge UP, 1990. Cambridge Applied Linguistics Series.

Swales, John M., and Christine B. Feak. *Academic Writing for Graduate Students*. 3rd ed., U of Michigan P, 2012.

Wingate, Ursula. "'Argument!' Helping Students Understand What Essay Writing Is About." *Journal of English for Academic Purposes*, vol. 11, no. 2, 2012, pp. 145–54, doi:https://doi.org/10.1016/j.jeap.2011.11.001.

Notes

1. For the academic paper in example 1, see "Social Networking's Good and Bad Impacts." This press release discusses and quotes a conference presentation by Larry D. Rosen, "Poke Me: How Social Networks Can Both Help and Harm Our Kids," plenary session 3378 of the 119th Annual Convention of the American Psychological Association, Walter E. Washington Convention Center, Washington, DC, 4–7 Aug. 2011. For the online essay in example 2, see Baron.

2. See Barton, "Evidentials"; Hyland, *Metadiscourse*.

3. Examples in this section of the afterword are from the Michigan Corpus of Upper-Level Student Papers (MICUSP) and are cited using their MICUSP paper tags; see MICUSP for more examples and the full papers.

4. Another passage from this paper appears in chapter 4 as argumentative example (C), and the introductory paragraph appears in the next section of the afterword.

5. This passage also appears in example (4) of chapter 4.

Appendix: Additional Corpus Analysis Information

Additional Detail about Keyword Analysis

Two aspects of the methodology in this book facilitated the keyword analysis. One is that student writing is part-of-speech-tagged (POS-tagged), meaning that in the corpora used in the keyword analysis, the grammatical function of each word is identified and noted in its textual context. This, in turn, means that both functional patterns and prominent lexical patterns can be identified using corpus analysis. The POS-tagger used was the *CLAWS 7 Tagset*, the same tagset used by the Brigham Young University (BYU) family of corpora. (See more information on the BYU family of corpora at corpus.byu.edu/. An excellent resource for POS-tagged corpora and information is Brown's *Grammar Lab* www.thegrammarlab.com.)

In the POS-tagged corpora, the tags are embedded in the texts. For instance, the following sentence from an annotated bibliography in the first-year corpus used in chapter 3 is untagged:

> From gaining knowledge about the political candidates, to running for a position in the government, this organization believes that equality can be attained through a political standpoint.

The POS-tagged version of the same sentence follows:

> From_II gaining_VVG knowledge_NN1 about_II the_AT political_JJ candidates_NN2 ,_, to_II running_VVG for_IF a_AT1 position_NN1

in_II the_AT government_NN1 ,_, this_DD1 organization_NN1 believes_VVZ that_DD1 equality_NN1 can_VM be_VBI attained_VVN through_II a_AT1 political_JJ standpoint_NN1 ._.

As this example shows, the POS-tags are descriptive and functional; they identify the function of the tagged words in their given textual context in that part of the corpus. The tags do not indicate prescriptive grammatical information (for instance, they would not note that the above sentence opens with what would be considered a dangling participle or dangling modifier, according to prescriptive grammatical rules for standardized edited English).

The other methodological tool is keyness, which is used in both the keyword analysis and that of stance word frequency. Keyness is calculated in this study using log-likelihood (LL), which compares observed versus expected frequencies and is useful because it does not assume the normal distribution of words across a corpus (Brown and Aull 399; see also Hardie). The greater the LL value, the more evidence there is for the significance of a particular difference, and the higher the keyness value, the more evidence that a word or tag occurs more often in the target corpus than would be expected by chance in comparison with the reference corpus. Per the first point, in this study, keyness is used to identify significant differences in frequencies of lexical items as well as POS-tags (or functional items). In both cases, the principle and the measure are the same, but rather than compare counts of individual words, the calculations account for nouns, verbs, or other part-of-speech categories and subcategories that are surfaced though key POS-tags (Brown and Aull 399–400).

Log-likelihood and keyness were calculated using *WordSmith Tools* 6.0 (Scott) as well as an LL calculator in *Excel* (created using the equations described in Rayson; Rayson and Garside). Conventional thresholds for significance (for $df = 1$) occur at 3.84 ($p < 0.05$), 6.63 ($p < 0.01$), and 10.83 ($p < 0.001$). All keyword patterns that I discuss in the book are highly significant, meaning that the likelihood that they are due to chance is less than 1 in 1,000. The significance of each stance word pattern discussed is noted in the text and more precisely in the appendix tables. Finally, as noted in the analysis chapters, each keyword pattern discussed in the study appears in at least 90% of the texts in each corpus, to avoid a keyword that is significant because it overpopulates many of the texts but is not representative of the majority of the texts.

The persistence of stance word patterns across each corpus was also calculated using *WordSmith Tools* 6.0. As in the keyword analysis, all stance word patterns analyzed appeared in at least 90% of the texts analyzed; in contrast to the keyword analysis, I specify which stance word patterns are statistically significant in a given analysis according to LL tests.

Tables with Additional Detail

The tables below complement the tables in the book but provide additional information. The additional keyword analysis tables include keyness values. The additional stance analysis tables include detail about stance word frequency according to raw frequency (far left columns), log-likelihood (LL), normalized frequency (Norm), and percent difference (Rayson and Garside). The frequencies are normalized by 10,000 words in order to make them comparable across corpora of different sizes.

Chapter 3 Additional Tables with Keyness and Log-Likelihood Values

Tables A1–A3, which supplement chapter 3, include additional keyword patterns in first-year argumentative and explanatory writing, and offer a comparison of stance word frequency in first-year writing.

First-Year Argumentative Keyword Patterns

Table A1 presents additional keyword patterns in first-year argumentative writing and includes keyness values.

First-Year Explanatory Keyword Patterns

Table A2 adds detail about keyword patterns in first-year explanatory writing and includes keyness values.

First-Year Argumentative and Explanatory Stance Word Patterns

Table A3 offers more detail about stance word pattern frequency in first-year argumentative writing (corpus 1, or C1) versus first-year explanatory writing (corpus 2, or C2). Note that *** indicates highly significant log-likelihood values ($p < 0.001$).

Chapter 4 Additional Tables with Keyness and Log-Likelihood Values

Tables A4–A6, which supplement chapter 4, include additional keyword patterns in upper-level argumentative and explanatory writing, and offer a comparison of stance word frequency in upper-level writing.

Upper-Level Argumentative Keyword Patterns

Table A4 presents additional keyword patterns in upper-level argumentative writing and includes keyness values.

Upper-Level Explanatory Keyword Patterns

Table A5 adds detail about keyword patterns in upper-level explanatory writing and includes keyness values.

Upper-Level Argumentative and Explanatory Stance Word Patterns

Table A6 offers more detail about stance word frequency in upper-level argumentative writing (C1) versus upper-level explanatory writing (C2). Note that *** indicates highly significant log-likelihood values ($p < 0.001$); * denotes moderately significant differences ($p<0.05$); *ns* identifies those distinctions that are not significant.

Chapter 5 Additional Tables with Common Clusters

Tables A7–A12, which supplement chapter 5, present information about genre- and level-specific key and stance word patterns.

Genre-Specific Keyword Patterns

Table A7 gives details about argumentative writing listed by keyness and including common clusters. Table A8 offers details of explanatory writing organized by keyness and including common clusters.

Genre-Specific Stance Word Patterns

In addition, table A9 offers more detail about stance word frequency in all the argumentative writing (first-year and upper-level) in C1 versus all the explanatory writing (first-year and upper-level) in C2, according to raw frequency (far left columns), log-likelihood (LL), normalized frequency (Norm) and percent difference (Rayson and Garside). The frequencies are normalized by 10,000 words in order to make them comparable across corpora of different sizes. Note that *** indicates highly significant log-likelihood values ($p < 0.001$) and * denotes moderately significant differences ($p<0.95$).

Level-Specific Keyword Patterns

Table A10, on first-year writing (vs. upper-level writing), is organized by keyness and includes common clusters. Table A11, on upper-level writing (vs. first-year writing), is organized by keyness and includes common clusters.

Level-Specific Stance Word Patterns

Table A12 offers more detail about stance word frequency in all the first-year writing in C1 versus all the upper-level writing in C2, according to raw frequency (far left columns). Note that *** indicates highly significant log-likelihood (LL) values ($p < 0.001$).

Genre- and Level-Specific Stance Word Patterns

Genre- and level-specific stance word patterns are represented graphically in figure 6.

Table A1. Keyword Patterns in First-Year Argumentative Writing, with Keyness Values

FIRST-YEAR ARGUMENTATIVE KEYWORD PATTERNS	KEYNESS
Modal verbs (**can/will/should/would** [be/not/have])	814.29
Infinitive verbs (**to /can/not** . . . help/make/get)	325.4
Infinitive *to be* verbs	259.4
Negation (***is/do/are not/n't only/be/have***)	251.9
Can as modal verb (**can *be/not/have/help***)	242.8
For as preposition	214.8
Are (***they/there are not/the/many***)	213.7
Have (***to/they/not have been/a/to***)	144.2
Adverb (general) (***also/only/however/even***)	158.9
After- or postdeterminer (***some/any/enough*** [of/people]s)	144.2
Common nouns (*people* [67% of common nouns], *media*)	122.7
Subordinating conjunction	
More (***more than/people/likely***)	105.5
Or (***whether or not, or even, his or her***)	76.1
These ([of] ***these animals/are/companies***)	59.9
Adjective (***other/social/human/new*** [and/the/health/people])	51.1
But as countering conjunction (**but** *also/the/it/they*)	45.0
Degree adverb ([it is] ***very/as/so /too***)	40.7
Prepositional adverb in phrasal verb (*go* **on** / *stand* **up** / ***stand out*** / *end* **up**)	24.7

Table A2. Keyword Patterns in First-Year Explanatory Writing, with Keyness Values

FIRST-YEAR EXPLANATORY KEYWORD PATTERNS	KEYNESS
Articles (94% the: ***the audience/image/article/use***)	1196.1
Lexical verb, third person singular *(shows/uses/makes/gives/states)*	956.0
This as determiner (***this article/image/is/source/study***)	403.0
Is (***it/this/there is a/the/an***)	181.3
Numbers (dates, percentages, number of years/images/organizations)	130.3
Of as preposition (***use/one/university of the/a/this***)	129.1
Prepositions (***in/to/on/by*** [the/a/this/their])	80.5
Also as adverb (***is/but/they also the/be/a***)	79.4
Wh- determiner (***which/what*** [the/is/they])	57.1

Table A3. Stance Word Patterns in First-Year Writing, with LL Values

	C1: FY ARG	C2: FY EXPL	C1 vs. C2 USE	LL	NORM C1	NORM C2	% DIFF
Hedges	2333	1982	ARG> EXPL	13.14***	56.32	50.42	11.69% more Arg
Boosters	3938	2670	ARG> EXPL	182.86***	95.06	67.93	39.95% more Arg
Generality Words	4171	6266	ARG> EXPL	320.68***	151.26	106.11	42.55% more Arg
Counters	2224	3101	ARG> EXPL	102.76***	74.86	56.58	32.31% more Arg
Reformulation Words	1275	1663	ARG> EXPL	33.06***	40.15	32.44	23.77% more Arg

Table A4. Keyword Patterns in Upper-Level Argumentative Writing, with Keyness Values

KEYWORD PATTERNS	KEYNESS
-s form of lexical verb *(**seems**, **makes**, **says**, **becomes**, **gives**)*	1867.7
possessive, pre-nominal pronouns *(**his** [32%], **their**, **her** [18%], **its**, **our**, **my**, **your** own/life/family, father, mother)*	1274.5
Genitive marker *'s* (59% singular proper nouns, 29% singular common nouns)	1052.4
is as main verb *(it/there/this **is** a/the/not)*	323.5
After- or postdeterminer *(**such**, **own**, **same**, **former**, **latter** a, time, an, way)*	263.9
that as conjunction (81%) or singular determiner *(the fact is **that** the / **that** is)*	242.5
general adverbs *(**also**, **only**, **however**, **even** the/in/to/as)*	235.9
negation *(it is **not**, people do **not**)*	226.5
countering conjunction **but** *(**but** the/also/it)*	208.94
It *(**it** is [31.6%], **it** seems/was/would)*	168.5
Wh- determiners *(**which**, **what** is/the/he/we)*	164.1
as as conjunction *(just/much **as**)*,	156.5
of *as preposition (idea/part/one/because **of** the/a/his/their)*	82.2
Infinitive verbs *(**to make**/**say**/**take**/**see**)*	78.1
One as indefinite pronoun (48.6% ***one's*** *own* / ***one*** *can*); 45.2% as single cardinal number *(of **one** / **one** of / that)*	67.2
wh- adverb *(**when**, **why**, **where** the/to/he/we/they)*	55.6
adverb of time *(and/is/would/can **then**, **now**, **again**, **today** the/it//is/we)*	34.6
Only as adverb (80%, ***only*** *to/in/a)* and as adjective (20%) *(**only** one)*	33.3
Which as determiner *(in/of/to **which** the/is/to/they)*	27.5

Table A5. Keyword Patterns in Upper-Level Explanatory Writing, with Keyness Values

KEYWORD PATTERNS	KEYNESS
Cardinal number (citations, number of people, years)	1597.9
Past participle of lexical verb (*was/were* [not] ***used/able/found***)	518.2
Lexical verb, past tense (***found/used/showed/included***)	357.6
Comparative adjectives (***higher/lower/greater/larger/better***)	294.4
Adjective (***other*, *social*, *different*, *new*, *important***); mostly attributive adjectives in noun phrases (***other important effects***); occasionally in predicate (e.g., *is* ***anxious*** *to deploy*)	177.6
Common nouns (***data/people/species/dynamics/media***)	128.5
For as preposition (***for*** *each/the/a/this*)	57.8
Also as adverb (*is/but/are/can* ***also*** *be/the/have*)	48.8
Infinitive ***to be*** verb (***to be a/used/the/seen/more/able***)	48.1
And as coordinating conjunction (mostly between nouns and attributive adjectives, e.g., ***ability and output***)	40.7
On as preposition (96.2%) and verb particle	39.6
More as comparative degree adverb (67.3%) and comparative after-determiner	30.9

Table A6. Stance Word Patterns in Upper-Level Writing, with LL Values

	C1: UL ARG	C2: UL EXPL	C1 vs. C2	LL	NORM C1	NORM C2	% DIFF
Hedges	4887	11927	EXPL> ARG	13.80**	84.27	89.73	6.09% more Expl
Boosters	4539	9995	ARG> EXPL	4.98*	78.27	75.20	4.08% more Arg
Generality Words	5258	8801	ARG> EXPL	315.56***	90.67	66.22	36.93% more Arg
Counters	5806	10477	ARG> EXPL	208.37***	100.12	78.82	27.01% more Arg
Reformulation Words	2372	5375	ns	0.21	40.90	40.44	ns

Table A7. Discourse Patterns in Argumentative Writing

KEYWORD PATTERNS	COMMON ITERATIONS AND COLLOCATIONS	COMMON CLUSTERS
Possessive pronouns	*their* (36.5%), *his* (23%), *her* (12.6%), *its, our, your [own/life/family, father, mother]*	*his or her, because of their, in their own, their ability to*
Infinitive verbs	*to make/say/take/see*	*to make a, to make the, to say that, can lead to*
Negation	*it is* ***not****, people do* ***not***	*it is not, should not be, is not a, this is not [to say]*
Modal verbs	*[singular noun] can/will/would/should [not/have/ also]*	*should not be / it would be / that can be / it can be*
Lexical verb, present tense	*seems, makes, says, becomes, gives*	*needs to be, seems to be, it seems that, [when] it comes to*
That as conjunction (~82%) and determiner; as adverb (1%)	[singular noun] ***that*** the/they/are/there	*the fact that, the idea that, is that the, it seems that*
To as infinitive marker (76.5%) and as preposition	*to make/have/help/take*	*in order to, to be able to, the ability to, needs to be*
Adverbs (general)	*also, only, however, even [the/and/more/that]*	*it is also, to do so, is not only*
But as countering conjunction	[singular noun] *but [also/the/not]*	*but it is, but also the, but in the, but it is, but it also*
It (third person singular pronoun)	***it*** is (31.6%), ***it*** *seems/was/would*	*it is also, to do so, is not only*
Is as main verb	*it/there/this* ***is*** *not/the/that*	*there is a, there is no, it is not, that it is*
Are *as main verb*	[plural common noun] ***are*** *not/the/more*	*there are many, that they are, that there are, because they are*
Prepositional adverb as particle in phrasal verb	[infinitive verb / lexical verb, present participle] *out/back/down/off [the/and/for]*	*[holding/giving] back to the, goes on to, points out that*
They (third person plural pronoun)	[singular noun, *that* as conjunction] ***they*** *are/have/ can/were*	*that they are, because they are, in which they, that they have is that they*
Subordinating conjunction	[singular noun, plural noun] *because, when, while, since [the, they, there, this]*	*because they are, because it is, when it comes to, this is because, if it is*

Present participle of lexical verb	[singular noun, plural noun] *making, using, taking, trying, looking, going [the/that/and]*	*looking at the, are trying to, living in the, is trying to*
As as conjunction (45.5%), preposition (20.6%), adverb	[singular noun, preposition] ***as*** *the/well/they/much*	[singular noun, plural noun] *as well as, such as the*
One as indefinite pronoun (48.6%) and cardinal number (45.2%)	*one's own, one can; of one, one of, one that*	*is one of (the), on the one hand, more than one*
Have	[plural noun], *they* ***have*** *been/the/not/shown*	*to have a, do / does not have (the), that have been, not have to*
After- or postdeterminer	[infinitive verb, present participle] *some, any, enough [other, people, sort, time]*	*some of the, in some cases, some sort of, there are some, any of the, some of these*
Wh- determiners	[singular noun, plural noun] *which, what [the/they/are]*	*way(s) in which the/they/he, which in turn, which is why*
Or	[singular noun, plural noun, infinitive verb] ***or*** *not/the/even*	*whether or not, his or her, he or he, right or wrong, whether or not they*
Be	*can/should/would/will/not* ***be*** *the/able/used*	*to be a, needs to be, should not be, cannot be, it would be, be able to*
STANCE WORD PATTERNS	COMMON ITERATIONS AND COLLOCATIONS	COMMON CLUSTERS
Significantly more boosters	*very/must/clearly/quite/really/ extremely/sure*	*is a very, it is very, to be very*
Significantly fewer hedges	*likely, perhaps, almost, usually, generally, relatively*	*more likely to, are more likely to, the possibility of*
Significantly more generality words	*all, people, any, human, society*	*the people of, of the people, of all the, all of the*
Significantly more counters	*but, however, while, till, although, though*	*even though the, it is still, but it is (still), rather than the, there is still*
Similar use of reformulation words	*especially, specifically, particularly, called, i.e., e.g., namely, to illustrate*	*this is especially (true), especially in the, is especially important, (and) more specifically*

Table A8. Discourse Patterns in Explanatory Writing

KEYWORD PATTERNS	COMMON ITERATIONS AND COLLOCATIONS	COMMON CLUSTERS
Cardinal numbers	figure and table numbers, citations, number of people/ years in event or study	*between the two, of the two, there are two*
Lexical verb, past tense	*found/used/showed/made [the/ that/from]*	*they found that, showed that the*
The as article	**the** *same/first/most/United*	*the United States, the use of, one of the, due to the, the fact that*
Past participle of lexical verb	*[was/were / were not] used/ able/found, used, shows, made, came*	*found that the, they found that, and found that, showed that they*
Adjective (usually attributive adjectives)	*other, social, different, new, important [effects/ideas]*	
Also as adverb	*is/but/are/can* **also** *be/the/have*	*it is also, can also be, is also a, has also been, there is also*
This as determiner	[infinitive verb, *that* as conjunction] **this** *article, study, image, paper, was*	*in this case, in this study, in this image, in this article, in this paper*
Coordinating conjunction ***and***	[singular noun, plural noun, proper noun] **and** *the, that, their, other*	*men and women, pathos ad logos, a and b, United States and*
On as preposition (96.2%) and verb particle	[singular noun, past participle] *based/focus/research* **on** *the/a/ their/this*	*based on the, impact on the, depending on the, is based on, effect on the, focuses on the*
STANCE WORD PATTERNS	COMMON ITERATIONS AND COLLOCATIONS	COMMON CLUSTERS
Significantly more hedges (17.6% more)	*(more/the) likely, perhaps, almost, possibility, usually*	*(are) more likely (to), the possibility of, less likely to, are likely to (be)*
Significantly fewer boosters	[singular noun, plural noun] *must, very, really, clearly, fully*	*it must be, is a very, it is very, there must be, is very important*
Significantly fewer generality words	*people, all, society, any, human, every, never*	*of the people, the people of, the people who, of all the*
Significantly fewer counters	*but, however, while, still, rather, although*	*is still a, it is still, even though the, rather than the, but it is*
Similar use of reformulation words	*especially, specifically, called, particularly, e.g., i.e., namely*	*(this) is especially important, especially in the, is called the*

Table A9. Stance Word Patterns in Argumentative Writing and Explanatory Writing, with LL Values

	ARG (FY+UL)	EXPL (FY+UL)	C1 vs. C2 USE	LL	NORM C1	NORM C2	% DIFF
Hedges	7220	13909	EXPL> ARG	54.19***	72.62	80.76	10.08% more Expl
Boosters	8477	12665	ARG> EXPL	110.04***	85.27	73.54	15.95% more Arg
Generality Words	11524	12972	ARG> EXPL	1116.17***	115.92	75.32	53.90% more Arg
Counters	8907	12701	ARG> EXPL	195.79***	89.59	73.75	21.49% more Arg
Reformulation Words	4035	6650	ARG> EXPL	6.22*	40.59	38.61	5.11% more Arg

Table A10. Keyword Patterns in First-Year Writing, with Common Clusters

KEYWORD PATTERNS	COMMON ITERATIONS AND COLLOCATIONS	COMMON CLUSTERS
To in infinitive verb form and as preposition	**to** make/help/get/have; **to** the/their/this	*in order to / the audience to / be able to / needs to be / due to the / is trying to / need to be / according to the*
Present participle of lexical verb	using/making/trying/taking/getting	*[noun] is trying to / are trying to / looking at the / by appealing to / texting while driving / by using the*
They as 3rd person plural subjective personal pronoun	that/because/what/and **they** are/have/can/will	*that they are / because they are / what they are / what they are / that they have / so that they*
Common nouns	*people* (64%) / *media/ data/statistics/species* (equally common before *people* are determiners and infinitive verbs)	*in the media / people do not / people who are, of the people, people need to, of social media, the people who*
Their as 3rd person possessive, prenominal pronoun	[infinitive verb / present participle of lexical verb] ***their*** *own/children/lives*	*on their Web site / to get their / due to their / in their advertisements / based on their / because of their / to make their*
Infinitive verb	to help/make/get/take	*to make the (audience), to persuade the, to appeal to, to take action, to help/support/lead/*
Are as verb	[noun/pronoun] **are** not/the/more/being	*there are many / that they are / that there are / because they are / those who are / they are not*
Is as verb	[noun/pronoun/it] **is** the/not/that/also	*There is a / that it is / this article is / it is a / there is no / that there is / this is a / it is important / because it is*
Can as modal verb	[singular noun / plural noun / pronoun *it*] ***can*** *not/help/also/make*	*[singular noun] that can be / it can be / that they can / the audience can / this can be / and can be*
Has	[singular noun / proper noun]/ *it* ***has*** *been/become/the/not*	*it has been / there has been / that has been / United States has / [singular noun] that has been / [singular noun] has become*
Prepositional adverb or verb particle	[infinitive verb] out, down, back/off [and/the/for]	*in regards to / back to the / has been around / out to the / to stand up / goes on to / up in the*

It as subject of clause	[because/that] [singular noun] ***it*** *was/has/can*	*that it is / when it comes to / because it is / and it is / as it is / and how it*
This as determiner	[infinitive verb / singular noun]/*that* **this** *article/image/issue*	*in this image / in this article / [singular noun] of this article / in this case / [singular noun] of this image / that this is / purpose of this*
Have	[plural noun]/they **have** been/the/not	*to have a / do not have / [plural noun] that have been / there have been / that they have / not have to*
That as conjunction (84%) and determiner	[singular noun / plural noun / lexical verb, present tense] ***that*** *the/they/are*	*[preposition] the fact that / the idea that / the audience that / that have been / an organization that / that can be*
On	[singular noun / present participle of lexical verb / plural noun] ***on*** *the/their/how/this*	*based on the / impact on the / focuses on the / effects on the / [effect/s] on the issue / based on their / negative effects on / depending on the [topic]*
Also	[singular noun]/is/but **also** the/has/uses	*it is also (a) / can also be / but also the / has also been / the image also / there is also*
More	as comparative degree adverb (~42%), comparative after- determiner (41%), and comparative adverb (~17%) [infinitive verb / present participle of lexical verb / singular noun] ***more*** *than/likely/people*	*are more likely to / to be more / they are more / more and more / it is more / will be more / there are more*
Modal verbs	can (~33%) / will (19.5%) / would (~13%) / should (~12%) / could/may/must [not/have/help/also]	*that can be / should not be / it can be / can be used / cannot be / can lead to / will continue to / it would be / can be seen / will not be*
By as preposition	[past participle of lexical verb / singular noun / plural noun] ***by*** *the/using/showing/making/their*	*the audience by / affected by the / as stated by / are affected by / the audience by demonstrating / used by the / was written by*
Lexical verb, present tense	[singular noun]/it shows/uses/makes/states	*needs to be / when it comes to / makes the audience / needs to be / shows that they / this means that*

Table A11. Keyword Patterns in Upper-Level Writing, with Common Clusters

KEYWORD PATTERNS	COMMON ITERATIONS AND COLLOCATIONS	COMMON CLUSTERS
Genitive markers	Possessive use of common noun, e.g., women's/one's/children's/ people's [and, theory, life, own]	*Women's movement, [noun]'s ability to, an individual's [life] / the world's [population]*
Adjective	In attributive position; Other/ social/different/important/new [and/for/that/with]	*On the other hand / more likely to / it is important to [note] / in other words / it is possible*
Lexical verb, past tense	(and/they/that/who/which) found/used/showed/made/ became (the/that)	*[they/and] found that / seemed to be / showed that the / we used the*
Of as preposition	Prepositional phrases used to specify quantity and attributes; e.g., *Number/one/part/use/ because/amount of the/this/ these/their)*	*One of the / the number of / the use of / part of the / some of the / the amount of*
As as conjunction	Usually noun precedes (and some lexical verbs), as part of identifying, classifying, defining *as the/they/one/shown*	*as shown in / as it is / as well as / as much as [possible] / as in the*
Adverb	Wide range of adverbs including sentence adverbs (*also/however/ thus*), specifiers (*even/both/ especially*), hedges (*perhaps*), intensifiers (*extremely*)	*It is also / can also be / to do so / however it is / as well as*
After- or postdeterminer	same/such/own/former/latter [time/way/and/the]	*At the same [time], of the same / the same way / in such a [way]*
Past participle of lexical verb	passive constructions (47%) and perfect aspect (10%), as well as *used/based/found/given/shown [with/and/the/for/that]*	*Based on the / can be [seen / used to] / compared to the / shown in figure / is based on / is related to*
Which as determiner	usually following noun and introducing relative clause; *which* the/are/was/they/would	*[noun] in which the / way(s) in which [they] / extent to which*
With as preposition	mostly follows nouns (and sometimes past participle of lexical verb), *with the/their/his/ this/other*	*Associated with the / along with the / to do with / in conjunction [/accordance] with / consistent with*
Comparative adjective	usually in noun phrase or infinitive verb phrase; *higher/ greater/lower/larger/better/ further*	*higher levels of / greater than the / in the lower / better understanding [of]*
Articles	The (94% of articles) the same/ first/most/other	*The United States / one of the / the fact that / the number of / due to the / the use of*

Table A11. (*continued*)

KEYWORD PATTERNS	COMMON ITERATIONS AND COLLOCATIONS	COMMON CLUSTERS
In and ***from*** as prepositions	*In/from* follow nouns, participles, and infinitive verbs; often elaborates via description of attributes, purpose, or origin (*in the/this/order/which, from the/this/their/his/her/each*)	*in order to / in which the / in terms of / an increase in / away from the / different from the / the transition from / removed from [the] / results from the*
But as countering conjunction	[plural nouns / singular nouns / proper nouns] *but the / also/not*	[singular noun, plural noun] *but it is, but also the, but in the, but does not, but there is, but this is, but also to, but also in*

Table A12. Stance Word Patterns in First-Year and Upper-Level Writing, with LL Values

	C1: FY (ALL)	C2: UL (ALL)	C1 vs. C2 USE	LL	NORM C1	NORM C2	% DIFF
Hedges	4315	16814	UL> FY	940.33***	53.45	88.07	39.31% more UL
Boosters	6608	14534	FY> UL	23.62***	81.85	76.13	7.51% more FY
Generality words	10437	14059	FY> UL	1822.94***	129.28	73.64	75.55% more FY
Counters	5325	16283	UL> FY	276.47***	65.96	85.29	22.67% more UL
Reformulations	2938	7746	UL> FY	25.62***	36.39	40.57	10.31% more UL

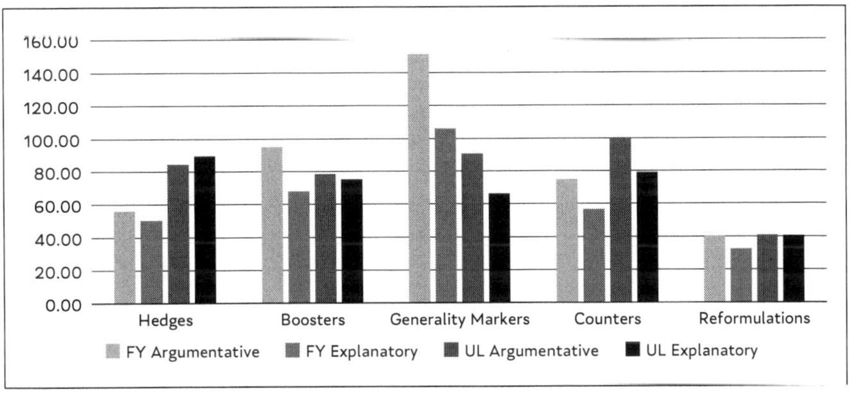

Figure 6. Stance Word Patterns by Genre and Level, Instances per 10,000 Words

Works Cited

"About USF." U of South Florida, 2019, www.usf.edu/about-usf/facts-statistics.aspx.

Accuplacer: Sample Questions for Students. The College Board, 2016, secure-media.collegeboard.org/digitalServices/pdf/accuplacer/accuplacer-sample-questions-for-students.pdf.

Ädel, Annelie. *Metadiscourse in L1 and L2 English*. John Benjamins Publishing, 2006. Studies in Corpus Linguistics 24.

Ädel, Annelie, and Ute Römer. "Research on Advanced Student Writing across Disciplines and Levels: Introducing the Michigan Corpus of Upper-Level Student Papers." *International Journal of Corpus Linguistics*, vol. 17, no. 1, 2012, pp. 3–34.

Adler-Kassner, Linda, and Peggy O'Neill. *Reframing Writing Assessment to Improve Teaching and Learning*. Utah State UP, 2010.

America's Best Value Colleges. "University of South Florida." *Forbes*, Forbes Media, 2019, www.forbes.com/colleges/university-of-south-florida.

Anderson, Paul, et al. "The Contributions of Writing to Learning and Development: Results from a Large-Scale Multi-Institutional Study." *Research in the Teaching of English*, vol. 50, no. 2, 2015, pp. 199–235.

Anderson, Virginia. "Confrontational Teaching and Rhetorical Practice." *College Composition and Communication*, vol. 48, no. 2, 1997, pp. 197–214.

Anson, Chris M., and Deanna P. Dannels. "Developing Rubrics for Instruction and Evaluation." *Strategies for Teaching First-Year Composition*, edited by Duane Roen et al., National Council of Teachers of English (NCTE), 2002, pp. 387–400. ED459476. *ERIC*, sjsucompprogram.pbworks.com/f/Grading+with+Rubrics.pdf.

Applebee, Arthur N., and Judith A. Langer. *Writing Instruction That Works: Proven Methods for Middle and High School Classrooms*. Teachers College Press, 2013.

"Argument/Opinion Writing: On Demand." 2013. *Achieve the Core*, 2016, achievethecore.org/page/1271/argument-opinion-writing-on-demand.

Aull, Laura Louise. "A Civil Style: Reexamining Discourse and Ethical Principles in Composition." *Style and the Future of Composition Studies*, edited by Paul Butler et al., Utah State UP, forthcoming.

———. "Connecting Writing and Language in Assessment: Examining Style, Tone, and Argument in the US Common Core Standards and in Exemplary Student Writing." *Assessing Writing*, vol. 24, 2015, pp. 59–73.

———. "Corpus Analysis of Argumentative Versus Explanatory Discourse in Writing Task Genres." *Journal of Writing Analytics*, vol. 1, no. 1, 2017, pp. 1–47.

———. *First-Year University Writing: A Corpus-Based Study with Implications for Pedagogy*. Palgrave Macmillan, 2015.

———. "Linguistic Attention in Rhetorical Genre Studies and First-Year Writing." *Composition Forum*, vol. 31, special issue on rhetorical genre studies, edited by Dylan Dryer, 2015, compositionforum.com/issue/31/linguistic-attention.php.

———. "Tools and Tech." *Assessing Writing*, vol. 33, 2017, pp. A2–A7.

Aull, Laura Louise, and Zak Lancaster. "Linguistic Markers of Stance in Early and Advanced Academic Writing: A Corpus-Based Comparison." *Written Communication*, vol. 1, no. 33, 2014, pp. 151–83.

Aull, Laura Louise, and Valerie Ross. "From Cowpaths to Conversation." *Pedagogy*, forthcoming.

Aull, Laura Louise, et al. "Generality in Student and Expert Epistemic Stance: A Corpus Analysis of First-Year, Upper-Level, and Published Academic Writing." *Journal of English for Academic Purposes*, vol. 26, 2017, pp. 29–41, doi:10.1016/j.jeap.2017.01.005.

Bacon, Nora. "Style in Academic Writing." Duncan and Vanguri, pp. 173–90.

Baker, Paul. "Querying Keywords Questions of Difference, Frequency, and Sense in Keywords Analysis." *Journal of English Linguistics*, vol. 32, no. 4, 2004, pp. 346–59.

Bakhtin, M. M. "The Problem of Speech Genres." *Speech Genres and Other Late Essays*, edited by Caryl Emerson and Michael Holquist, translated by Vern W. McGee, U of Texas P, 1986, pp. 60–102.

Barlow, M. "Software for Corpus Access and Analysis." *How to Use Corpora in Language Teaching*, edited by J. M. Sinclair, John Benjamins, 2004, pp. 205–21.

Baron, Dennis. "Facebook and Your Health: A Dr. Grammar Special Report." *The Web of Language: Dennis Baron's Go-to Site for Language and Technology in the News*, 10 Aug. 2011, illinois.edu/blog/view/25/57626.

Bartholomae, David. "Inventing the University." *Journal of Basic Writing*, no. 5, 1986, pp. 4–23.

Barton, Ellen L. "Contrastive and Non-contrastive Connectives: Metadiscourse Functions in Argumentation." *Written Communication*, vol. 12, no. 2, 1995, pp. 219–39.

———. "Evidentials, Argumentation, and Epistemological Stance." *College English*, vol. 55, no. 7, 1993, pp. 745–69.

Barton, Ellen L., and Gail Stygall. *Discourse Studies in Composition*. Hampton Press, 2002.

Bastian, Heather. "Capturing Individual Uptake: Toward a Disruptive Research Methodology." *Composition Forum*, vol. 31, 2015, compositionforum.com/issue/31/individual-uptake.php.

Bawarshi, Anis. *Genre and the Invention of the Writer: Reconsidering the Place of Invention in Composition*. Utah State UP, 2003.

———. "The Genre Function." *College English*, vol. 62, no. 3, 2000, pp. 335–60. *JSTOR*, www.jstor.org/stable/378935.

———. "Sites of Invention: Genre and the Enactment of First Year Writing." *Relations, Locations, Positions: Composition Theory for Writing Teachers*, edited by Peter Vandenberg et al., National Council of Teachers of English (NCTE), 2006, pp. 103–37.

Bawarshi, Anis, and Mary Jo Reiff. *Genre: An Introduction to History, Theory, Research, and Pedagogy*. WAC Clearinghouse / Parlor Press, 2010.

Bazerman, Charles. *Shaping Written Knowledge: The Genre and Activity of the Experimental Article in Science*. U of Wisconsin P, 1988.

Bazerman, Charles, et al. "Taking the Long View on Writing Development." *Research in the Teaching of English*, vol. 51, no. 3, 2017, pp. 351–60.

Bean, John C. *Engaging Ideas: The Professor's Guide to Integrating Writing, Critical Thinking, and Active Learning in the Classroom*. Wiley, 2011.

Beaufort, Anne. *College Writing and Beyond: A New Framework for University Writing Instruction*. Utah State UP, 2007.

Beck, Sarah W., and Jill V. Jeffery. "Genres of High-Stakes Writing Assessments and the Construct of Writing Competence." *Assessing Writing*, vol. 12, no. 1, 2007, pp. 60–79.

Bennett, Randy Elliot. *On the Meanings of Constructed Response*. Educational Testing Service (ETS), 1991. *Wiley*, onlinelibrary.wiley.com/doi/pdf/10.1002/j.2333-8504.1991.tb01429.x.

Berkenkotter, Carol, and Thomas Huckin. *Genre Knowledge in Disciplinary Communities*. Lawrence Erlbaum, 1995.

Berlin, James. *Rhetoric and Reality : Writing Instruction in American Colleges, 1900–1985*. Southern Illinois UP, 1987. Conference on College Composition and Communication.

———. *Writing Instruction in Nineteenth-Century American Colleges*. Southern Illinois UP, 1984.

Bernstein, Charles. "Ninety-Five Theses." *Profession*, Modern Language Association, Oct. 2016, profession.mla.org/95-theses/.

Best Colleges and National Universities. "University of Michigan." *U.S. News and World Report*, 2019, www.usnews.com/best-colleges/university-of-michigan-9092.

———. "University of South Florida." *U.S. News and World Report*, 2019, www.usnews.com/best-colleges/usf-1537.

Biber, Douglas. *Variation across Speech and Writing*. Cambridge UP, 1988.

Biber, Douglas, and Jesse Egbert. *Register Variation Online*. Cambridge UP, 2018.

Biber, Douglas, and Bethany Gray. "Challenging Stereotypes about Academic Writing: Complexity, Elaboration, Explicitness." *Journal of English for Academic Purposes*, vol. 9, no. 1, 2010, pp. 2–20.

Biber, Douglas, et al. *Longman Grammar of Spoken and Written English*. Vol. 2, MIT Press, 1999.

Biber, Douglas, et al. "Speaking and Writing in the University: A Multidimensional Comparison." *TESOL Quarterly*, vol. 36, no. 1, 2002, pp. 9–48.

Bitzer, Lloyd F. "The Rhetorical Situation." *Philosophy and Rhetoric*, vol. 1, no. 1, 1992, pp. 1–14.

Bizzell, Patricia. "College Composition: Initiation into the Academic Discourse Community." *Curriculum Inquiry*, vol. 12, no. 2, 1982, pp. 191–207.

Bloom, Lynn Z. "The Essay Canon." *College English*, vol. 61, no. 4, 1999, pp. 401–30.

Boettger, Ryan K., and Stefanie Wulff. "Using Authentic Language Data to Teach Discipline-Specific Writing Patterns to STEM Students." IEEE International Professional Communication Conference, 2–5 Oct. 2016, Austin, TX.

Bourdieu, Pierre, and Jean-Claude Passeron. *Reproduction in Education, Society and Culture*. Translated by Richard Nice, Sage Publications, 1977.

Brereton, John. "A Closer Look at the Harvard Entrance Examinations in the 1870s." *Writing Assessment in the Twenty-First Century: Essays in Honor of Edward M. White*, edited by Norbert Elliot and Les Perelman, Hampton Press, 2012, pp. 31–43.

———. *The Origins of Composition Studies in the American College, 1875–1925*. U of Pittsburgh P, 1996.

Brown, David West, and Laura Louise Aull. "Elaborated Specificity vs. Emphatic Generality: A Corpus-Based Comparison of Higher and Lower Scoring Advanced Placement Exams in English." *Research in the Teaching of English*, vol. 51, no. 4, 2017, pp. 394–417.

Brown, David West, and Chris C. Palmer. "The Phrasal Verb in American English: Using Corpora to Track Down Historical Trends in Particle Distribution, Register Variation, and Noun Collocations." *Studies in the History of the English Language VI: Evidence and Method in Histories of English*, edited by Michael Adams et al., De Gruyter, 2015, pp. 71–97.

Burstein, Jill, et al. "Informing Automated Writing Evaluation Using the Lens of Genre: Two Studies." *Calico Journal*, vol. 33, no. 1, 2016, pp. 117–41.

Butler, Paul. *Out of Style: Reanimating Stylistic Study in Composition and Rhetoric*. Utah State UP, 2008.

CAHSPE (California High School Proficiency Examination). Sacramento County Office of Education for the California Department of Education, 2019, www.chspe.net/about/writing/.

Carillo, Ellen C. "Creating Mindful Readers in First-Year Composition Courses: A Strategy to Facilitate Transfer." *Pedagogy*, vol. 16, no. 1, 2016, pp. 9–22.

Cassidy, L., et al. *Classroom Trials: A Study of Instruction with Writing Software*. SRI International, 2016.

CCCC (Conference on College Composition and Communication). "Bibliography of Resources on Labor in College Composition." National Council of Teachers of English (NCTE), 1998–2018, cccc.ncte.org/cccc/labor/bibliography.

———. "CCCC Statement on Working Conditions for Non-Tenure-Track Writing Faculty." National Council of Teachers of English (NCTE), Apr. 2016, cccc.ncte.org/cccc/resources/positions/working-conditions-ntt.

Civic Learning and Democratic Engagement National Task Force. "A Crucible Moment: College Learning and Democracy's Future." Report submitted to the United States Department of Education, American Association of Colleges and Universities, 2011.

Clark, Irene L., and Andrea Hernandez. "Genre Awareness, Academic Argument, and Transferability." *The WAC Journal*, vol. 22, 2011, pp. 65–78.

CLAWS 7 Tagset. University Centre for Computer Corpus Research on Language, Lancaster University, 1993–2014, ucrel.lancs.ac.uk/claws7tags.html.

Coffin, Caroline, and A. Hewings. "IELTS as Preparation for Tertiary Writing: Distinctive Interpersonal and Textual Strategies." *Analysing Academic Writing: Contextualized Frameworks*, edited by Louise Ravelli and Robert A. Ellis, A&C Black, 2005, pp. 153–71.

"Collaborative Research: The Role of Instructor and Peer Feedback in Improving the Cognitive, Interpersonal, and Intrapersonal Competencies of Student Writers in STEM Courses." Principal investigator, Joseph Moxley. Award 1544239, National Science Foundation, 2015–19, www.nsf.gov/awardsearch/showAward?AWD_ID=1544239.

Condon, William. "Large-Scale Assessment, Locally-Developed Measures, and Automated Scoring of Essays: Fishing for Red Herrings?" *Assessing Writing*, vol. 18, no. 1, 2013, pp. 100–08.

Connors, Robert J. *Composition-Rhetoric: Backgrounds, Theory, and Pedagogy*. U of Pittsburgh P, 1997.

———. "The Erasure of the Sentence." *College Composition and Communication*, vol. 52, no. 1, 2000, pp. 96–128. *JSTOR*, www.jstor.org/stable/358546.

———. "Personal Writing Assignments." *College Composition and Communication*, vol. 38, no. 2, 1987, pp. 166–83.

Conrad, Susan M. "Investigating Academic Texts with Corpus-Based Techniques: An Example from Biology." *Linguistics and Education*, vol. 8, no. 3, 1996, pp. 299–326.

Crismore, Avon. *Metadiscourse: What It Is and How It Is Used in School and Non-school Social Science Texts*. Technical Report 273, Center for the Study of Reading, University of Illinois, 1983.

Crismore, Avon, and Rodney Farnsworth. "Metadiscourse in Popular and Professional Science Discourse." *The Writing Scholar: Studies in the Language and Conventions of Academic Discourse*, edited by Crismore and Farnsworth, Sage, 1990, pp. 45–68.

Crossley, Scott A., et al. "The Development and Use of Cohesive Devices in L2 Writing and Their Relations to Judgments of Essay Quality." *Journal of Second Language Writing*, vol. 32, 2016, pp. 1–16.

Crossley, Scott, et al. "What Is Successful Writing? An Investigation into the Multiple Ways Writers Can Write Successful Essays." *Written Communication*, vol. 31, no. 2, 2014, pp. 184–214.

Crosswhite, James. *The Rhetoric of Reason: Writing and the Attractions of Argument*. U of Wisconsin P, 2012.

Crowley, Sharon. "Linguistics and Composition Instruction, 1950–1980." *Written Communication*, vol. 6, no. 4, 1989, pp. 480–505.

———. *Toward a Civil Discourse: Rhetoric and Fundamentalism*. U of Pittsburgh P, 2006.

Crusius, Timothy W. *Kenneth Burke and the Conversation after Philosophy*. Southern Illinois UP, 1999.

Cumming, Alister, et al. "Differences in Written Discourse in Independent and Integrated Prototype Tasks for Next Generation TOEFL." *Assessing Writing*, vol. 10, no. 1, 2005, pp. 5–43.

Cushman, Ellen. "The Rhetorician as an Agent of Social Change." *College Composition and Communication*, vol. 47, no. 1, 1996, pp. 7–28.

Davies, William. "The Age of Post-Truth Politics." *The New York Times*, vol. 24, 2016, www.nytimes.com/2016/08/24/opinion/campaign-stops/the-age-of-post-truth-politics.html.

Deacon, Roger. "Truth, Power, and Pedagogy: Michel Foucault on the Rise of the Disciplines." *Educational Philosophy and Theory*, vol. 34, no. 4, 2002, pp. 435–58.

Deane, Paul. "On the Relation between Automated Essay Scoring and Modern Views of the Writing Construct." *Assessing Writing*, vol. 18, no. 1, 2013, pp. 7–24.

Deans, Thomas. "Shifting Locations, Genres, and Motives: An Activity Theory Analysis of Service-Learning Writing Pedagogies." *The Locations of Composition*, edited by Christopher J. Keller and Christian Weisser, State U of New York P, 2007, pp. 289–306.

DeStigter, Todd. "On the Ascendance of Argument: A Critique of the Assumptions of Academe's Dominant Form." *Research in the Teaching of English*, vol. 50, no. 1, 2015, pp. 11–34.

Devitt, Amy J. "Generalizing About Genre: New Conceptions of an Old Concept." *College Composition and Communication*, vol. 44, no. 4, 1993, pp. 573–86. *JSTOR*, www.jstor.org/stable/358391.

———. "Genre Performances: John Swales' Genre Analysis and Rhetorical-Linguistic Genre Studies." *Journal of English for Academic Purposes*, vol. 19, 2015, pp. 44–51.

———. "Re-fusing Form in Genre Study." *Genres in the Internet: Issues in the Theory of Genre*, vol. 188, 2009, pp. 27–47.

———. *Writing Genres.* Southern Illinois UP, 2004. Rhetorical Philosophy and Theory.

———. "Written Language in Use." *Contours of English and English Language Studies*, edited by Michael Adams and Anne Curzan, U of Michigan P, 2011, pp. 298–314.

Devitt, Amy J., et al. *Scenes of Writing: Strategies for Composing with Genres*. Pearson / Longman, 2004.

Dijk, Teun A. van. *Discourse and Context: A Sociocognitive Approach.* Cambridge UP, 2008.

Doolan, Stephen M. "Generation 1.5 Writing Compared to L1 and L2 Writing in First-Year Composition." *Written Communication*, vol. 30, no. 2, 2013, pp. 135–63.

Downs, Douglas, and Elizabeth Wardle. "Teaching About Writing, Righting Misconceptions: (Re)Envisioning 'First-Year Composition' as 'Introduction to Writing Studies.'" *College Composition and Communication*, vol. 58, no. 4, 2007, pp. 552–84.

Driscoll, Dana Lynn, and Roger Powell. "States, Traits, and Dispositions: The Impact of Emotion on Writing Development and Writing Transfer across College Courses and Beyond." *Composition Forum*, vol. 34, 2016, compositionforum.com/issue/34/states-traits.php

Dryer, Dylan B. "Scaling Writing Ability: A Corpus-Driven Inquiry." *Written Communication*, vol. 30, no. 1, 2013, pp. 3–35.

Duffy, John. "The Good Writer: Virtue Ethics and the Teaching of Writing." *College English*, vol. 79, no. 3, 2017, pp. 229–50.

———. "Post-Truth and First-Year Writing." *Inside Higher Education*, 8 May 2017, www.insidehighered.com/views/2017/05/08/first-year-writing-classes-can-teach-students-how-make-fact-based-arguments-essay.

Duncan, Mike, and Star Medzerian Vanguri, editors. *The Centrality of Style*. WAC Clearinghouse / Parlor Press, 2013. Perspectives on Writing.

Elliot, Norbert, and David M. Williamson. "Assessing Writing Special Issue: Assessing Writing with Automated Scoring Systems." *Assessing Writing*, vol. 18, no. 1, 2013, pp. 1–6, doi.org/10.1016/j.asw.2012.11.002.

Elliot, Norbert, et al. Textual Transactions: A Review of the Empirical Tradition in Writing Studies Research. Modern Language Association Annual Convention, 5 Jan. 2019, Chicago, IL. Panel.

Ervin, Elizabeth. "Encouraging Civic Participation among First-Year Writing Students; or, Why Composition Class Should Be More Like a Bowling Team." *Rhetoric Review*, vol. 15, no. 2, 1997, pp. 382–99.

"Essay: Example Two of Two." SAT, The College Board, collegereadiness.collegeboard .org/sample-questions/essay/2.

"Ethnicity Reports." Office of the Registrar, Regents of the U of Michigan, 2019, ro.umich.edu/reports/ethnicity.

Fahnestock, Jeanne, and Marie Secor. "The Rhetoric of Literary Criticism." *Textual Dynamics of the Professions: Historical and Contemporary Studies of Writing in Professional Communities*, edited by Charles Bazerman and James G. Paradis, U of Wisconsin P, 1991, pp. 76–96.

Flowerdew, John. "Genre in the Classroom: A Linguistic Approach." Johns, *Genre*, pp. 91–102.

Foucault, Michel. *Power/Knowledge: Selected Interviews and Other Writings, 1972–1977*. Pantheon, 1980.

Framework for Success in Postsecondary Writing. Council of Writing Program Administrators (CWPA) / National Council of Teachers of English (NCTE) / National Writing Project (NWP), 2011.

Friend, Christy. "Ethics in the Writing Classroom: A Nondistributive Approach." *College English*, vol. 56, no. 5, 1994, pp. 548–67.

Frow, John. "'Reproducibles, Rubrics, and Everything You Need': Genre Theory Today." *PMLA*, vol. 122, no. 5, 2007, pp. 1626–34.

Gabrielson, Stephen, et al. "The Effects of Task Choice on the Quality of Writing Obtained in a Statewide Assessment." *Applied Measurement in Education*, vol. 8, no. 4, 1995, pp. 273–90.

Gee, James Paul. *An Introduction to Discourse Analysis: Theory and Method*. Routledge, 2014.

George, Diana. "From Analysis to Design: Visual Communication in the Teaching of Writing." *College Composition and Communication*, vol. 54, no. 1, 2002, pp. 11–39.

Gere, Anne Ruggles, et al. "Local Assessment: Using Genre Analysis to Validate Directed Self-Placement." *College Composition and Communication*, vol. 4, no. 64, 2013, pp. 605–33.

Good, Graham. *The Observing Self: Rediscovering the Essay*. Taylor and Francis, 2014.

Grabe, William. "Narrative and Expository Macro-genres." Johns, *Genre*, pp. 249–67.

Graham, George Frederick. *English; or, the Art of Composition, Explained in a Series of Instructions and Examples*. London, 1842.

Graham, Steve, et al. "Writing: Importance, Development, and Instruction." *Reading and Writing*, vol. 26, no. 1, 2013, pp. 1–15.

Guillory, John. "The Common Core and the Evasion of Curriculum." *PMLA*, vol. 130, no. 3, 2015, pp. 666–72.

Haefner, Joel. "Democracy, Pedagogy, and the Personal Essay." *College English*, vol. 54, no. 2, 1992, pp. 127–37. Also published in *Cross-Talk in Comp Theory: A Reader*, edited by Victor Villanueva Jr., National Council of Teachers of English (NCTE), 2003, pp. 509–19.

Hamp-Lyons, Liz, and Sheila Prochnow Mathias. "Examining Expert Judgments of Task Difficulty on Essay Tests." *Journal of Second Language Writing*, vol. 3, no. 1, 1994, pp. 49–68.

Hardie, Andrew. "Log Ratio: An Informal Introduction." *ESRC Centre for Corpus Approaches to Social Science (CASS)*, 2014, cass.lancs.ac.uk/log-ratio-an-informal-introduction/.

Hardy, Jack A., and Eric Friginal. "Genre Variation in Student Writing: A Multi-dimensional Analysis." *Journal of English for Academic Purposes*, vol. 22, 2016, pp. 119–31.

Hardy, Jack A., and Ute Römer. "Revealing Disciplinary Variation in Student Writing: A Multi-dimensional Analysis of the Michigan Corpus of Upper-Level Student Papers (MICUSP)." *Corpora*, vol. 8, no. 2, 2013, pp. 183–207.

Harrington, David V. "Teaching Ethical Writing." *Freshman English News*, vol. 10, no. 1, 1981, pp. 13–16. *JSTOR*, www.jstor.org/stable/i40139714.

Harrington, Susanmarie, et al. "Revising FYC Outcomes for a Multimodal, Digitally Composed World: The WPA Outcomes Statement for First-Year Composition (Version 3.0)." *WPA: Writing Program Administration*, vol. 38, no. 1, 2014, pp. 129–43.

Hart-Davidson, Bill. "Genres Are Enacted by Writers and Readers." *Naming What We Know: Threshold Concepts of Writing Studies*, edited by Linda Adler-Kassner and Elizabeth Wardle, UP of Colorado, 2015, pp. 39–40.

Harvey, Gordon. "Presence in the Essay." *College English*, vol. 56, no. 6, 1994, pp. 642–54, doi:10.2307/378310.

Heath, Shirley Brice. "Rethinking the Sense of the Past: The Essay as Legacy of the Epigram." *Theory and Practice in the Teaching of Writing: Rethinking the Discipline*, edited by Lee Odell, Southern Illinois UP, 1993, pp. 105–31.

Herrington, Anne, and Charles Moran. "What Happens When Machines Read Our Students' Writing?" *College English*, vol. 63, no. 4, 2001, pp. 480–99.

Hesse, Douglas. "The Place of Creative Nonfiction." *College English*, vol. 65, no. 3, 2003, pp. 237–41.

Hinkel, Eli. "Hedging, Inflating, and Persuading in L2 Academic Writing." *Applied Language Learning*, vol. 15, nos. 1–2, 2006, pp. 29–53.

———. "Simplicity without Elegance: Features of Sentences in L1 and L2 Academic Texts." *TESOL Quarterly*, vol. 37, no. 2, 2003, pp. 275–301.

Hunston, S., and G. Thompson. *Evaluation in Text: Authorial Stance and the Construction of Discourse*. Oxford UP, 2001.

Huot, Brian. "The Literature of Direct Writing Assessment: Major Concerns and Prevailing Trends." *Review of Educational Research*, vol. 60, no. 2, 1990, pp. 237–63.

———. *Rearticulating Writing Assessment for Teaching and Learning*. UP of Colorado, 2003.

Huot, Brian, and Michael Neal. "Writing Assessment: A Techno-history." MacArthur et al., pp. 417–32.

Hyland, Ken. *Disciplinary Discourses: Social Interactions in Academic Writing*. U of Michigan P, 2004.

———. *Metadiscourse: Exploring Interaction in Writing*. Continuum, 2005. Continuum Discourse Series.

———. "Persuasion and Context: The Pragmatics of Academic Metadiscourse." *Journal of Pragmatics*, vol. 30, no. 4, 1998, pp. 437–55, doi:10.1016/S0378-2166(98)00009-5.

———. "Stance and Engagement: A Model of Interaction in Academic Discourse." *Discourse Studies*, vol. 7, no. 2, 2005, pp. 173–92.

Hyland, Ken, and Carmen Sancho Guinda. *Stance and Voice in Written Academic Genres*. Springer, 2012.

Hyland, Ken, and Polly Tse. "Metadiscourse in Academic Writing: A Reappraisal." *Applied Linguistics*, vol. 25, no. 2, 2004, pp. 156–77, doi:10.1093/applin/25.2.156.

Hyon, Sunny. "Using Genre Analysis to Teach Writing in the Disciplines." *Discipline-Specific Writing: Theory into Practice*, edited by John Flowerdew and Tracey Costley, Taylor and Francis, 2016.

James, William. "The Social Value of the College-Bred." *William James*, www.uky.edu/~eushe2/Pajares/jaCollegeBred.html.

Jockers, Matthew L. *Macroanalysis: Digital Methods and Literary History.* U of Illinois P, 2013.

Johns, Ann M. "Genre Awareness for the Novice Academic Student: An Ongoing Quest." *Language Teaching,* vol. 41, no. 2, 2008, pp. 237–52.

———, editor. *Genre in the Classroom: Multiple Perspectives.* Taylor and Francis, 2002.

June, Audrey Williams. "With Postelection Tensions Running High, College Presidents Carefully Choose Their Words." *The Chronicle of Higher Education,* 16 Nov. 2016, www.chronicle.com/article/With-Postelection-Tensions/238423.

Kane, Michael T. "Validation." *Educational Measurement,* edited by Robert L. Brennan, 4th ed., American Council on Education, 2006, pp. 17–64.

Kitzhaber, Albert. "Themes, Theories, and Therapy: The Teaching of Writing in College. The Report of the Dartmouth Study of Student Writing." 1963.

Klein, Perry D. "The Challenges of Scientific Literacy: From the Viewpoint of Second-Generation Cognitive Science." *International Journal of Science Education,* vol. 28, nos. 2–3, 2006, pp. 143–78.

Kolln, Martha, and Craig Hancock. "The Story of English Grammar in United States Schools." *English Teaching,* vol. 4, no. 3, 2005, pp. 11–31.

Kuhi, Davud, and Biook Behnam. "Generic Variations and Metadiscourse Use in the Writing of Applied Linguists: A Comparative Study and Preliminary Framework." *Written Communication,* vol. 28, no. 1, 2011, pp. 97–141, doi:10.1177/0741088310387259.

Kyle, Kristopher, and Scott A. Crossley. "Automatically Assessing Lexical Sophistication: Indices, Tools, Findings, and Application." *TESOL Quarterly,* vol. 49, no. 4, 2015, pp. 757–86.

Lancaster, Zak. "Do Academics Really Write This Way? A Corpus Investigation of Moves and Templates in 'They Say / I Say.'" *College Composition and Communication,* vol. 67, no. 3, 2016, pp. 437–64.

———. "Exploring Valued Patterns of Stance in Upper-Level Student Writing in the Disciplines." *Written Communication,* vol. 31, no. 1, 2014, pp. 27–57, doi:10.1177/0741088313515170.

———. "Interpersonal Stance in L1 and L2 Students' Argumentative Writing in Economics: Implications for Faculty Development in WAC/WID Programs." *Across the Disciplines,* vol. 4, no. 8, 2011, pp. 1–23. WAC Clearinghouse / Colorado State University, wac.colostate.edu/atd/ell/lancaster.cfm.

———. "Tracking Interpersonal Style." Duncan and Vanguri, pp. 191–212.

———. "Using Corpus Results to Guide the Discourse-Based Interview." *Journal of Writing Research,* vol. 1, no. 8, 2016, pp. 119–48.

Lea, Mary R., and Brian V. Street. "Student Writing in Higher Education: An Academic Literacies Approach." *Studies in Higher Education*, vol. 23, no. 2, 1998, pp. 157–72.

Lee, Gerald Stanley. *The Lost Art of Reading*. G. P. Putnam's Sons, 1902.

Leskes, Andrea. "A Plea for Civil Discourse: Needed, the Academy's Leadership." *Liberal Education*, vol. 99, no. 4, 2013. *Association of American Colleges and Universities*, www.aacu.org/publications-research/periodicals/plea-civil-discourse-needed-academys-leadership.

Li, Ting, and Sue Wharton. "Metadiscourse Repertoire of L1 Mandarin Undergraduates Writing in English: A Cross-Contextual, Cross-Disciplinary Study." *Journal of English for Academic Purposes*, vol. 11, no. 4, 2012, pp. 345–56.

Lunsford, Andrea A. "The Nature of Composition Studies." *An Introduction to Composition Studies*, edited by Erika Lindemann and Gary Tate, Oxford UP, 1991, pp. 3–14.

MacArthur, Charles A., et al. *Handbook of Writing Research*. Guilford Press, 2008.

MacDonald, Susan Peck. "The Erasure of Language." *College Composition and Communication*, vol. 58, no. 4, 2007, pp. 585–625.

———. *Professional Academic Writing in the Humanities and Social Sciences*. Southern Illinois UP, 1994.

Mangrum, Benjamin. "Aggregation, Public Criticism, and the History of Reading Big Data." *PMLA*, vol. 133, no. 5, 2018, pp. 1207–24.

Martin, E. "WAC Paradoxes Revisited: A Program Director's Response." *Pedagogy: Critical Approaches to Teaching Literature, Language, Composition, and Culture*, vol. 1, no. 2, 2001, pp. 275–86.

Martin, James. "Genre and Language Learning: A Social Semiotic Perspective." *Linguistics and Education*, vol. 20, no. 1, 2009, pp. 10–21.

———. "A Universe of Meaning—How Many Practices." Johns, *Genre*, pp. 269–78.

Matsuda, Paul, and Jill V. Jeffery. "Voice in Student Essays." *Stance and Voice in Written Academic Genres*, edited by Ken Hyland and Carmen Sancho Guinda, Palgrave Macmillan, 2012.

Matthews, Catherine, and Beverly B. Zimmerman. "Integrating Service Learning and Technical Communication: Benefits and Challenges." *Technical Communication Quarterly*, vol. 8, no. 4, 1999, pp. 383–404.

McNamara, Danielle S., et al. "Linguistic Features of Writing Quality." *Written Communication*, vol. 27, no. 1, 2010, pp. 57–86.

Medway, Peter. "Fuzzy Genres and Community Identities: The Case of Architecture Students' Sketchbooks." *The Rhetoric and Ideology of Genre*, edited by Richard Coe et al., Hampton, 2002, pp. 123–53.

Melzer, Dan. "Writing Assignments across the Curriculum: A National Study of College Writing." *College Composition and Communication*, vol. 61, no. 2, 2009, pp. W240–W261.

Micciche, Laura R. "Making a Case for Rhetorical Grammar." *College Composition and Communication*, vol. 5, no. 4. 2004, pp. 716–37.

MICUSP (Michigan Corpus of Upper-Level Student Papers). Regents of the U of Michigan, 2009, micusp.elicorpora.info.

Miller, Carolyn R. "Genre as Social Action." *Quarterly Journal of Speech*, vol. 70, no. 2, 1984, pp. 151–67.

———. "Genre as Social Action (1984), Revisited Thirty Years Later (2014)." *Letras & Letras*, vol. 31, no. 3, 2015, pp. 56–72.

———. "Rhetorical Community: The Cultural Basis of Genre." *Genre in the New Rhetoric*, edited by Aviva Freedman and Peter Medway, Routledge, 2003, pp. 57–66.

Miller, Susan. *Textual Carnivals: The Politics of Composition*. Southern Illinois UP, 1991.

Mooney, Christopher. "The Vital Role of Scholarship in Public Discourse." *The Chronicle of Higher Education*, 3 Dec. 2017, www.chronicle.com/article/The-Vital-Role-of-Scholarship/241956.

Moore, Tim, and Janne Morton. "Dimensions of Difference: A Comparison of University Writing and IELTS Writing." *Journal of English for Academic Purposes*, vol. 4, no. 1, 2005, pp. 43–66.

Moxley, Joe. "Big Data, Learning Analytics, and Social Assessment." *The Journal of Writing Assessment*, vol. 6, no. 1, 2013, pp. 1–10.

Mur-Duenas, P. "An Intercultural Analysis of Metadiscourse Features in Research Articles Written in English and in Spanish." *Journal of Pragmatics*, vol. 43, no. 12, 2011, pp. 3068–79, doi:10.1016/j.pragma.2011.05.002.

Nesi, Hilary, and Sheena Gardner. *Genres across the Disciplines: Student Writing in Higher Education*. Cambridge UP, 2012.

Nilsen, Alleen Pace. "Civility: The Right Thing to Teach in Contentious Times." *English Journal*, vol. 97, no. 6, 2008, pp. 65–69.

North, Sarah. "Disciplinary Variation in the Use of Theme in Undergraduate Essays." *Applied Linguistics*, vol. 26, no. 3, 2005, pp. 431–52.

Nunes, Matthew J. *The Theme System: Current-Traditionalism, Writing Assignments, and the Development of First-Year Composition*. 2015. Ohio U, PhD dissertation.

Odell, Lee, and Susan M. Katz. *Writing Now: Shaping Words and Images*. Bedford/St. Martin's, 2010.

Odell, Lee, et al. "The Discourse-Based Interview: A Procedure for Exploring the Tacit Knowledge of Writers in Nonacademic Settings." *Research on Writing: Principles and Methods*, edited by Peter Mosenthal et al., Longman, 1986, pp. 221–36.

Ohmann, Richard Malin. *Selling Culture: Magazines, Markets, and Class at the Turn of the Century*. Verso, 1996.

"Overview of the Analytical Writing Measure." GRE General Test, Educational Testing Service (ETS), 2019, www.ets.org/gre/revised_general/prepare/analytical_writing.

Payne, William Morton. *English in American Universities*. D. C. Heath, 1895.

Poe, Mya. "The Consequences of Writing Assessment." *Research in the Teaching of English*, vol. 48, no. 3, 2014, pp. 271–75.

Poe, Mya, et al. *Learning to Communicate in Science and Engineering: Case Studies from MIT*. MIT Press, 2010.

Poe, Mya, et al., editors. *Writing Assessment, Social Justice, and the Advancement of Opportunity*. WAC Clearinghouse / UP of Colorado, 2018.

"Post-Truth Politics." *The Economist*, 10 September 2016.

"Prepare for the GRE General Test." Educational Testing Service (ETS), 2019, www.ets.org/gre/revised_general/prepare.

"Presidents' Message to President-Elect." *Inside Higher Education*, 18 Nov. 2016, www.insidehighered.com/news/2016/11/18/110-college-presidents-issue-letter-trump-urging-him-speak-out-against-harassment.

Puma, Vincent D. "Relationships between Writer-Audience Proximity, Register, and Quality in the Essays of First-Year College Students." Report from the Department of English, Flagler College. *ERIC*, files.eric.ed.gov/fulltext/ED282217.pdf. Accessed 2 Feb. 2018.

Quirk, Randolph, et al. *A Comprehensive Grammar of the English Language*. Longman, 1985.

Ramage, John D., et al. *The Allyn and Bacon Guide to Writing*. 5th ed., Pearson, 2008.

Ratcliffe, Krista. *Rhetorical Listening: Identification, Gender, Whiteness*. Southern Illinois UP, 2005.

Ray, Brian. *Style: An Introduction to History, Theory, Research, and Pedagogy*. Parlor Press, 2015.

Rayson, Paul. *Log-Likelihood Calculator*. 2009, University of Lancaster, ucrel.lancs.ac.uk/llwizard.html.

Rayson, Paul, and Roger Garside. "Comparing Corpora Using Frequency Profiling." *Proceedings of the Workshop on Comparing Corpora*, Association for Computational Linguistics, 2000, pp. 1–6.

Reiff, Mary Jo, and Anis Bawarshi. "Tracing Discursive Resources: How Students Use Prior Genre Knowledge to Negotiate New Writing Contexts in First-Year Composition." *Written Communication*, vol. 28, no. 3, 2011, pp. 312–37, doi:10.1177/0741088311410183.

Reynolds, Tom. "Selling College Literacy: The Mass-Market Magazine as Early Twentieth Century Literacy Sponsor." *American Periodicals: A Journal of History and Criticism*, vol. 15, no. 2, 2005, pp. 163–77.

Rodin, Judith, and Stephen P. Steinberg, editors. *Public Discourse in America: Conversation and Community in the Twenty-First Century*. U of Pennsylvania P, 2003.

Roemer, Marjorie, et al. "Reframing the Great Debate on First-Year Writing." *College Composition and Communication*, vol. 50, no. 3, 1999, pp. 377–92.

Römer, Ute, and Matthew Brook O'Donnell. "From Student Hard Drive to Web Corpus (Part 1): The Design, Compilation and Genre Classification of the Michigan Corpus of Upper-Level Student Papers (MICUSP)." *Corpora*, vol. 6, no. 2, 2011, pp. 159–77.

Römer, Ute, and Stefanie Wulff. "Applying Corpus Methods to Written Academic Texts: Explorations of MICUSP." *Journal of Writing Research*, vol. 2, no. 2, 2010, pp. 99–127.

Russell, David. "Activity Theory and Its Implications for Writing Instruction." *Reconceiving Writing, Rethinking Writing Instruction*, edited by Joseph Petraglia, Routledge, 1995, pp. 51–78.

———. "Rethinking Genre in School and Society: An Activity Theory Analysis." *Written Communication*, vol. 14, no. 4, 1997, pp. 504–54.

———. "Writing and Genre in Higher Education and Workplaces: A Review of Studies That Use Cultural-Historical Activity Theory." *Mind, Culture, and Activity*, vol. 4, no. 4, 1997, pp. 224–37.

———. *Writing in the Academic Disciplines, 1870–1990: A Curricular History*. Southern Illinois UP, 1991.

Scheffler, Israel. "Philosophical Models of Teaching." *Harvard Educational Review*, vol. 35, no. 2, 1965, pp. 131–43.

Scott, Mike. *Wordsmith Tools*. 6.0 ed., Oxford UP, 2014, www.lexically.net/wordsmith/.

Silver, Marc. "The Stance of Stance: A Critical Look at Ways Stance Is Expressed and Modeled in Academic Discourse." *Journal of English for Academic Purposes*, vol. 2, no. 4, 2003, pp. 359–74, doi:10.1016/s1475-1585(03)00051-1.

Simpson-Vlach, Rita, and Nick C. Ellis. "An Academic Formulas List: New Methods in Phraseology Research." *Applied Linguistics*, vol. 31, no. 4, 2010, pp. 487–512.

Slomp, David H. "Challenges in Assessing the Development of Writing Ability: Theories, Constructs and Methods." *Assessing Writing*, vol. 17, no. 2, 2012, pp. 81–91.

Smagorinsky, Peter. *Research on Composition: Multiple Perspectives on Two Decades of Change*. Teachers College Press, 2006.

Smit, David W. *The End of Composition Studies*. Southern Illinois UP, 2004.

"Social Networking's Good and Bad Impacts on Kids." American Psychological Association, 6 Aug. 2011, www.apa.org/news/press/releases/2011/08/social-kids.

Soliday, Mary. *Everyday Genres: Writing Assignments across the Disciplines*. Southern Illinois UP, 2011.

Sommers, N., and L. Saltz. "The Novice as Expert: Writing the Freshman Year." *College Composition and Communication*, vol. 56, no. 1, 2004, pp. 124–49.

Staples, Shelley, et al. "Academic Writing Development at the University Level: Phrasal and Clausal Complexity across Level of Study, Discipline, and Genre." *Written Communication*, vol. 33, no. 2, 2016, pp. 149–83.

Stotsky, Sandra. "Conceptualizing Writing as Moral and Civic Thinking." *College English*, vol. 54, no. 7, 1992, pp. 794–808.

Stuckey-French, Ned. *The American Essay in the American Century*. U of Missouri P, 2011.

Sullivan, Patrick. "The Unessay: Making Room for Creativity in the Composition Classroom." *College Composition and Communication*, vol. 67, no. 1, 2015, pp. 6–34.

Swales, John M. "Attended and Unattended 'This' in Academic Writing: A Long and Unfinished Story." *ESP Malaysia*, vol. 11, no. 1, 2005, pp. 1–15.

———. *Genre Analysis: English in Academic and Research Settings*. Cambridge UP, 1990. Cambridge Applied Linguistics.

———. *Research Genres: Explorations and Applications*. Cambridge UP, 2004.

Swales, John M., and Christine B. Feak. *Academic Writing for Graduate Students: Essential Tasks and Skills*. Vol. 1, U of Michigan P, 2004.

Tardy, Christine M. *Beyond Convention: Genre Innovation in Academic Writing*. U of Michigan P, 2015.

Tassoni, John Paul, and William H. Thelin. *Blundering for a Change: Errors and Expectations in Critical Pedagogy*. Boynton/Cook, 2000.

Tedick, Diane J. "ESL Writing Assessment: Subject-Matter Knowledge and Its Impact on Performance." *English for Specific Purposes*, vol. 9, no. 2, 1990, pp. 123–43.

Thaiss, Chris, and Tara Porter. "The State of WAC/WID in 2010: Methods and Results of the US Survey of the International WAC/WID Mapping Project." *College Composition and Communication*, vol. 61, no. 3, 2010, pp. 534–70.

Thaiss, Chris, and Terry Myers Zawacki. *Engaged Writers, Dynamic Disciplines*. Boynton/Cook, 2006.

Thompson, Geoff. "Interaction in Academic Writing: Learning to Argue with the Reader." *Applied Linguistics*, vol. 22, no. 1, 2001, pp. 58–78.

Thompson, Geoff, and Yiyun Ye. "Evaluation in the Reporting Verbs Used in Academic Papers." *Applied Linguistics*, vol. 12, no. 4, 1991, pp. 365–82.

Thornburg, Aaron. *Writing across the Curriculum (WAC): First Findings: June 2013–June 2016, Internal Report 1*. Eastern Oregon University, 2016, www.eou.edu/writing-center/files/2011/08/WAC-First-Findings-2015-2016_FINAL.pdf. Accessed 1 Oct. 2018.

Toth, Christie, and Laura Aull. "Directed Self-Placement Questionnaire Design: Practices, Problems, Possibilities." *Assessing Writing*, vol. 20, no. 0, 2014, pp. 1 18, doi:10.1016/j.asw.2013.11.006.

Toulmin, Stephen. *The Uses of Argument*. Cambridge UP, 1958.

Trimbur, John. *The Call to Write*. Cengage Learning, 2013.

Trollinger, William Vance, Jr., and Carl F. Kaestle. "Seven Highbrow and Middlebrow Magazines in 1920." *Literacy in the United States: Readers and Reading Since 1880*, 1993, pp. 204–24.

"Undergraduate Admissions." Office of Undergraduate Admissions, Regents of the U of Michigan, 2019, admissions.umich.edu/apply/freshmen-applicants/student-profile.

Vande Kopple, William J. "Metadiscourse, Discourse, and Issues in Composition and Rhetoric." Barton and Stygall, pp. 91–113.

———. "Some Exploratory Discourse on Metadiscourse." *College Composition and Communication*, vol. 36, no. 1, 1985, pp. 82–93.

Vojak, Colleen, et al. "New Spaces and Old Places: An Analysis of Writing Assessment Software." *Computers and Composition*, vol. 28, no. 2, 2011, pp. 97–111.

Walvoord, Barbara E. "The Future of WAC." *College English*, vol. 58, no. 1, 1996, pp. 58–79. *JSTOR*, www.jstor.org/stable/378534.

Wardle, Elizabeth. "'Mutt Genres' and the Goal of FYC: Can We Help Students Write the Genres of the University?" *College Composition and Communication*, vol. 60, no. 4, 2009, pp. 765–89.

White, Edward M., et al. *Very Like a Whale: The Assessment of Writing Programs*. UP of Colorado, 2015.

Wilcox, K., and Jill V. Jeffery. "Adolescents' Writing in the Content Areas: National Study Results." *Research in the Teaching of English*, vol. 49, no. 2, 2014, pp. 168–76.

Wilder, Laura, and Joanna Wolfe. "Sharing the Tacit Rhetorical Knowledge of the Literary Scholar: The Effects of Making Disciplinary Conventions Explicit in Undergraduate Writing About Literature Courses." *Research in the Teaching of English*, vol. 44, no. 2, 2009, pp. 170–209.

Wingate, Ursula. "'Argument!' Helping Students Understand What Essay Writing Is about." *Journal of English for Academic Purposes*, vol. 11, no. 2, 2012, pp. 145–54, doi:10.1016/j.jeap.2011.11.001.

Wodak, Ruth, and Michael Meyer. *Methods for Critical Discourse Analysis*. Sage, 2009.

WPA Outcomes Statement for First-Year Composition. 14 July 2014. *Council of Writing Program Administrators*, wpacouncil.org/positions/outcomes.html. Accessed 15 Mar. 2018.

"Writing Assignments across the Curriculum." U of Maryland, www.english.umd.edu/academics/writingcenter/faculty/type.

"Writing Sample Essays." ACT, 2019, www.act.org/content/act/en/products-and-services/the-act/test-preparation/writing-sample-essays.html?page=0&chapter=0.

Wysocki, Anne Frances. "Impossibly Distinct: On Form / Content and Word / Image in Two Pieces of Computer-Based Interactive Multimedia." *Computers and Composition*, vol. 18, no. 2, 2001, pp. 137–62, doi:10.1016/s8755-4615(01)00053-6.

Yancey, Kathleen Blake. "Looking Back as We Look Forward: Historicizing Writing Assessment." *College Composition and Communication*, vol. 50, no. 3, 1999, pp. 483–503.

Zanders, Crystal J., and Emily Wilson. "Holistic, Local, and Process-Oriented: What Makes the University of Utah's Writing Placement Exam Work." *Assessing Writing*, vol. 41, 2019, pp. 84–87.

Zhu, Wei. "Writing in Business Courses: An Analysis of Assignment Types, Their Characteristics, and Required Skills." *English for Specific Purposes*, vol. 23, no. 2, 2004, pp. 111–35.